AF739770

Women and Sustainable Development

Sustainable development has been recognized as a paradigm for considering a future in which environmental, social, and economic concerns are balanced in the pursuit of improving quality of life. The ideals and principles behind this paradigm are based on the concepts of generational and gender equality, social tolerance, poverty reduction, environmental protection and restoration, natural resource conservation, and the building of fair and peaceful societies. This book identifies and characterizes selected aspects of women's functioning in modern societies, in the context of the goals, assumptions, and challenges of sustainable development. It offers an innovative, multidimensional perspective on the potential and role of women in the context of sustainable development.

The book is divided into five chapters. The first chapter is dedicated to the role of women in the modern economy and their demographic and social characteristics in the European Union. The second chapter focuses on the role of women in meeting the sustainable development goals (SDGs), including the perspective of EU horizontal policies. The third chapter offers an analysis of women's living conditions in the EU, in terms of their social, professional, and economic situation, and leisure time management. The next chapter considers female entrepreneurship in the EU in terms of social and geopolitical changes, while the final one is devoted to the analysis of the situation of women in selected industry markets.

The book summarizes interdisciplinary research questions, focusing on sustainability, gender, human rights, and the economy and the trends, tendencies, and dependencies, and results will be an important source of comparison for academic researchers and a starting point for further in-depth analyses.

Agata Niemczyk is an Associate Professor in the Department of Tourism at the Krakow University of Economics, Poland.

Zofia Gródek-Szostak is an Assistant Professor in the Department of Economics and Enterprise Organization at Krakow University of Economics, Poland.

Renata Seweryn is an Associate Professor in the Department of Tourism at the Krakow University of Economics, Poland.

Urszula Grzega is an Associate Professor in the Department of Consumer Research at the University of Economics in Katowice, Poland.

Routledge Studies in Gender and Economics

The Economics of Women and Work in the Global Economy
Edited by Reyna Elizabeth Rodríguez Pérez and David Castro Lugo

The Economics of Gender and Sport
A Quantitative Analysis of Women's Cricket
Vani Kant Borooah

The Economics of Gender in China
Women, Work and the Glass Ceiling
Sisi Sung

Women's Productive and Reproductive Labour
Class and Gender Inequalities in Turkey
Ayşe Arslan

Identity Economics
Multidisciplinary Insights into Decision-Making Behavior
Edited by Meral Uzunöz Altan, Meltem İnce-Yenilmez, Oğuzhan Altınkoz and Sinem Bağçe

Gender Inequality in the Global Labor Market
A Feminist Economics Approach
Edited by Reyna Elizabeth Rodríguez Pérez and David Castro Lugo

Women and Sustainable Development
A European Cross-Country Analysis
Agata Niemczyk, Zofia Gródek-Szostak, Renata Seweryn and Urszula Grzega

For more information about this series, please visit www.routledge.com/Routledge-Studies-in-Gender-and-Economics/book-series/RSGENECON

Women and Sustainable Development

A European Cross-Country Analysis

Agata Niemczyk, Zofia Gródek-Szostak, Renata Seweryn and Urszula Grzega

Routledge
Taylor & Francis Group
LONDON AND NEW YORK

First published 2025
by Routledge
4 Park Square, Milton Park, Abingdon, Oxon OX14 4RN

and by Routledge
605 Third Avenue, New York, NY 10158

Routledge is an imprint of the Taylor & Francis Group, an informa business

© 2025 Agata Niemczyk, Zofia Gródek-Szostak, Renata Seweryn and Urszula Grzega

The right of Agata Niemczyk, Zofia Gródek-Szostak, Renata Seweryn and Urszula Grzega to be identified as authors of this work has been asserted in accordance with sections 77 and 78 of the Copyright, Designs and Patents Act 1988.

All rights reserved. No part of this book may be reprinted or reproduced or utilised in any form or by any electronic, mechanical, or other means, now known or hereafter invented, including photocopying and recording, or in any information storage or retrieval system, without permission in writing from the publishers.

Trademark notice: Product or corporate names may be trademarks or registered trademarks, and are used only for identification and explanation without intent to infringe.

British Library Cataloguing-in-Publication Data
A catalogue record for this book is available from the British Library

ISBN: 978-1-032-76200-5 (hbk)
ISBN: 978-1-032-76202-9 (pbk)
ISBN: 978-1-003-47753-2 (ebk)

DOI: 10.4324/9781003477532

Typeset in Times New Roman
by SPi Technologies India Pvt Ltd (Straive)

The publication presents the result of the Project no. 093/ZIE/2023/DOS financed from the subsidy granted to the Krakow University of Economics.

Contents

Figures

Tables

Authors' biographies

Zofia Gródek-Szostak (ORCiD: 0000-0001-6283-6952) is an Assistant Professor in the Department of Economics and Business at the Krakow University of Economics. She is an accredited consultant of the Polish Agency for Enterprise Development (PARP) in the field of proinnovative consulting services of the National Innovation Network (KSI) and general consulting services of the National Service System (KSU). She is the author of papers on public financing of investments and R&D works and on implementing innovative solutions in enterprises. Additionally, she is member of the Regional Studies Association (RSA) and The Polish Economic Society (PTE).

Urszula Grzega (ORCiD: 0000-0002-1220-7880) is an Associate Professor in the Department of Consumer Research at the University of Economics in Katowice. She researches, writes, and lectures on the consumption economics, household economics, household finances, consumer behavior, behavioral economics, sustainable consumption, and standard of living. She is member of a number of national and international research teams. She is a member of the PTE. She is the author of more than 150 publications.

Agata Niemczyk (ORCiD: 0000-0002-5594-6296) is an Associate Professor in the Department of Tourism at the Krakow University of Economics. She researches, writes, and lectures on consumer behavior, cultural and business tourism, tourism marketing, territorial marketing, silver economy, green entrepreneurship, and sustainable development. She is member of national and international research teams. She is member of the RSA and the PTE. She is the author and co-author of more than 250 publications.

Renata Seweryn (ORCiD: 0000-0002-5124-668X) is an Associate Professor in the Department of Tourism at the Krakow University of Economics, and the Plenipotentiary of the CUE Rector for the Quality of Education. She is the author and co-author of over 230 publications in the fields of tourism economics, business tourism, tourism marketing, tourists' satisfaction and loyalty, youth tourism, senior tourism, and leisure and tourist behaviour. She is member of the Intercollegiate Team of Experts at the Małopolska Tourism Organisation (researching the tourist traffic in Krakow and Malopolska), the Expert Team of the Foundation of the Cracow University of Economics (researching the meetings industry in Krakow), and the Krakow Tourism Expert Team (researching the impact of tourism and the meetings industry on the economy of Krakow).

Preface

It cannot be denied that the position of women has changed significantly over the centuries. The prospects for women's development are currently the greatest in the history of civilization. However, there are still many barriers and problems related to gender stereotypes, the perception of women, and building their image in public opinion, in social life, on the labor market, and in the media.

The issues highlighted in the book are analyzed against the sustainable development goals. This has been recognized as a paradigm for thinking about the future in which environmental, social, and economic considerations are balanced in striving to improve the quality of life of every person in accordance with the 5P principle (People, Planet, Prosperity, Peace, and Partnership).

The work aims to identify and characterize selected aspects of women's functioning in modern societies, in the context of the goals, assumptions, and challenges of sustainable development. The scope of the work covers the following perspectives: subjective – women, objective – areas of women's functioning in the dimensions of sustainable development, spatial – EU countries, time frame – 2010–2022.

The inferences were divided into five parts, to answer the following research questions:

- Q1 How diverse is the demographic situation of European women?
- Q2 How diverse are the EU countries in terms of gender equality?
- Q3 How do the sustainable development goals relate to the socio-professional and economic situation of women?
- Q4 How much has the entrepreneurship syndrome of women living in the EU changed?
- Q5 What is the scale of women's migration in the EU? How does migrant women's entrepreneurship rank in the EU?
- Q6 What is the position of women in selected sectors of the European economy?

The first part discusses the role of women in the modern economy and their demographic and social characteristics in the EU. The next one locates women's positions in the sustainable development goals, including through the perspective of EU horizontal policies. The third chapter offers an analysis of the living conditions of women in the EU, in terms of their socio-professional and economic situation and the management of their leisure time. The next part of the monograph refers to the problem of women's entrepreneurship in the EU in the aspect of social and geopolitical changes, including migration. The work ends with a chapter analyzing the situation of women in selected industry markets.

The book is addressed to students, scientists, and economic practitioners responsible for sustainable development, as well as social policy entities. The content presented allows a better understanding of the role of women in society of the 21st century. The results of the analyses constitute a useful decision-making premise for various institutions in the implementation of activities and formulating instruments for the sustainable development of EU countries and the entire world.

1 Women in society at the turn of the 21st century

Transformations of the woman's position in society at the turn of the 21st century

The transformation of the position of women in society at the turn of the 21st century is an important, interdisciplinary issue, which requires in-depth analysis of the literature on the subject. Scientific sources clearly show how the key issues of gender position as a determinant of social change have changed, along with cultural, social, and economic developments. Identifying the specific role of women in social development at the turn of the century became one of the key issues for understanding the changes taking place in modern civilization (Carter, 2021). Recognizing the benefits resulting from the feminization of social, political, and cultural life allows for understanding social transformations for broad participation of women in the economy, internationally and globally (Lundberg & Stearns, 2019). The consequence of these changes is the growing influence of women on the economy and the increasing importance of their role in social and political life. From an economic perspective, this fact is associated with many direct and indirect social and economic benefits. On the most recent published list of the most powerful women by McGrath (2023), the first four places are occupied by personalities holding high positions in politics, that is, Ursula von der Leyen, the first woman to lead the European Commission, age 65, from Belgium; Krystina Lagarde, age 67, from Germany; Kamala Harris, age 59, an American and the youngest in this group, as well as the 46-year-old Italian Giorgia Meloni (McGrath, 2023). The fact that their gender was not an obstacle to taking up such important functions as supervising government and EU authorities, or the most important international institutions and organizations, is an irrefutable proof of the enormous transformations that have occurred in the situation of women in Europe and the world at the turn of the 21st century. The literature indicates that leaders often share characteristics traditionally associated with masculinity, such as competitiveness, self-confidence, ambition, and aggressiveness (Koenig et al., 2011). This allows associating the image of women with attributes such as power, money, and social control. Currently, women's sphere of influence has a broad social scope. No longer are only men who shape the

DOI: 10.4324/9781003477532-1

trends and policies that define the world. The path to the current situation has historically been complicated and has required many individual and social efforts.

The observed change in the social paradigm, which is based on the increase in the role and position of women in the 21st century, requires analysis of its conditions, causes, and effects. The retrospective points to the beginnings outlined in classic feminist philosophy, which emphasized social and cultural constructions of gender and the importance of women's emancipation. It was then developed by gender studies, queer theory, cultural feminism, postfeminism, and the concept of gender performativity against the background of social theories of identity and power (Butler, 1999; Madsen, 2000). We are talking about the achievements of activists and authors such as Simone de Beauvoir, Michel Foucault, Judith Butler, Rozalinda Gill, Hélène Cixous, Luce Irigaray, and Julia Kristeva.

When discussing the issue of transformation of the situation of women, the most important thing is undoubtedly the granting of passive and active voting rights to women, which equaled the rights of men and women. Although the first countries began to introduce them only at the end of the 19th century (US Wyoming Territory, New Zealand, Australia), it was only in the 10th century that the democratization of women's political life flourished. This was largely due to the suffrage movement (Gidlow, 2021). These changes brought about questioning of the gender-based social order and are called the first wave of feminism (Mohajan, 2022). The male paradigm was understood as abstract, disembodied, rational, impartial, and independent, while women were assigned maternal roles associated with the domestic and not the public sphere. The norm was that a woman belonged to a man (her husband). She did not own property as a resource that would allow her to support herself independently. The economic dependence of a woman was one of the main factors that inhibited her influence in the social arena (Rubio-Marín, 2014).

As emphasized in the literature, in the years 1890–1930, the number of national women's political organizations that demanded the extension of women's suffrage in a country largely determined the likelihood of its female citizens obtaining the right to vote (Ramirez, Soysal, & Shanahan, 1997). In Europe, the first country to grant women passive and active suffrage was Finland (Grand Duchy of Finland), which at the time was an autonomous Russian province with its own parliament. This took place in 1906 and in 1908 Denmark followed Finland. The breakthrough came during World War I, when the situation of women changed dramatically. They took the place of men in the social sphere as they fought at the front. Work that provides financial independence has largely contributed to the emancipation of women (Rubio-Marín, 2014). The vote, partial or full, has been granted in a large number of European countries around the world, such as Norway, Iceland, Canada, Netherlands, Russia, Latvia, Estonia, Poland, Lithuania, Germany, Austria, Great Britain, Azerbaijan, Armenia, Kyrgyzstan, Uruguay, Sweden, Hungary, Belgium, Luxembourg, Georgia, Belarus, Ukraine, and the United States.

However, this process was very long and in fact continues to this day. Only at the end of the 20th century were these countries joined by (in chronological order): Iraq, Liechtenstein, Kuwait, Namibia, and Qatar. In addition, there are countries in the world where these women obtained the vote only in the 21st century. These are Bahrain, Oman, and the United Arab Emirates. The last country to introduce equal voting rights is Saudi Arabia, which introduced this legislation only in 2015 (Welch, 2015).

It is clear that the turn of the 21st century brought many opportunities to strengthen the position of women in society in the economic, social, psychological, educational, and political dimensions. These can be considered at multiple scales: self, family, community, and society. These issues are discussed in more detail in the subsequent chapters of this book. This does not change the fact that all these aspects currently spur economic transformation toward adopting and reinforcing policies and effective legislation that promote gender equality and empower women and girls at all levels (Reshi & Sudha, 2022). This fits the concept of sustainable development, especially Goal 5. From the point of view of social and economic sciences, the issue of gender equality deserves in-depth analysis in such categories as employment, education, health, politics, and culture (Fukui, Nakamura, & Steinsson, 2023). What is noteworthy here is the study of women's and men's access to education, the possibility to choose career paths, their promotion criteria, salary levels, and work–life balance, due to the social roles they perform (Jost & Möser, 2023). Defining gender as a social construct rather than a biological determination (men and women) was revolutionary.

When discussing the issue of transformations in the position of contemporary women, it is impossible not to discuss the role of mother, to which women are predestined due to their natural procreative function. Having been identified in previous centuries mainly with social expectations regarding the birth and upbringing of children, women do not feel such strong pressure to fulfill this mission these days. Especially in highly developed countries, women have fewer children at an increasingly later age, prioritizing their education and career. This also results in decreasing natural growth, especially in Europe. The current changes mean a decline in births and even the emergence of a new trend of not having children (child-free). It is accompanied by socially accepted hedonism, consumerism, and a reluctance to start families and get married. Services in the tourism, recreation, catering, and development industries that cannot be used by people with children are offered most often not for rational reasons, but rather to ensure the peace of mind of other clients (Kupriianova & Kupriianova, 2023). This change in the situation of women can be called discrimination based on having children. These aspects require interdisciplinary scientific analysis in ethics and morality, philosophy, biology, sociology, psychology, and demography.

The above-described transformations of the role of women in contemporary society are related to cultural conditions and social, family, and social policies pursued by the Member States. The literature on the subject raises the issue of two periods in women's lives that have a strong impact on their economic situation and determine their quality of life: the period of maternity leave and old age (Herbst-Debby & Achouche, 2023). The first of these periods is associated with the concepts of "motherhood penalty" and "fatherhood premium", or – more generally – "the family wage gap", that is, the pay gap that is a consequence of fulfilling the role of a parent. It appears during maternity leave and increases throughout women's professional lives. In turn, the period of old age is associated with the fact that women statistically live longer than men, which is associated with loneliness, psychological and physical failure, as well as poverty (Herbst-Debby & Achouche, 2023).

On the one hand, the feminization of social life seems to be a natural phenomenon today. On the other hand, gender inequalities are still observed in employment policy. The labor market and women's professional opportunities in building their career path are still one of the areas that require improvement when it comes to equal rights (Papangkorn, Chatjuthamard & Jiraporn, 2022). The mechanism of reward based on affiliation to a certain demographic group, rather than on the basis of their skills and abilities, is still valid, even in European countries that are considered to be the least discriminatory towards women. Therefore, a number of legislative provisions are being introduced, developed by the European Union and its bodies. These are the EU Strategy for Gender Equality 2020–2025 and Directive 2006/54/EC (Directive 2006/54/EC, 2006), for which the EU adopted binding measures on March 4, 2021. On the other hand, on 8 March 2022, the European Commission adopted a new EU-wide proposal for a directive on combating violence against women and domestic violence. On 22 November 2022, after 10 years of negotiations, the directive on gender balance on corporate boards was also adopted (Veldman, 2023). It aims to improve gender balance in corporate management positions in the largest listed companies in the EU. Moreover, the problem of gender discrimination is evidenced by the fact that on 8 March 2023 the European Commission launched a pan-European campaign to break down gender stereotypes (#EndGenderStereotypes, n.d.). It must still be emphasized that gender cannot influence career choices, the division of caregiving responsibilities, and the perception of a person's potential and limitations on the labor market. Gender diversity is one of the main sustainable development goals recommended for implementation (Czapran, 2023). The 20th and 21st centuries have introduced a major change in the scope of problems modern women face. While voting rights seem to be a natural privilege of women these days, the right to equal pay for the same work, stereotypical expectations regarding the roles played in society, which are shaped in the socialization process, and the values with which the female gender should identify are still the subject of social and scientific discourse.

This analysis of the literature on the subject leads to the question whether the world is still male-dominated? Women are still overrepresented in lower paid sectors and underrepresented in leadership positions. In this context, Directive 2019/1158/EU on work–life balance and the latest changes in the representation of women on company boards (Gender Balance on Management Boards Directive) also play an important role (Belova & Ivanova, 2022). From mid-2026, nonexecutive management boards of large companies will be required to have at least 40% of women, and in executive management boards and director positions, 33%. This applies to large companies with at least 250 employees (Belova & Ivanova, 2022). The introduction of quotas to protect the underrepresented gender, that is, women, is intended to counteract the "glass ceiling effect" (Dowling, 2017). Women who are as qualified as men, or often better, cannot be treated worse in recruitment, promotions, or remuneration policy. Research conducted by M. Zaccone (2023) shows that women are more likely to be promoted to the position of general director in enterprises that employ a large number of women and which value the principles of sustainable development and an organizational culture based on values and ethics.

Only during the COVID-19 pandemic was the discriminatory position of women in the European labor market become more evident. Of the 49 million healthcare workers in the EU, 76% are women (Rayner & Rayner, 2022), so they were overwhelmingly directly involved in combating the pandemic. It was a time-consuming physical and emotional burden for them, which had implications for their families and loved ones. Second, it should be noted that women, as the main staff of industries most exposed to quarantine and a drop in income, such as hotel industry, education, paid housework/cleaning services, have suffered the economic repercussions of this situation to a greater extent than men (Belova & Ivanova, 2022). Moreover, the apparent disproportionality in overall working hours in EU member states is highlighted. Women typically spend 13 hours more per week on unpaid care and housework, and 85% of single parents are women (Belova & Ivanova, 2022).

All these elements are currently of great importance on the labor market and affect the functioning of both the demand side of the market, for example, households, and the supply side, including enterprises and other organizations. Ultimately, these translate into economic development and competitiveness of economies. Similar effects have been noticed in the world of politics. Based on research conducted in European countries, it was found that a larger number of women in public institutions contribute to a better quality of management. Moreover, higher-quality government services contribute to women's political empowerment. Therefore, it is a two-way relationship. Factors such as the level of economic development, education, and social trust were taken into account in the study (Rios et al., 2023).

The appropriate phrase: "economy of the future is female" results mainly from the increased professional activity of women and their "economical contribution" of knowledge, commitment, special organizational and communication skills, the ability to compromise, flexibility, and other soft skills enabling the creation of beneficial business relationships (Lechman, 2019). Research shows that women-led microenterprises are committed to a business model in which the difference lies in providing value through relationships based on emotions and experiences. Social capital is not only about knowledge and business skills. Interpersonal relationships are also necessary, which is why certain personal and/or soft competencies, such as language skills, creativity, innovation, and empathy, can also contribute to its growth. These characteristics are attributed to the female gender and can determine the competitiveness of women in business (Aracil-Jordá et al., 2023).

The prospects for women's development are currently undoubtedly the greatest in the history of civilization, although there are still many barriers and problems related to gender stereotypes, the perception of women, and the creation of their image in public opinion, in social life, on the labor market and in the media (Ye, 2023). The female gender is invariably associated with multifactorial social exclusions, violence, mobbing, as well as economic discrimination and a greater risk of poverty (Hughes et al., 2015).

Despite the development of civilization, women still have to face the common problems of violence and sexual abuse, sexism, gaslighting, depreciation, humiliation, and object treatment, both in the family and professional environment. This also includes highly developed countries as well as Europe. Mass migrations and the cultural and religious changes that accompany them, on the one hand, contribute to highlighting customs and norms that are unfair to women. On the other hand, they cause cultural diffusion, also to the detriment of countries that receive refugees and migrants. An issue assigned only to the female sex is abortion legislation. In takes liberal or radical forms, depending on a country, putting women in a situation of moral, health-related, and legislative dilemmas. It is women who must face emotional, psychological and health consequences, moral trauma, victim syndrome, hypersensitivity, and a sense of helplessness. And societies bear the long-term costs, including the costs of support and specialized treatment to victims and their caregivers (Kupriianova & Kupriianova, 2023).

In recent years, that is, since 2017, a civil movement called #MeToo has emerged, raising the issue of sexual abuse against women in the workplace. This issue is also explored in the literature on the subject. A broad analysis of this problem was conducted by, among others, Zimerman, Rotenstein, and Anupam (2023). They pointed out the importance of persistent gender stereotypes in the workplace and considered whether public discussion on this topic brings more benefits or losses to the image and role of women in the professional arena in various industries.

The development of new technologies and artificial intelligence presents new categories of challenges that modern women face. The so-called fourth-wave feminism begins around 2012 and relies heavily on social media such as Facebook, Twitter, Instagram, or YouTube. There is emerging research on gender-neutral language in new media, on gender bias in virtual messengers, algorithms, and chat GPT, as well as on introducing feminatives into native languages (Đorđević, 2023).

The topic of transformations in the role of women in the 20th and 21st centuries is best concluded with the current motif of the pop culture icon, Barbie. Since 1958, the famous doll has been shaping the image and image of women in society. In the 2020s, it became synonymous with postfeminist criticism. The latest publications now emphasize the influence of this symbol on the questioning of the current expectations of women's permanent physical and social perfection, as well as their unlimited potential, in favor of an unrealistic, stereotypical image of femininity. It emphasizes the complex roles women play and the range of their life aspirations. Modern Barbie represents women's constant fight for freedom from stereotypes and expectations (Tang, 2023; Yakali, 2023). This makes it all the more necessary to study the contemporary image of women on an interdisciplinary basis, which requires an in-depth analysis. This point in history, in which the world and Europe find themselves will require further changes in social roles and relationships. Gender as a determinant of social, professional, and political activity plays a role in the context of the theory of needs, motivation, decision-making, quality of life, economic, and nonmaterial reasons (Bishu, Sabharwal & Reyes, 2023).

Womenomics

The term womenomics, which is a combination of the words "women" and "economics", in the simplest sense means women's economics. It is most often used in the context of the growing role of women in national economic and social life (Maitland & Wittenberg-Cox, 2013). The history of womenomics started in Japan in the early 1990s. It was then that Kathy Matsui, vice president and chief specialist for Japanese strategy at Goldman Sachs Japan, addressed the problem of women's advancement in society and professional life in her scientific research, in the perspective of the country's economic development. Kathy Matsui and her team pointed to the potential for economic growth resulting from women's greater involvement in professional work. Based on the results of their research, conducted from a macro and microeconomic perspective, the authors found that countries where women have equal status to men in government, work, and social position cope better with professional and economic problems compared to men. Kathy Matsui's theory, original at the time, was based on the assumption that removing structural obstacles in the women's labor market could stimulate GDP growth. Furthermore, allowing women to have equal access to economic participation could provide not only economic but also social benefits (Macnaughtan, 2015). Following this line of thinking, in 2013, Japanese Prime Minister Shinzo Abe initiated a progressive plan aimed at increasing employment and strengthening the position of women in the Japanese labor market, among other things. This policy was called "Womenomics" and was intended to be one of the pillars of Abe's economic growth strategy. Japan, although it achieved high rates of economic growth in the postwar period, has struggled with recurring financial crises, recessions, and deflation since the end of the 20th century. Public debt was also a big problem, accounting for 226% of annual GDP in 2013. On top of all that, the country was aging rapidly (Schad-Seifert, 2019). Part of Prime Minister Abe's goal to strengthen the position of women in the economy was a structural reform in which a woman's life would not be dictated only by marriage, childbirth, and raising children but would also focus on fulfilling her aspirations and professional goals. The prime minister had a vision of creating a society in which women would have the opportunity to "shine". He saw a clear need to build businesses that exploited the economic potential of women, among others, to offset the shrinking labor force. The assumptions Abe made were very correct and, as it turns out, they were verified in various places and times, but not in Japan itself. The conservatism that prevails in the country was indicated as the main factor that hampers the development of the Japanese economy by increasing the diversity of genders on the labor market. The role of women was still associated primarily with the role of wife, mother, and homemaker, although over time the patriarchy prevailing in society increasingly overwhelmed men as well (Bintang & Kurniawaty, 2021).

Japan's neoliberal policies have certainly provided women with a range of opportunities in terms of work, but the country's deep-rooted culture has not allowed them to "shine." In hindsight, it can be assessed that despite the efforts of the then and subsequent Japanese governments to create a gender-equal environment, not much progress was made in this area. Unfortunately, it probably would have ensured faster results in terms of economic growth. However, it should be added that over the last few years, gradual, slow but positive changes in women's social and professional life have been observed in Japan. Evidence of positive changes that can be observed was the election of a woman to the position of mayor of a city in Kyoto Prefecture in 2023 (Popko, 2024). In Japan and elsewhere, women's equal participation in economic life progresses too slowly, leading media and scholars to criticize womenomics as an unrealistic political concept lacking effective tools. Many women face obstacles to full-time employment and those in the labor market often hold secondary positions with limited promotion and earning opportunities, exacerbated by a lack of female role models in management (Elysia, Juniari & Devi, 2023).

As already mentioned, although the assumptions of womenomics encountered considerable resistance in Japan itself, over time they have gained importance in many global economies. Currently, they are a valid and extremely important subject of interest for researchers representing various scientific disciplines, including not only economics but also management. Currently, the concept of womenomics has a broad meaning and can be applied to various research perspectives, including macro and microeconomics. It is most often considered in the context of:

1 State policy and women's influence on the economy.
2 The importance of women in the labor market and their place in business.
3 Trends in women's purchasing behavior.

Starting with the macroeconomic role of women, it should be noted that in this context, womenomics is treated as a phenomenon that signifies the growing role of women in the national economic and social life. As scholars Vera

Mackie and Ayako Kano expressed it in a speech before UN members: "Feminism is a policy aimed at strengthening the economy and the nation, not only improving the situation of women" (Schieder, 2024). Gender equality and the full use of women's potential in the economy are becoming crucial for social and economic development. The insufficient representation of women in the national socioeconomic and political life in the period preceding the end of the 20th century resulted from the belief that these were the domains of men's lives. However, the 21st century brought an end to the perception of women as passive participants in these areas of life and contributed to the emergence of many initiatives involving women in development projects.

In 2006, "The Economist" stated that the future of the global economy lies with women. Reihan Salam, in "Foreign Policy," echoed this, suggesting the end of the "macho era" and attributing the economic collapse to male-driven high-risk ventures. Salam coined the term "hecession" to describe the recession caused by traditional male-dominated sectors like construction and heavy industry failing (Woźniak, 2013). With women making up about 60% of university graduates in developed countries, the concept of "womenomics" emerges, highlighting women's growing role in shaping the economy due to their education, talents, and skills.

Today, womenomics is a widely discussed topic in the context of economic, social, and educational policy. The efforts to promote it cover a wide range of initiatives, from gender equality legislation, educational programs, to investments in child and elder care. The main assumption of womenomics as a national policy is to use the full potential of women in the economy by promoting gender parity, supporting women at work, and working to eliminate obstacles hindering women's professional advancement (Schad-Seifert, 2019). However, it is important to remember that much remains to be done to implement specific solutions to the problems. This includes resolving the issues of wage differences, social stigma, and the double burden of being a homemaker and full-time mother and employee, as well as other demands placed on women. Furthermore, supportive policies are needed to ensure women have equal opportunities in their career paths (Elysia, Juniari & Devi, 2023). The interest in women's professional activity in the context of economic development is evidenced by awarding the Nobel Prize in Economics to Claudia Goldin. She is the third woman to receive this award in economics and the first to be honored exclusively in this category. Claudia Goldin studied the gender pay gap over two centuries. Her research shows that gender inequality hinders economic growth. Women earn less for the same work, which limits their opportunities and the economy's ability to fully utilize human resources. Goldin emphasizes that time spent raising children should be viewed as an economic investment. Including women's work in economic calculations is crucial because it affects social capital and retirement security. Goldin highlights the challenges women face in balancing home and work, advocating for equal career opportunities and social support. In countries that value empathy and cooperation, such as Finland and Sweden, the employment rate of women is higher. Conversely, in countries where masculine values such as activity, rivalry, competitiveness, and aggressiveness are prioritized, women's participation in the labor market decreases, as seen in Romania. Gender parity not only leads to social justice but also influences sustainable and long-term economic development (Perrin, 2024).

To sum up the importance of women in macroeconomics, note that in every society women are an important element of GDP growth. They constitute 50% of the population, and by entering the labor market, they are able to contribute to greater productivity and higher GDP. In the United Kingdom, a government-appointed commission reported that the country could gain an additional 2% of GDP by leveraging women's skills better. Raising women's participation in the labor market to the same level as men could significantly increase GDP (by as much as 9% to 21%), said the head of the IMF, Christine Lagarde, and the Prime Minister of Norway, Erna Solberg, in a joint document. Gender parity in the economy could increase the UK's GDP by USD 250 billion, the US GDP by USD 1,750 billion, Japan's GDP by USD 550 billion, France's GDP by USD 320 billion, and the Germany's GDP by USD 310 billion. Furthermore, it is estimated that the world as a whole could increase global GDP by 5.3 trillion USD by 2025, reducing the gender gap in labor force participation by 25% over the same period (Urs, 2018).

When looking at the other side of womenomics, that is, business, we should start with the fact that women were often employed in companies due to the policy of diversity and equal opportunities. Over time, company managers began to view women as individuals employed for profit. There are a number of studies conducted by scientists and specialists in the employment industry, from Michigan to California to Norway, that confirm the reality of the phenomenon called the "asset-to-estrogen ratio". Some research authors wrote more than a decade ago that women are not only valuable as employees, but in many cases even irreplaceable (Shipman & Kay, 2010). Therefore, in 2019, Griffin presented evidence that companies that promote women in management positions are more profitable, better organized, more responsible, motivated, and innovative (Griffin, 2019). There are studies showing that women are less prone to risk and aggressive behavior compared to their male counterparts and increasing the employment of women "inhibits the crazy risks taken by men, heads of corporations, and financial institutions" (Eisenstein, 2017, p. 38). The aforementioned Matsui, Suzuki, and Tatebe (2019) provided evidence of a positive relationship between having a gender-diverse leadership team and positive company performance. In the months after the US financial crisis, this research was cited as evidence that the crisis could have been avoided if more women worked in the financial sector. It was also pointed out that women's skills may be crucial in overcoming the crisis (Prügl, 2012). In 2001, Professor Roy Adler from Pepperdine University discovered in his study published in the Harvard Business Review that companies that promoted more women also performed better financially. These results were quite revolutionary at the time. The research cited specific numbers related to the employment of women and the increase in company profitability. Roy Adler and his colleagues examined data from more than two hundred Fortune 500 companies and found that the 25 companies that employ the highest percentage of women, relative to all entities surveyed, achieved above-industry median results (Urs, 2018). There is also a famous saying of Professor Harvey Wagner from the University of North Carolina, who wrote based on his research: "If you analyse a company with no women on its management board, you will find a company with problems". Also noteworthy are two separate studies conducted in 2007 by the business research companies McKinsey and Catalyst. They have shown that companies in Europe and the United States with as many women on their boards as possible are more profitable than others. The banking crisis and the collapse of Lehman Brothers sparked a debate about whether more women in leadership positions would help improve corporate governance. It was often said: "If Lehman had more sisters instead of brothers, it would probably survive". Practically, since the beginning of the crisis, various theories have emerged regarding the inclusion of more women in the world of finance and formal matters. It was assumed that women could protect the economy against the risk of another global financial collapse but would also stimulate economies struggling after the crisis (Strauß, 2023). McKinsey's research has once again confirmed that a larger number of women in management positions improves financial results. Following his research results, the Zurich-based Swiss investment firm Naissance Capital launched the Women's Leadership Fund ($2 billion) in January 2018 to invest in companies with women on management boards. In Norway, the government was so convinced of women's contribution to economic success that it mandated that 40% of every company's board members be women. And in this case, it was not so much about political correctness, but rather about ensuring that companies were competitive and profitable. From research conducted in the United Kingdom, Cranfield University School of Management also shows that companies with women on the board perform better than their less diverse competitors. A study by Leeds Business School found that having at least one woman on the board reduced the risk of company liquidation by 20% and having two or three women directors further reduced the risk of bankruptcy (based on data from 17,000 UK companies) (Urs, 2018).

These studies, as well as other, created the theoretical framework that led to the development of business feminism. Financial institutions, non-governmental organizations, and multinational corporations increasingly view women as an "untapped resource" that can provide high returns on investment (Eisenstein, 2017). Therefore, it is once again important to empower women by including them in the market economy. Investing in women and providing them with the opportunity to apply for loans and greater investment in human capital (i.e., education, health care, etc.) will bring tangible benefits to the entire business (Roberts, 2012). According to Eisenstein, including women in solving economic problems can help repair and ensure the future of existing business structures (Calkin, 2018). Fodor, Glass and Nagy (2018) believe that the more women there are in top positions in corporate hierarchies, the more society will become equal as a whole. Yet another advantage of employing women is the diversity of opinions that women bring.

Based on the above research, it can also be concluded that the time for employing and retaining women due to political correctness or good appearance is irrevocably over. Women add value in every way. As employees, they are conscientious, efficient, and effective, bringing a different perspective and work style. Greater saturation with the "feminine element" brings about a qualitative change in organization and management. Women are characterized by a more democratic style of managing the work of their subordinates, and, compared to men, they attach greater importance to the harmony of interpersonal relations. They also strive for strong group integration and eliminate conflicts in the group. Importantly, women managers tolerate failure better than men and are characterized by greater flexibility and greater adaptability. A higher percentage of women in high management positions can also influence the culture of the organization in terms of ethics. This could impact, for example, more fair trade principle-based ventures or reduce the share of those that involve involvement in morally reprehensible, corruption-related processes.

Combining the above threads and referring to the previously discussed womenomics, it is noteworthy that from an economic perspective, the growing participation of women in professional life is associated with many direct and indirect social and economic benefits. The accurate phrase: "the economy of the future is women" stems mainly from the increased professional activity of women who contribute their knowledge, commitment, special organizational, and communication skills, the ability to compromise, flexibility, and other soft skills, which foster beneficial business relationships (Lechman, 2019). All these elements are currently of great importance on the labor market and affect the functioning of both the demand side of the market, for example, households, and the supply side. This includes enterprises and other organizations and ultimately brings economic development and competitiveness of economies.

The third approach to womenomics refers to a woman as an active consumer responsible for purchasing products to meet her personal needs and the needs of her family. Marketing experts, citing data from the world's largest economies, emphasize that the woman is the most important consumer in the 21st century as well as the driving force of the modern economy. Research from Boston Consulting Group shows that American women are responsible for 94% of home furnishings spending. The choice of holiday offers, purchase of a house or apartment, and a car is also her domain, 92%, 91%, and 60%, respectively. This is because more and more women are professionally active and and therefore they willingly choose products that emphasize their value and strength. The global consulting company EY in its report "The role of women in global economic growth" predicts that by 2028, women will be responsible for decisions involving up to 75% of consumer spending. Therefore, brands that want to appeal to women's tastes should be like a mobile app. They should provide products that will help women organize their daily schedule and optimize their time (Stopyra-Fiedorowicz, 2018). It is worth emphasizing that an increasing number of women are achieving the status of financially independent consumers who decide on the household budget. Kathy Matsui noticed this trend a decade ago, creating a basket of 115 companies whose activities are largely focused on female customers. This group included, among others: representatives of companies in the textile industry, beauty industry, financial services, and retail (Woźniak, 2013). Taking into account the above, the concept of womenomics should be identified with the active role of women in the market of consumer goods and services. It should also be treated as a growing trend in consumer purchasing behavior. As the most frequent shoppers in their households, women shop not only for themselves but for the entire family. They choose products for children, husbands, or partners, for the home, for animals, for distant relatives, etc. Men more often act as influencers of these purchases than those responsible for making them. Therefore, taking into account this large and growing female power in making purchasing decisions, what needs to be taken into account, for example, is the increasing popularity of bio, food, cosmetic, and chemical products, the so-called clean labels. These are products with a simple and understandable product composition, not only in terms of health but also in terms of environmental protection. This approach to women as a growing consumer power can also help companies deal with climate dilemmas, diversity, and corporate responsibility standards (Heins, 2023).

The growing purchasing power of women combined with their increasing decision-making in their households once again shows their influence on stimulating the economy, this time through consumption.

Finally, it should be emphasized that the women's economy is the economy of the future. Every year, the quantitative and qualitative impact and contribution of women to the economy increase, at every possible level. A future marked by greater and growing participation of women in socioeconomic life seems inevitable. Their importance is now greater than ever (Tse et al., 2024).

Statistics on women in the EU

The following section presents basic demographic statistics of women in the European Union. Comparative research in this area enables the identification of demographic and social differences in spatial arrangements, including by gender. This facilitates monitoring the progress toward achieving gender equality and pinpointing where inequalities exist. Such research undoubtedly supports the development of scientific knowledge on gender differences and allows for the indirect identification of factors influencing these differences. Comparative research on gender differences also allows for better adaptation of public and social policies to the needs of both women and men in individual market sectors and in living conditions in general. Gender statistics is an area that crosses traditional statistical fields to identify, collect, and disseminate knowledge on the actual living conditions of women and men. It thus raises policy issues relating to gender equality (UNECE, 2010).

Eurostat data shows that in 2022, the total population of the EU-27 was 446.8 million people. The population, although it decreased slightly compared to 2020, increased over the years 2010–2022. In 2010, it numbered 440.6 million, that is, it was 6 million lower than in the year closing the analysis period (Figure 1.1). Although the overall population of the EU has increased, not all Member States have seen growth. A total of eight countries saw population decline, the rest saw population growth or stagnation. The population of individual EU countries in 2022 ranged from 0.5 million in Malta to 83.2 million in Germany. Germany, France, and Italy accounted for almost half (47%) of the total EU population in 2022 (Eurostat, 2023a).

In the years 2010–2022, the total number of women in the EU increased, but in the three years of the analysed period, it was lower than the year before (Figure 1.2). The first slight decline was recorded in 2011, and the next two in 2021–2022. In 2022, the number of women living in the EU amounted to 228.4 million and was higher by 2.6 million compared to 2010. At the same time, the number of women was higher than the number of men by 10 million, which means almost 5% more women than men, and 51.1% of the total EU population in 2022 were women.

The greatest advantage in the number of women over the number of men was observed in Latvia and Lithuania where there were 116 and 115 women per 100 men, respectively (Figure 1.3). A large predominance of the number of women in relation to the number of men, that is, over 6 percent, was also noted in: Estonia, Portugal, Hungary, Croatia, Poland, France, Bulgaria, and Romania. In a group of countries such as Malta, Luxembourg, Sweden, and Slovenia, a predominance of men over women was recorded in 2022. The most significant difference can be seen in Malta, where there are 93 women per 100 men (Eurostat, 2024a). In the case of other countries not mentioned

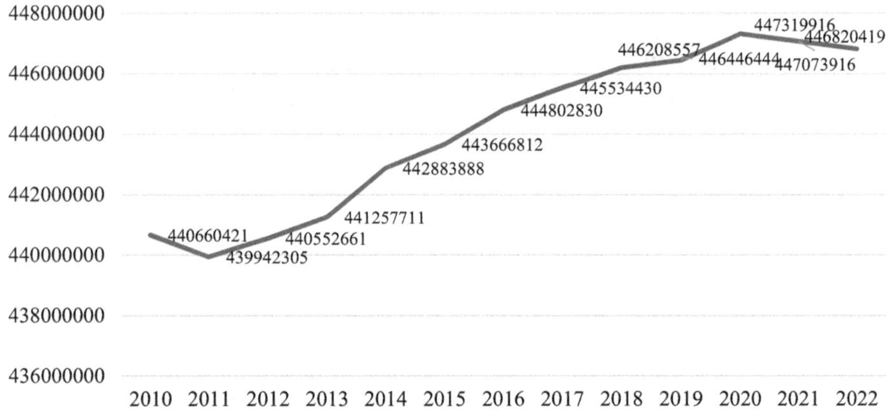

Figure 1.1 Population in the European Union in 2010–2022.

Source: Eurostat (2024a).

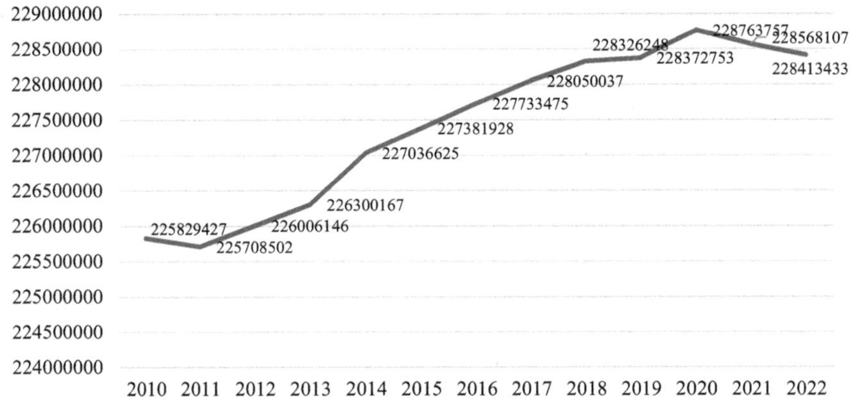

Figure 1.2 Number of women in the European Union in 2010–2022.

Source: Eurostat (2024a).

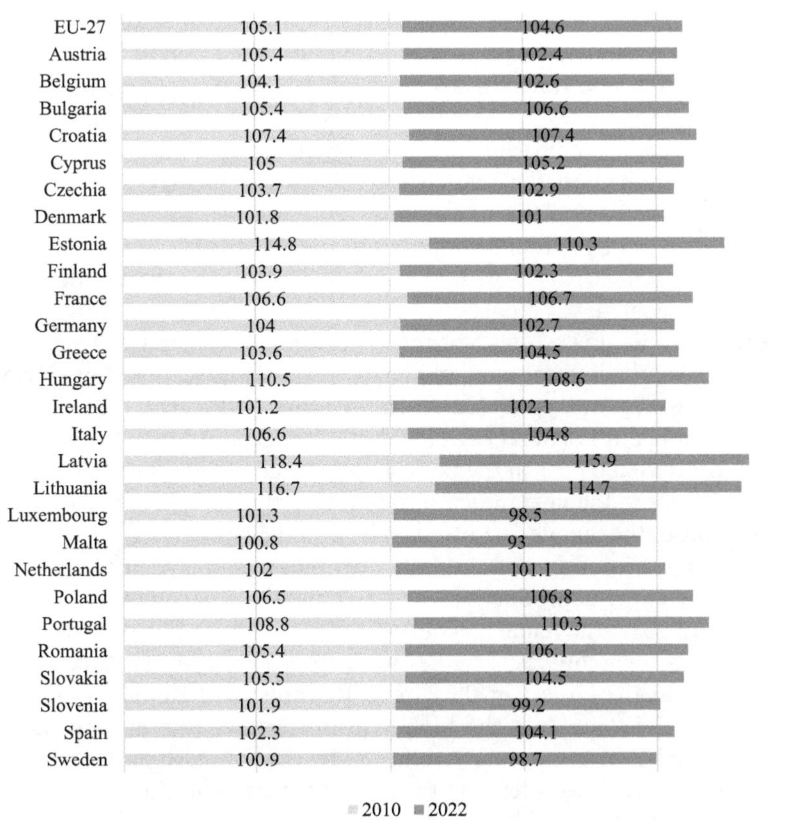

Figure 1.3 Women per men in European Union in 2010 and 2022.

Source: Eurostat (2024a).

earlier, it was observed that women slightly outnumber men, which is now treated as a normal phenomenon.

The relatively small changes in numbers and gender structure of the population that took place in the EU-27 in the years 2010–2022 were mainly caused by natural increase and migration. Some negative changes in the population, including the number of women, observed at the end of the period under study were most likely the result of the COVID-19 pandemic. They resulted in an increased number of deaths in some EU regions, a decline in fertility, limited migration related to the closure of borders, and difficulties economic related to job loss or job instability. Note that the age structure of the EU population has changed over the analysed period. Eurostat research shows that in the years 2010–2022, the share of the population aged 80+, as well as the share of people aged 65 and over, increased (Niemczyk et al., 2023). This observation applies to all Member States (in 2022, the 65+ age group accounted for as much as 21% of the total population). The highest share of seniors in the total population was recorded in Italy and Portugal (24% each), as well as in Finland and Greece (23% each), and the lowest in Ireland and Luxembourg (15% each). Similarly, a decline in the share of young people (aged 0–19) was observed. In 2022, the highest percentage of young people was recorded in Ireland (26%), the lowest in Malta and Italy (18%) (Eurostat, 2023b). Society aging is a problem that affects both sexes, but it is known that statistically, women live longer than men. This means that there are more women than men in an aging society. An indicator confirming the fact in the EU is the median age of women (Table 1.1).

The average age of the female population in the EU in 2022 was 46 years, 3 years higher than in 2010. In 2022, among the EU Member States, the highest median age of women was recorded in Italy (49.4 years), followed by Portugal (48.3 years), and the lowest in Cyprus (39 years) and Ireland (39.4). For comparison, in 2010, the highest median age of women was recorded in Germany (45.3) and the lowest in Cyprus (36.4). In the years 2010–2022, the median age increased the most in Portugal (by 5.5 years), the least in Malta (0.3), while in Sweden, it decreased by 0.1 in the period under study (Eurostat, 2024d).

When it comes to the next indicator describing the demographics of women in the EU, that is, the female fertility rate, it should be noted that this is a measure determining the number of children a woman would give birth to on average during her entire reproductive period. This value declined in 2010–2021 (Figure 1.4). In 2010, the female fertility rate for the entire EU was 1.57, and in 2021, it was 1.53. The highest declines were recorded in Malta, Luxembourg, and Finland and the largest in the Czech Republic and Romania (Eurostat, 2024b). In 2021, France had the highest total fertility rate among Member States (1.84 live births per woman), followed by the Czech Republic (1.83) and Romania (1.81). The lowest fertility rates were recorded in Malta (1.13), Spain (1.19), and Italy (1.25) – Table 1.1. In general, the value of the female fertility rate in the EU is so low that it does not ensure a level of reproduction that guarantees simple replacement of generations. For this level to be maintained

Table 1.1 Women in the European Union (EU = 27) – demographic characteristics

Subject/Geo	*Women in M.*		*Median age of females*		*Total fertility rate*		*Mean age of women at birth of first child*		*Mean age at first marriage women*		*Life expectancy*	
	2010	*2022*	*2010*	*2022*	*2010*	*2021*	*2010*	*2021*	*2010*	*2021*	*2010*	*2022*
EU-27	225.9	228.4	42.7	45.9	1.57	1.53		29.7			82.9	83.4
Austria	4.3	4. 6	42.8	45.2	1.44	1.48	28.2	29.9			83.5	83.5
Belgium	5.5	5.9	42.1	43.0	1.86	1.60	28.0	29.5	29.4	32.2	83.0	83.9
Bulgaria	3.8	3.5	44.5	47.1	1.57	1.58	25.6	26.5	26.6	28.3	77.4	78.1
Croatia	2.2	2.0	43.9	47.4	1.55	1.58	27.5	29.2	27.1	28.8	79.9	80.8
Cyprus	0.4	0.5	36.4	39.0	1.44	1.39	28.5	30.3			83.9	83.6
Czechia	5.3	5.3	41.3	45.1	1.51	1.83	27.6	28.8	27.9	29.9	80.9	82.0
Denmark	2.8	3.0	41.4	43.4	1.87	1.72		30.0	31.2	33.0	81.4	83.2
Estonia	0.7	0.7	43.7	45.8	1.72	1.61	26.3	28.5	28.0		80.8	82.4
Finland	2.7	2.8	43.5	45.0	1.87	1.46	28.3	29.8	30.2	32.1	83.5	83.8
France	33.4	35.0	41.2	43.7	2.03	1.84		29.1	30.7		85.3	85.2
Germany	41.7	42.2	45.3	47.6	1.39	1.58	28.9	30.1			83.0	83.3[a]
Greece	5.7	5.3	42.4	47.5	1.48	1.43	29.1	31.0	29.3	30.9	83.3	83.3
Hungary	5.3	5.0	42.3	45.8	1.25	1.61	27.7	28.6	28.3	29.7	78.6	79.5
Ireland	2.3	2.6	34.4	39.4	2.05	1.78	26.9	31.2	31.3		83.1	84.3[a]
Italy	30.5	30.2	44.7	49.4	1.46	1.25		31.6	30.3	33.0	84.7	85.0
Latvia	1.1	1.0	44.3	47.7	1.36	1.57	26.0	27.7	27.1	30.0	78.0	79.6
Lithuania	1.7	1.5	43.2	47.9	1.50	1.36	26.4	28.3	26.5	28.6	78.9	80.3
Luxembourg	0.3	0.3	39.6	40.2	1.63	1.38	29.5	31.3	30.2	32.4	83.5	85.3
Malta	0.2	0.3	41.3	41.6	1.36	1.13	27.4	29.5	28.6		83.6	84.8
Netherlands	8.4	8.8	41.4	43.7	1.79	1.62	29.2	30.3	29.8	32.0	83.0	83.2
Poland	19.6	19.4	39.9	43.7	1.41	1.33	26.5	28.1	26.1		80.7	81.3
Portugal	5.5	5.4	42.8	48.3	1.39	1.35	28.1	30.4	27.7	32.0	83.2	84.5
Romania	10.4	9.8	41.7	45.3	1.59	1.81	25.5	27.1	25.6	27.5	77.7	79.3
Slovakia	2.8	2.8	38.7	43.3	1.43	1.63	27.0	27.3	27.2	28.9	79.3	80.6
Slovenia	1.0	1.0	43.2	46.3	1.57	1.64	28.4	29.0	29.0	31.4	83.1	84.1
Spain	23.5	24.2	41.1	46.2	1.37	1.19	29.8	31.6	30.9	34.7	85.5	85.9
Sweden	4.7	5.2	41.8	41.7	1.98	1.67	28.9	29.8	32.7		83.6	84.8

Source: Eurostat (2024a, 2024b, 2024c, 2024d, 2024e, 2024f).

[a] 2021.

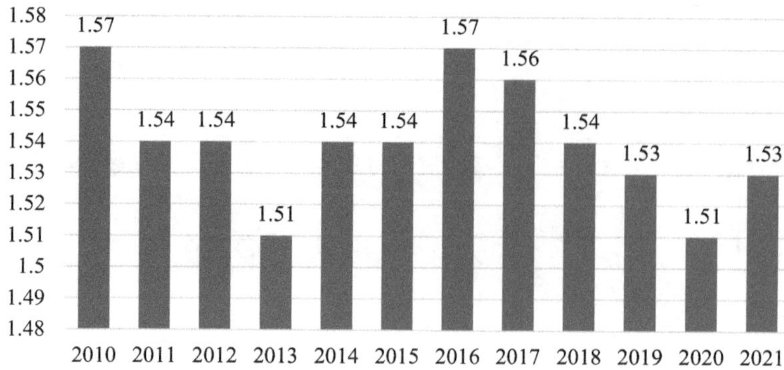

Figure 1.4 Total fertility rate in the European Union in 2010–2021.

Source: Eurostat (2024b).

and to ensure the natural replacement of generations, the fertility rate should range from 2.1 to 2.15 (GUS, 2011). The above situation has put the EU community in the area of the so-called narrowed population reproduction, as evidenced by the net and gross reproduction rates, the natural growth rate and the number of live births (Eurostat, 2023b). For years, demographic factors (including the number of marriages entered into and dissolved) and social factors (including lack of work, poverty, concerns about social exclusion) have been mentioned among the reasons for the lower fertility rate among women. The main economic reason for the low fertility rate of women is the poor financial situation of families. Sociologists define the state related to the current demographic situation of the population as the crisis of the family in Western culture (Grzega, 2012).

When analysing the demographic situation of women in the EU, note the age of women giving birth to their first child and the age of women entering their first marriage (Table 1.1). Despite incomplete data for all Member States, the trend that could be observed was the increasing age of women at the time of giving birth to their first child and entering marriage for the first time. Data on the age of mothers at first birth from 2013 shows that the rate was 28.8 years for the EU-27. This number has increased every year, reaching 29.7 in 2021. Between 2010 and 2021, the average age of mothers giving birth to their first child increased in all Member States under study. The highest increase occurred in Estonia and Lithuania, while the lowest in France. In 2021, the oldest mothers giving birth to their first child were residents of Italy and Spain (31.6 years), and the youngest were from Bulgaria (26.5) and Romania (27.1). Eurostat data also shows that the age of women at first marriage has increased in all EU Member States for which data were available. The greatest increase was observed in Portugal (from 27.7 years in 2010 to 32 in 2021) and Spain (from 30.9 to 34.7), the least – in Hungary (from 28.3 to 29.7). In 2021, the highest average age of women at first marriage was recorded in Spain (34.7) and the youngest in Romania (27.5) (Eurostat, 2024e).

Life expectancy is an indicator expressing a person's average number of years to live at the time of birth. Note that this indicator is treated as a synthetic measure of the standard of living and is also a reflection of the overall living conditions of society. This includes working conditions, social and environmental conditions, housing, educational and other personal conditions, and even diet. Assessment of the standard of living using the average life expectancy index is primarily used to determine the health status of the population, the effects of health-related activities, and the level of civilization development of societies, especially in the long term. It is also an important element of the demographic characteristics of the population or its part due to selected characteristics, for example, gender.

Data in Figure 1.5 shows that in the period 2010–2022, women's life expectancy at birth increased by 0.5 years. The life expectancy index reached its highest value in 2019 and was 84 years. Then, it decreased for the next two years, compared to the previous year, by 0.8 and 0.3, respectively.

These declines were most likely the result of an increase in mortality due to the COVID-19 pandemic. Eurostat data shows that in 2022, the life expectancy for women in the EU was 83.4 years and for men 78 years, which means that women live on average 5.4 years longer than men. Longer life expectancy for women applies to all EU Member States, with the largest differences between men and women in Latvia (9.8) and Lithuania (8.8), and the smallest in the Netherlands (2.9). In 2022, the highest life expectancy at birth for women was estimated in Spain (85.9) and Luxembourg (85.3), and the lowest in Bulgaria (78.1) and Romania (79.3). Life expectancy, although it decreased in the period 2020–2021, still shows an increasing trend in the long term. The increase in this value over a long period of time is due to many factors, such as reduced infant

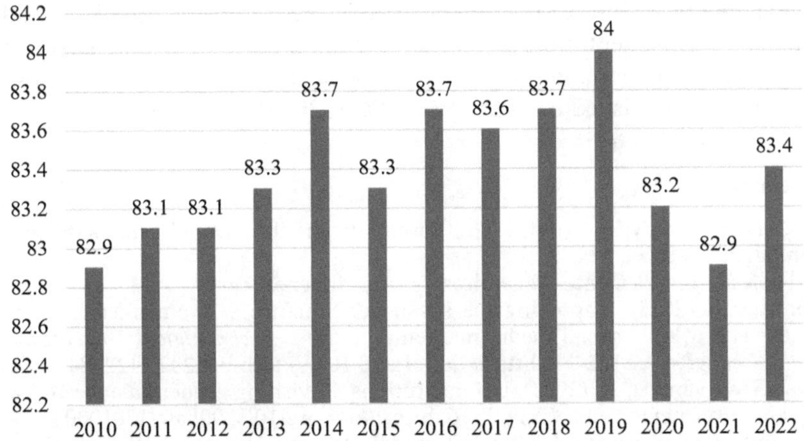

Figure 1.5 Women's life expectancy at birth in EU in 2010–2022.

Source: Eurostat (2024f).

mortality, increasing living standards, improved lifestyles and better education, as well as advancement in health care and medicine.

Conclusions

The summary states that the feminization of social life is a natural phenomenon today. This is not only due to the domination of women, who prevail in almost all EU countries, but also due to their inclusion in development projects, political, business, and economic life. There is no denying that in every society, women are an important contributor to GDP growth. The prospects for women's development are currently the greatest in the history of civilization.

However, on the other hand, inequalities in employment policies based on gender are emphasized, and women with equal, if not better qualifications than men cannot be treated worse in recruitment, promotions, and remuneration policies. The pursuit of equal rights is part of the sustainable development goals (Goal 5). This means the right to equal pay for the same work as men, but also gender equality in the areas of education, health, politics, and culture.

In this perspective, a new order in the economy is ahead, where women will decide and resolve important social and economic matters much more effectively than before. This fulfills the idea of womenomics, which states that the economy of the future is a woman, as reflected in the saying "*if Lehman had more sisters instead of brothers, he would probably survive*" (and the 2008 economic crisis could have been avoided). In addition, the coexistence of women and men in management is an opportunity for better development of a company or organization, both in theory and in practice. Diverse teams make better decisions because they take into account many different perspectives. Thus, they generate more ideas, are more creative, more innovative, and better adapt decisions to implementation options in a specific place and time. Diversity in management supports adapting to the needs of different audience groups and helps achieve established business goals (POT, 2023).

References

#EndGenderStereotypes (n.d.). Retrieved from https://end-gender-stereotypes.campaign.europa.eu

Aracil-Jordá, J., Clemente-Almendros, J.-A., Jiménez-Zarco, A.-I. & González-González I. (2023). Improving the social performance of women-led microenterprises: The role of social media marketing actions. *Technological Forecasting and Social Change*, *191*, 122484. https://doi.org/10.1016/j.techfore.2023.122484

Belova, G. & Ivanova, A. (2022). EU institutions: Revisiting gender balance and women's empowerment. *Laws*, *12*(1), 1–16. https://doi.org/10.3390/laws12010003

Bintang, A. & Kurniawaty, I. (2021). Towards sustainable society: Womenomics and women employment in Japan. Bintang Aulia and Kurniawaty Iskandar 2021. *IOP Conference Series: Earth and Environmental Science*, *716*(1), 012103. https://doi.org/10.1088/1755-1315/716/1/012103

Bishu, S. G., Sabharwal, M. & Reyes, R. (2023). Careers of women public managers: Career needs of women public managers across generations. *Public Administration Review*, *83*(1), 163–180.

Butler, J. (1999). *Gender trouble*. New York: Routledge.

Calkin, S. (2018). The World Bank and the challenge of 'the business case' for feminist IPE. In J. Elias & A. Roberts (Eds.), *Handbook on the international political economy of gender*. Cheltenham, United Kingdom: Edward Elgar Publishing. 311–322.

Carter, L. (2021). Women historians in the twentieth century. In H. Egginton & Z. Thomas (Eds.), *Precarious professionals: Gender, identities and social change in modern Britain*. University of London Press. 263–286. http://www.jstor.org/stable/j.ctvz0hcf9.16

Czapran, T. (2023). *Applying the concept of diversity management in IT and robotics organisations*. Sofia: The Bulgarian Academy of Science.

Directive 2006/54/EC. (2006). Retrieved from https://eur-lex.europa.eu/legal-content/EN/TXT/?uri=celex:32006L0054

Dorđević, J. (2023). Debiasing Europe with ChatGPT: Using the new 'device' to reduce the impact of gender bias in AI-generated discourse. *Conference – Observatory of the discourses of/on Europe "Europe's devices, European devices?"*, 16–17 November 2023, GRIPIC- CELSA Sorbonne Université, Paris-Neuilly, France.

Dowling, G. (2017). The glass ceiling: Fact or a misguided metaphor? *Annals in Social Responsibility*, *3*, 23–41. https://doi.org/10.1108/ASR-05-2017-0002. https://www.emerald.com/insight/content/doi/10.1108/ASR-05-2017-0002/full/pdf?title=the-glass-ceiling-fact-or-a-misguided-metaphor

Eisenstein, H. (2017). Hegemonic feminism, neoliberalism and womenomics: 'Empowerment' instead of liberation? *New Formations: A Journal of Culture/Theory/Politics*, 91, 35–49.

Elysia, J., Juniari, N. & Devi, N. (2023). Womenenomics: Gender inclusivity as a grow strategy in Japan. *Journal Transformasi Global*, *10*(5), 47–58.

Eurostat. (2023a). EU population increases again after two years decrease 11 July 2023. Retrieved from https://ec.europa.eu/eurostat/en/web/products-eurostat-news/w/edn-20230711-1

Eurostat. (2023b). Demography 2023 edition, Interactive publications. Retrieved from https://ec.europa.eu/eurostat/web/interactive-publications/demography-2023

Eurostat. (2024a). Population in k. in 2022; Females in k. in 2022; Women per men in 2022. Retrieved from https://ec.europa.eu/eurostat/databrowser/view/demo_pjan__custom_9548541/default/table?lang=en

Eurostat. (2024b). Total fertility rate in 2021 - wpółczynnik dzietności. Retrieved from https://ec.europa.eu/eurostat/databrowser/view/tps00199/default/table?lang=en

Eurostat. (2024c). Mean age of women at birth of first child in 2021 – średni wiek kobiet rodzących pierwsze dziecko. Retrieved from https://ec.europa.eu/eurostat/databrowser/view/tps00017/default/table?lang=en

Eurostat. (2024d). Median age of females in 2022. Retrieved from https://ec.europa.eu/eurostat/databrowser/view/demo_pjanind/default/table?lang=en

Eurostat. (2024e). Mean age at first marriage women in 2021. Retrieved from https://ec.europa.eu/eurostat/databrowser/view/DEMO_NIND__custom_9565652/default/table?lang=en

Eurostat. (2024f). Life expectancy by age and sex. Retrieved from https://ec.europa.eu/eurostat/databrowser/view/DEMO_MLEXPEC__custom_3842762/bookmark/table?lang=en&bookmarkId=ec51edd8-75d3-44ea-9389-6c60199a1c5f

Fodor, E., Glass, C., & Nagy, B. (2018). Transnational business feminism: Exporting feminism in the global economy. *Gender, Work and Organization*, *26*(8), 1117–1137.

Fukui, M., Nakamura E., & Steinsson J. (2023). Women, wealth effects, and slow recoveries. *American Economic Journal: Macroeconomics*, *15*(1), 269–313. https://doi.org/10.1257/mac.20200312

Gidlow, L. (2021). Woman suffrage, women's votes. In N. A. Hewitt & A. M. Valk (Eds.), *A companion to American women's history*, chapter twelve. John Wiley & Sons Ltd. https://doi.org/10.1002/9781119522690.ch12

Griffin, P. (2019). The everyday practices of global finance: Gender and regulatory politics of 'diversity'. *International Affairs*, *95*(6), 1215–1233.

Grzega, U. (2012). Sytuacja społeczno-zawodowa i ekonomiczna kobiet w Polsce [The social, professional, and economic situation of women in Poland]. In E. Kieżel & S. Smyczek (Eds.) *Zachowania rynkowe kobiet. Wybory i determinanty*. Warszawa: Placet.

GUS. (2011). *Wskaźniki zrównoważonego rozwoju Polski* [*Sustainable development indicators of Poland*]. Katowice: Wydawnictwo GUS i Urzędu Statystycznego w Katowicach. s. 21.

Heins, M. (2023). The development of "transnational business feminism" in global finance: Contextualizing Japan's "womenomics" policies in times of crisis. *Studies in Risk and Sustainable Development*, *397*, 1–10.

Herbst-Debby A. & Achouche N. (2023). Double jeopardy: Gendered social policy for two risky life periods in six welfare state contexts. *Women's Studies International Forum*, *100*, 102814. https://doi.org/10.1016/j.wsif.2023.102814

Hughes, C., Bolis, M., Fries, R., & Finigan, S. (2015). Women's economic inequality and domestic violence: Exploring the links and empowering women. *Gender and Development*, *23*(2), 279–297. https://doi.org/10.1080/13552074.2015.1053216

Jost, M. & Möser, S. (2023). Salary, flexibility or career opportunity? A choice experiment on gender specific job preferences. *Frontiers in Sociology*, *8*(17), 1154324. https://doi.org/10.3389/fsoc.2023.1154324. PMID: 37139224; PMCID: PMC10150105.

Koenig, A. M., Eagly, A. H., Mitchell, A. A. & Ristikari, T. (2011). Are leader stereotypesmasculine? A meta-analysis of three research paradigms. *Psychological Bulletin*, *137*(4), 616–642. https://doi.org/10.1037/A0023557

Kupriianova, L. & Kupriianova, D. (2023). Medical, legal, philosophical and socioeconomical prerequisites of decrease of the fertility rate in Europe. *Grail of Science*, 459–471. https://doi.org/10.36074/grail-of-science.15.09.2023.73

Lechman, E. (2019). Still 'few, slow and low'? On the female dimension of technology, labour markets and economic activity: Evidence for the period of 1990–2017. *Economics and Sociology*, *12*(1), 11–38. https://doi.org/10.14254/2071-789X.2019/12-1/1

Lundberg, S. & Stearns, J. (2019). Women in economics: Stalled progress. *Journal of Economic Perspectives*, *33*(1), 3–22. https://doi.org/10.1257/jep.33.1.3

Macnaughtan, H. (2015). Womenomics for Japan: Is the Abe policy for gendered employment viable in an era of precarity? *The Asia-Pacific Journal*, *12/1*(13), 1–23.

Madsen, D. L. (2000). *Feminist theory and literary practice*. Pluto Press. https://doi.org/10.2307/j.ctt18fs482

Maitland, A., & Wittenberg-Cox, A. (2013). *Kobiety i ich wpływ na biznes. Nowa rewolucja gospodarcza* [*Women and their impact on business: A new economic revolution*]. Warszawa: Oficyna a Wolters Kluwer business.

Matsui, K., Suzuki, H., & Tatebe, K. (2019). *Report: Womenomics 5.0*. Goldman Sachs Bank. https://www.goldmansachs.com/intelligence/pages/womenomics-5.0/multimedia/womenomics-5.0-report.pdf 22.04.2024

McGrath, M. (2023). The world's most powerful women. *Forbes*. Retrieved from https://www.forbes.com/lists/power-women/?sh=395c465a958f

Mohajan, H. (2022). Four waves of feminism: A blessing for global humanity. *Studies in Social Science & Humanities*, *1*, 1–8. https://doi.org/10.56397/SSSH.2022.09.01

Niemczyk, A., Szalonka, K., Gardocka-Jałowiec, A., Nowak, W., Seweryn, R. & Gródek-Szostak, Z. (2023). *The silver economy an ageing society in the European Union*. London: Routledge.

Papangkorn, S., Chatjuthamard, P., & Jiraporn, P. (2022). *Gender diversity and corporate governance*. IntechOpen. https://doi.org/10.5772/intechopen.101189

Perrin, F. (2024). *Claudia Goldin: Nobel Prize 2023 paving the way for women and gender perspectives in economics*. Retrieved from https://link.springer.com/article/10.1007/s11698-024-00282-717.04.2024

Popko, I. (2024). Mężczyźni w Japonii przechodzą kryzys tożsamości. Jakie mają dzisiaj oczekiwania wobec kobiet? [Men in Japan are going through an identity crisis. What expectations do they have towards women today?], *Rzeczpospolita* 07.03.2024. https://kobieta.rp.pl/styl-zycia/art39930261-mezczyzni-w-japonii-przechodza-kryzys-tozsamosci-jakie-maja-dzisiaj-oczekiwania-wobec-kobiet

POT. (2023). *Kobiece liderki w turystyce: Jak osiągnąć równość płci i zrównoważony rozwój?* [Women leaders in tourism: How to achieve gender equality and sustainable development?]. Retrieved from https://www.pot.gov.pl/pl/pcb/news/kobiece-liderki-w-turystyce-jak-osiagnac-rownosc-plci-i-zrownowazony-rozwoj

Prügl, E. (2012). 'If Lehman Brothers had been Lehman Sisters…': Gender and myth in the aftermath of the financial crisis. *International Political Sociology*, *6*(1), 21–35.

Ramirez, F. O., Soysal, Y. & Shanahan, S. (1997). The changing logic of political citizenship: Cross-national acquisition of women's suffrage rights, 1890 to 1990. *American Sociological Review*, *62*(5), 735–745.

Rayner, L., & Rayner, D. (2022). *Gender equality: Who cares? Do you?* European Policy Centre. Retrieved from https://www.epc.eu/en/publications/Gender-equality-Who-cares-Do-you~4680d4)

Reshi, I. A., & Sudha. T. (2022). Women empowerment: A literature review. *International Journal of Economic, Business, Accounting, Agriculture Management and Sharia Administration*, *2*(6), 1353–1359. https://doi.org/10.54443/ijebas.v2i6.753

Rios, V., Beltrán-Esteve, M., Gianmoena, L., Peiró-Palomino, J. & Picazo-Tadeo, A. J. (2023). Quality of government and women's political empowerment: Evidence from European regions. *Papers in Regional Science*, *102*(6), 1067–1097. https://doi.org/10.1111/pirs.12761

Roberts, A. (2012). Financial crisis, financial firms…and financial feminism? The rise of 'transnational business feminism' and the necessity of Marxist-Feminist IPE. *The Social Studies*, *8*(2), 85–108.

Rubio-Marín, R. (2014). The achievement of female suffrage in Europe: On women's citizenship. *International Journal of Constitutional Law*, *12*(1), 4–34. https://doi.org/10.1093/icon/mot067

Schad-Seifert, A. (2019). Womenomics: A model for a new family policy in Japan? In U. Meier-Gräwe, M. Motozawa, & A. Schad-Seifert (Eds.), *Family life in Japan and Germany*. Wiesbaden: Springer VS. https://doi.org/10.1007/978-3-658-26638-7_8

Schieder, C. S. (2024). Womenomics vs. women: Neoliberal cooptation of feminism in Japan. *Meiji Journal of Political Science and Economics*, *3*(1), 53–60.

Shipman, C. & Kay, K. (2010). *Womenomics: Work less, achieve more, live bett*er. New York: Harper Business.

Stopyra-Fiedorowicz, J. (2018). *Umacnia się pozycja kobiet w ekonomii i światowej gospodarce. Marki muszą to uwzględnić w stylu komunikacji* [The position of women in economics and the global economy is strengthening. Brands need to take this into account in their communication style]. Retrieved from https://biznes.newseria.pl/news/umacnia-sie-pozycja,p914926344 17.04.2024.

Strauß, N. (2023). Framing sustainable finance: A critical analysis of op-eds in the financial times. *International Journal of Business Communication*, *60*(4), 1427–1440. https://doi.org/10.1177/23294884211025982

Tang, K. (2023). Read the female values from the movie Barbie. *Advances in Education, Humanities and Social Science Research*, *7*, 569. https://doi.org/10.56028/aehssr.7.1.569.2023

Tse, C., Benyamini, A., Plancher, C. & Yao, F. (2024). The power of the Sheconomy. *Strategic Advisory Solutions*, March. https://am.gs.com/en-fr/advisors/insights/article/2024/the-power-of-the-sheconomy

UNECE. (2010). *Developing gender statistics: A practical tool.* Geneva: United Nations Publications. https://unece.org/DAM/stats/publications/Developing_Gender_Statistics.pdf

Urs, S. (2018). *Womenomics: Beyond empathy and equity, it is business.* Retrieved from https://www.linkedin.com/pulse/womenomics-beyond-empathy-equity-business-shalini-urs

Veldman, A. (2023). Gender quota for corporate directors: A task for the European Union? The revival of the directive on gender balanced company boards. *Utrecht Law Review, 19*(3), 44–56. https://doi.org/10.36633/ulr.913

Welch, G. (2015). Women and the vote: A world history JAD ADAMS. *Women's History Review, 24*(6), 1014–1017. https://doi.org/10.1080/09612025.2015.1060783

Woźniak, W. (2013). Womenomics, czyli o wpływie kobiet na światową gospodarkę [Womenomics: The impact of women on the global economy]. *Pomorski Przegląd Gospodarczy, 1*. https://ppg.ibngr.pl/pomorski-przeglad-gospodarczy/womenomics-czyli-o-wplywie-kobiet-na-swiatowa-gospodarke

Yakali, D. (2023). Is she a feminist icon now? Barbie 2023 movie and a critique of post-feminism. *Studies in Media and Communication, 12*(198). https://doi.org/10.11114/smc.v12i1.6478

Ye, X. (2023). The impact of gender stereotypes on women in the workplace. *Communications in Humanities Research, 13*, 125–130. https://doi.org/10.54254/2753-7064/13/20230257

Zaccone, M. (2023). Unveiling the relationship between women on board and woman CEO selection: What is the role of sustainability governance? *Sinergie Italian Journal of Management, 41*, 215–234. https://doi.org/10.7433/s122.2023.10

Zimerman, A., Rotenstein, L. & Anupam, J. (2023). Trends in scientific collaboration between men and women following the #MeToo Movement. *Journal of General Internal Medicine*. https://doi.org/10.1007/s11606-023-08441-8

2 The role of women in meeting the Sustainable Development Goals

The concept of sustainable development

The concept of sustainable development means the transformation of the economy toward a new, green paradigm. It has emerged in the last century, and its essence has evolved along with economic development.

The political and sociological perspective of this issue focuses on the analysis of historical progress and changes, as well as the development of economic and ecological thought. In the historical and economic context, the concept of growth was considered the most important. This idea was defined as the mutual interaction of legal, environmental and cultural factors in the economic space. It emphasizes the growing role of ecological awareness of subsequent generations regarding the use of resources during ongoing development. As the legal aspect became more important, legislative work in the field of sustainable development professionalized. The turning point came in the 20th century, when a number of international bodies began to address this topic as a priority in their agendas (Peters, 2023).

Classical economists such as David Ricardo, Thomas Robert Malthus, and John Stuart Mill created the foundations of the concept of sustainable development. In their works – the Ricardian theory of land rent, the Malthusian population doctrine, and the concept of diminishing returns in agriculture – they considered the limits of growth. This topic was later dealt with by representatives of neoclassical economics, Marxism, institutionalism, and Keynesian economics (Ditlev-Simonsen, 2022; Pelsa & Balina, 2022).

The second important trend in the literature on the subject, which is believed to be the origin of the idea of sustainable development, is the concept of corporate social responsibility (CSR). Howard Bowen is considered the father of this term. He first used this concept in 1953 in the book "Social Responsibility of Businessman", recognizing that it is the responsibility of managers to manage enterprises in a way that is consistent with goals and values of the entire society (Bowen, 1953). This author pointed to the responsibility of managers as decision-makers. Only later did enterprises as entire organizational systems begin to be recognized as socially responsible. This perspective was developed in 1979 in Carroll's CSR Pyramid, which is probably the most well-known

DOI: 10.4324/9781003477532-2

CSR model (Carroll, 2016; Ditlev-Simonsen, 2022). It points to the obligation of enterprises to respect legal and economic regulations and ethical codes. It also obliges them to support social goals with financial surpluses for philanthropic reasons. This understanding of CSR has changed in the following years, along with the development of the concept of sustainable development.

In the 1970s, environmental pollution and degradation became a leading topic in public opinion and scientific considerations. Already at the time, fuel industry companies declared, based on their research, that failure to take actions to neutralize and prevent further destruction would result in the depletion of natural resources and a climate catastrophe (Davidson & Kemp, 2024). In 1968, an international think-tank organization the Club of Rome was founded. It brought together scientists, politicians, and businessmen, dealing with research and publishing global world problems, including those related to environmental threats (Kuźniarska, Mania & Jedynak, 2023). "The Limits to Growth" was published by the Club of Rome in 1972. It was one of the first scientific publications to address the endangered future of humanity due to the increased number of people on Earth and natural resource depletion. In the same year, the announcement of the Stockholm Declaration was a breakthrough. It did not use the term "sustainable development", but the theses presented in the document constitute the foundations of this concept. This document emphasizes the right to preserve and use the natural environment equitably by all generations, which requires rational management and protection of resources. This is about the responsibility to protect and improve the environment for present and future generations (Principle 1) and to protect Earth's non-renewable resources from depletion so that all humanity can benefit from them (Principle 5). Rational resource management is a way to improving the environment (Principle 13), and rational planning is a tool for reconciling the needs of development with the needs of protecting and improving the environment (Principle 14). A new perspective was given to the concept of economic development: nature protection is given appropriate importance in planning economic development (Principle 4) and economic and social development is a necessary condition to foster human functioning and to create conditions to improve the quality of life on earth (Principle 8). Moreover, accelerated development (stimulated by transfer financial and technical assistance) of developing countries is to eliminate environmental deficiencies (Principle 9). Europe's environmental policy should increase the current (and future) development potential of developing countries (Principle 11). Moreover, price stabilization and revenues (for goods and raw materials) are prerequisites for environmental management (Principle 10) (Mensah & Ricart Casadevall, 2019).

Another significant breakthrough was the publication of the Report of the World Commission on Environment and Development, "Our Common Future" in 1987, in which the concept of sustainable development first appeared as an ideal for the global economy and corporations: "Sustainable development is development that meets the needs of the present without compromising the ability of future generations to meet their own needs" (Fischer et al., 2023).

Further work was undertaken five years later at the meeting of the United Nations Conference on Environment and Development in Rio de Janeiro from June 3 to 14, 1992. The issues discussed were: energy and raw material consumption, environmental impact, societal impact, employment structure, profit generation, entrepreneurship and economic structure, availability of goods and services, "environmental performance" of goods and services, agriculture, and infrastructure. It was then that the Business Charter for Sustainable Development was developed. The direction of changes needed to achieve a new order that will allow for sustainable development was highlighted. According to Matuszczak (2011), these are: reduction or elimination of unsustainable production and consumption trends, internalization of ecological costs, and implementation of economic instruments based on the "polluter pays" principle, using the best available techniques and methods of business management.

Based on the existing solutions, in 1994, John Elkington proposed the concept of sustainable development based on accounting principles, the so-called 3E rule, or the triple bottom line: economics, ecology, and ethics. Its foundation is the equality of the company's social, economic, and environmental activities, which should be defined similarly to financial plans: specifically, according to set direction of development, according to an adopted plan and in a measurable way (Księżak & Fischbach, 2018). This direction brought attention to non-financial indicators for measuring the activities of business organizations, which has evolved until contemporary times.

In July 2001, the European Commission presented its position on CSR in the Green Paper on CSR. It refers to the role of social responsibility as an integral part of management, embedded in everyday activities (Korontzis, 2013). The Commission emphasized that CSR can make a positive contribution to achieving the goal set out in the Lisbon Strategy. It assumed that the EU would become the most competitive and dynamic knowledge-based economy, capable of sustainable economic growth with more and better jobs and greater social cohesion. Moreover, it outlined a new role of the business sector in society.

In 2006, Michael E. Porter and Mark R. Kramer (2006) published a groundbreaking article in the Harvard Business Review titled "Strategy and Society: the Link Between Competitive Advantage and Corporate Social Responsibility". The publication emphasized the strategic approach to CSR, that is, linking CSR with other strategies implemented in the company – communication, personnel, and marketing strategies. Their views evolved toward the concept of creating shared value (Porter & Kramer, 2011), which is about redefining productivity in the supply chain, and at the same time generating profit and social value. It also is about a new approach to the goods and services offered. In this way, the relationship between economic and social development is highlighted, as sustainable development covers all stakeholder groups. To achieve sustainable development goals (SDGs), business goals should be combined with social ones to create competitive advantages on their basis. SDGs were set out in the United Nations 2030 Agenda for Sustainable Development in 2015. Its task is to meet challenges such as social inequalities, decent working and pay conditions, meeting basic human needs, and peace and justice. Currently, the idea of sustainable development has undergone a transformation toward the so concept of ESG (Environmental, Social, Governance), which are three priority areas (Hariram et al., 2023). It was noted that all these types of environment, for example, internal and external natural and social surroundings, which are influenced by the organization, are important. Coherence of three key elements – economic growth, social inclusion, and environmental protection – is essential for sustainable development.

Transformation of the economy toward the so-called green entrepreneurship, eco-development, sharing economy, bagel economy, or donut economy – not only encourages but also requires respecting the principles of sustainable development. Initially understood as charity, support, profit sharing, compliance with business ethics, and later expected as responsibility for damage caused in the external environment as a result of business activity, sustainable development has now taken the form of seeing business opportunities as green initiatives. New business models give opportunities to develop sustainable attitude toward customers. "Differentiate or Die" says a slogan which is well-known among marketers and that sounds like an easy recipe for success, but in practice it becomes more and more difficult to differentiate from competitors (Romanowski & Wieja, 2021). In agriculture, sustainability is concerned with solving problems like: greenhouse gas emission, freshwater irrigation, soil erosion, deforestation, and species extinctions. The industry must meet challenges such as greenhouse gas emission and SO_2 emission (exposure to toxic substances or high water withdrawal). For the service sector, the most important challenge is to counteract difficulties, for example, food waste, greenhouse gas emission, or particulate matter emission (Chen et al., 2022). Efforts to ensure sustainable development of the energy sector, which is a fundamental problem of the modern world, deserve special attention. Research and development work on developing various methods of renewable energy technologies are key investments in developed economies these days. Equally important are issues of environmental management, cybersecurity and circular economy planning (Cassotta & Sidortsov, 2019).

Globalization and the development of international markets are associated with the creation of international organizations that regulate market cooperation, including in the field of sustainable development. Since the 1990s, procedures for developing and implementing standards and guidelines relating to management systems, including environmental ones, have been initiated. The first environmental management standard was BS 7750 developed by the British Standards Institution, which gave rise to the ISO 14000 Environmental Management System. In 2010, the International Organization for Standardization introduced the ISO Standard ISO 26000 (Guidance on Social Responsibility). The following are also important for sustainable development: Quality Management System ISO 9000 (quality management system), Social Accountability SA 8000 (social responsibility management), AA 1000 – AA1000

SES – Stakeholder Engagement Standard, AA1000APS – Account Capability Principles Standard, and AA1000 SES – Stakeholder Engagement Standard. Noteworthy is the specific British Standard BS 8901 – an international standard specifying sustainable management of events, which applies to clients, organizers, and all service providers related to the event. This means that more and more industries are standardizing for consistent global sustainability.

As standards emerged, ways of measuring sustainable activities and non-financial indicators were created. The first guidelines constituting a global framework for reporting for sustainable development, the so-called Global Reporting Initiative (GRI) Guidelines were published in 2000 by the Global Reporting Initiative. Two years later, the GRI G2 Guidelines were created. In the years 2006–2013, subsequent versions of the guidelines came into force: G3, G3.1, and G4, respectively. In November 2016, the Global Sustainability Standards Board (GSSB) announced the latest version of the guidelines – the so-called GRI Standards. They are flexible, allowing companies to choose topics that are most relevant to their business and stakeholders. This approach encourages companies to focus on the issues that matter, providing a more tailored view of their sustainability performance. The European Sustainability Reporting Standards (ESRS) are also worth mentioning.

Initially, declaring and communicating these business activities was voluntary. Non-financial reports, published alongside financial ones, were perceived as means to building a positive image of the organization and PR campaigns. Recent years have brought major changes in the legislation in terms of compliance with the principles of sustainable development. More and more guidelines are changing from voluntary to mandatory. In 2019, the Green Deal was initiated by the European Commission (Sikora, 2021). It is a package of political initiatives aimed at putting the EU on the path of ecological transformation and, ultimately, achieving climate neutrality by 2050. The EU Fit for 55 package of climate regulations, which is part of the Green Deal, plays an important role as it aims at reducing greenhouse gas emissions in Europe by at least 55% by 2030 compared to the 1990 level and achieving climate neutrality by 2050. The transition toward climate neutrality will open up significant opportunities for economic growth, new business models and markets, job creation, and technological development. These modifications aim to transform the EU into a fair and prosperous society with a modern and competitive economy.

Revolutionary changes have occurred in sustainable development reporting. The Corporate Sustainability Reporting Directive (CSRD) was published on December 16, 2022, in the Official Journal of the EU. Directive (EU) 2022/2464 requires large entities and listed SMEs in the EU to report on environmental, social, human rights, and corporate governance issues in a fully audited report. This aims to increase transparency and provide a holistic view of company performance. The December 14, 2023 directive on corporate due diligence in sustainable development supports this policy. Sustainability indicators will be taken into account by potential financial investors when assessing the condition of enterprises.

What deserves attention is the social discourse for and against sustainable development policy. It is a green revolution, which, alongside the digital one, follows the industrial or agrarian model. The attitudes of social groups that bear its costs (e.g., farmers and miners) contribute to negative social moods, contestations and protests. They are counterbalanced by supporters and sympathizers of ecological movements, for example, Greta Thunberg, the Green Party, or Greenpeace.

Structural changes in the global and local economy are a long-term process. Developing new ways of creating value for stakeholders based on new technologies and innovative business models takes time and social acceptance. The fundamental challenge for decision-makers is to measure the level of well-being and analyse its redistribution, determining its durability, and degree of sustainability. The analysis of these values may be carried out through research on citizens' participation in economic growth (Sala, Ciuffo & Nijkamp, 2015).

Friederich and Symons (2023) emphasize, in turn, that taxonomies regarding sustainable investments will continue to be the subject of political disputes. It will be difficult to identify green practices that maximize the expected well-being of future generations and/or minimize catastrophic risk.

An interesting new model of a plan for a sustainable economy was presented by Hariram et al. (2023) in a simple equation format, where Sustainable Economy = Principles of Global Sustainability = Happiness + Well-being + Equality = Regenerative Practices + Climate and Biodiversity Protection + Ecological Restoration. This concept refers to the concept of "sustainalism" which is "a socio-political, economic, and environmental theory of global social organizations as a whole that advocates for the means of production, distribution, exchange, and symbiotic lifestyle to be owned or regulated by the worldwide community holistically" (Hariram et al., 2023). Undoubtedly, cooperation and participation of market players, cross-sectoral cooperation, as well as creating ecosystems, clusters and fostering dialogue, and valuing co-creation will be of great importance in further sustainable development initiatives (Peters & Lohse, 2023). EU countries also draw attention to the need for close integration of sectoral policies.

A paradigm shift toward sustainable development requires an adequate education system, to increase awareness and competences of the future (Niemczyk et al., 2023; Ochoa-Dąderska et al., 2024). Nelson Mandela stated, in 2003, that "education is the most powerful weapon we can use to change the world" (Kioupi & Voulvoulis, 2019), that's why it should be a priority in governments' green strategies. There should be a strong emphasis on disseminating the essence, content, and importance of the SDGs. Women's issues among these goals will constitute the next subchapter.

The sustainable development goals

Document *Transforming our world: the 2030 Agenda for Sustainable Development* was signed by the leaders of UN member countries at the summit in New York on September 25–27, 2015. The 17 SDGs (Figure 2.1) contained

Figure 2.1 Sustainable Development Goals.

Source: United Nations (2015).

in them constitute a roadmap for sustainable progress, including issues of gender equality. They focus on five areas: People, Planet, Prosperity, Peace, and Partnership (5xP). They are linked to specific 169 actions to be executed by all stakeholders, governments, international organizations, non-governmental organizations, the science and business sectors, as well as citizens. They aim to solve the most important problems of the modern world. These include reducing poverty in all its forms, ensuring access to education, food, and clean water, promoting equal opportunities, supporting human rights, peace and stability in the world, protecting the natural environment, and mitigating climate change and access to sustainable energy sources (Opoku, 2024).

From the point of view of the subject of this publication, the analysis of the SDGs through the perspective of the position of women revealed in them was considered important. Particular emphasis was placed on gender equality and women's empowerment, which are at the core of Goal 5, but also Goals 1 and 3. Belova and Ivanova (2022) pointed out the terminological aspect. By distinguishing the concepts of individual issues, they suggested that the terms have been understood differently in the European Community, the European Union, EU institutions and in EU strategic acts from different periods. In the Treaty establishing the European Economic Community in 1957, the EC/EU agenda raises the multifaceted issue of equality and highlights the complexity of the concept of gender for the first time. It can be concluded that in that period the first manifestation of the concept of gender equality appeared in the socio-economic space as the principle of non-discrimination and "equal pay for equal work". Even though almost 70 years have passed since then, gender equality is still a real challenge, depending on the geographical, historical, and theoretical context (GenderIndex of Inequalities) (Isakova & Luna 2021). The term is also understood differently by international organizations (EU, European Council, OECD, and UN). Gender deepens inequality.[1] By 2014, 143 countries around the world had included gender equality in their constitutions, but 52 countries did not (Montiel et al., 2021). Undoubtedly, Europe remains the continent of women, compared to other regions. Its legislative instruments ensure compliance with the SDGs and the implementation of the tasks included in them.

Gender equality is a cross-cutting objective and is the main focus of national policies, budgets, and European institutions. Goals 5, 10, 16, and 17 are reflected in the formulation of horizontal policies in EU policies,[2] and in the characteristics of the situation of women on industry markets.[3] Economic issues, which – apart from those indicated above – also appear in Goals 1, 2, 3, and 8. They have their counterparts in the presentation of the labor market. The latest Gender Equality Strategy, covering the period 2020–2025, sets out the policy objectives and actions that will make significant progress toward a gender-equal Europe by 2025. Examples of policies used under Goal 5 include: Strategic commitment to gender equality or Report on gender equality – in the area of equality between women and men; European Pillar of Social Rights – in the area of employment and social rights; EU cohesion policy (regional policy) ensuring coherence of the reform, or EU financing instruments in the area of economy. Beneficiaries implementing the activity under the European Funds for Social Development Program 2021–2027 (FERS) and European Social Fund Plus for 2021–2027 are required to comply with horizontal principles. These include two equality principles, that is, the principle of equal opportunities and nondiscrimination, including accessibility for people with disabilities, and the principle of gender equality. These strategies allow Europe to become one of the safest and fairest places in the world for women, although efforts are still needed to achieve greater progress toward the United Nations Sustainable Development Goal 5.

The situation is different in a global perspective. Goals 1, 5, and 8 address challenges directly related to the situation of women in societies worldwide. In terms of Goal 5, considered crucial in the latest Sustainable Development Goals Report (2023), the report indicates that changes occur very slowly. At the current pace, for example, it will take approximately 300 years to ban child marriage globally, 286 years to close gaps in legal protection and removal discriminatory laws, 140 years to achieve equality for women in managerial and leadership positions in the workplace, and 47 years to achieve equal representation of women and men in state authorities. The reason is the still unreorganized systemic barriers in international and national policies in various geographical zones.

In Goal 1, attention was paid to combating poverty. As evidenced by information from the Sustainable Development Goals Report (2023) by the end of 2022, nowcasting suggests that 8.4 per cent of the world's population, or as many as 670 million people, could still be living in extreme poverty. According to World Bank 2020 data (Montiel et al., 2021), the number of people living on less than USD 1.90 a day has steadily decreased from 1.9 billion, or 36% of the world's population, in 1990 to 734 million, or 10% in 2015. Unfortunately, the COVID-19 pandemic reversed this trend in 2020 and the scale of extreme poverty increased again. In 2020, almost half of the world's population still lived on less than USD 5.50 a day or USD 2,000 a year. The 2024 World Bank Report reports that approximately 700 million people live on less than USD 2.15 per day, which is the extreme poverty line. The SDG of ending extreme poverty by 2030 remains out of reach: an estimated 600 million people will live on less than USD 2.15 per day in 2030. Moreover, it still remains relevant that unequal treatment based on gender pushes women into poverty, deprives them of basic rights, and entraps them in poverty. Furthermore, statistically speaking, women have fewer savings and it is harder for them to overcome adversity. In this context, the economic situation of women in EU countries is worth highlighting.[4]

Goals 1, 5, and 8 are related to the situation of women in the labor market.[5] Employment opportunities directly address the problem of poverty, especially among women, since they have not yet achieved economic equality in many places around the world. Therefore, they are more likely than men to face economic poverty and a lower quality of life (Our World in Data Team, 2023;

Oxfam, 2024). In 2018, working women still earned 20% less than men globally (Montiel et al., 2021). According to the latest data published in the *Global Wage Report 2022–23* (ILO, 2023) and Desogus & Karthikeyan (2024)) women working in the EU earn on average 12.7% less per hour than men. In 2021, there were large differences between Member States in the gender pay gap in the EU. The largest was observed in Estonia (20.5%), Austria (18.8%), Germany (17.6%), Hungary (17.3%), and Slovakia (16.6%). On the other hand, Luxembourg has closed the gender pay gap. Other countries with a low gender pay gap in 2021 include: Romania (3.6%), Slovenia (3.8%), Poland (4.5%), Italy (5.0%), and Belgium (5.0%). The gender pay gap continues to persist in labor markets around the world, with women paid, on average, less than men (ILO, 2023).

In terms of Goal 8, decent work and economic growth, there is the issue of informal employment, in precarious jobs, without social protection. As reported in The Sustainable Development Goals Report (2023), before the pandemic, the number of informal employment cases worldwide slowly decreased from 58.6% in 2015 to 57.8% in 2019. However, preventive measures and quarantine conditions negatively affected this trend. The problem of job loss affected the overwhelming majority of informal workers, especially women. The subsequent economic recovery was supported by informal employment, which recorded a slight increase, reaching 58.0% in 2022. During the employment recovery period, the situation for women was worse. In 2022, four out of five jobs created for women were informal, compared to only two out of three jobs for men. In most cases, the change in the relative share of formal and informal employment between 2019 and 2021 (or 2022) was associated with an increase in wage inequality (ILO, 2023).

The method of implementing SDGs in the context of the situation of women on the labor market can also be considered: (1) from the point of view of the role of women and their career paths in enterprises and corporations, and (2) analysing the conditions for strengthening women's entrepreneurship, noting certain factors of their activity specific to the female gender. Implementing the goal of equal treatment of women and men in the workplace is an issue that is systemic, ambiguous, complex, and conflictual. To be effectively solved, it requires public–private partnerships (Eden & Wagstaff, 2021). The literature shows that women display different managerial behaviors. They tend to be more risk averse and tend to lead smaller companies (Wagner, 2007). International companies can strengthen the position of women in their organizations and actively promote their employees to managerial positions. Siegel, Pyun & Cheon (2019) suggest that corporations can introduce such trends as the norm in countries where gender equality policies are not yet developed. Therefore, they would help local businesses access skilled and underutilized labor, supporting personnel and organizational success.

The implementation of the goal of equal treatment of women and men in the labor market from the second proposed perspective, that is, gender-determined entrepreneurship, is associated with cultural gender and social archetypes (Aracil-Jordá et al., 2023; Opoku, Frimpong et al., 2024).

Entrepreneurial activity is perceived socially as masculine. There can also be gender bias in the education system regarding such activities. For these reasons, women-owned businesses are less likely to succeed. Here, discrimination involves a lower willingness of resource providers (e.g., lenders) to support women's entrepreneurship (Gupta et al., 2009), greater difficulty in obtaining access to external capital by companies run by women, or lower frequency of requests for financing by women entrepreneurs (Kwapisz & Hechavarría, 2018). Generally speaking, many authors emphasize that less gender discrimination in the labor market translates into organizational efficiency (Roh & Kim, 2016) and overall global growth (Woetzel et al., 2015) or economic development (Duflo, 2012). As Montiel et al. (2021) note, SDGs can be implemented by multinationals through subsidiaries' investments. However, multinationals can help create societal value in addition to profit. There are known examples of strengthening the position of women in the renewable energy sector and improving their skills in economic empowerment not only during crises but also pandemics.

Health status and, in the context of the previous areas, life satisfaction were found in Goal 3. Ensuring healthy lives for all people of all ages has a gender inclination. The most important problems considered here are reducing maternal mortality and expanding universal health coverage (The Sustainable, 2023). The next determinant of life satisfaction is access to education, that is, Goal 4. Constant learning broadens horizons and makes work more efficient. On the other hand, access to high-quality education brings benefits to society. Access to education for girls and women in many countries is still more difficult, and their role in society remains more related to their cultural role (taking care of the home, family, and giving birth to children) than to their presence on the labor market (Opoku, Ekung et al., 2024). Young women are more than twice as likely as young men to be out of education, employment, or training (The Sustainable, 2023). The position of women in higher education is also notable, as the percentage of women among scientists and graduate students of doctoral studies is still lower than that of men.[6] Investment in research and development is the key to progress in this area, which refers to supporting innovation in Goal 9. It is also very important for the quality of life to manage cities and human settlements to make them safe, stable, sustainable, and inclusive, thus achieving Goal 11. Attention should be paid to food consumption, indicating which countries are stronger and weaker in this respect.[7] This relates to Goal 2. These considerations also refer to Goal 12, which prioritizes, among others, sustainable consumption.

Organizations of all sectors, including national and local governments, as well as the commercial and business sectors, are required to implement the SDGs. From research conducted by Waal and Thijssens (2020) and Heras-Saizarbitoria et al. (2022) (1370 organizations from 97 countries), it follows that enterprises were very evasive or silent about their approach to tackling the SDGs in their social reports. In most cases, it was not explained whether the SDGs were prioritized, and there was rarely evidence of a significant prioritization process. The reports omitted or treated the issues related to the implementation of tasks within the SDGs superficially. For example, only a small number of organizations refer to specific strategies, goals, indicators, activities, or results. Therefore, the legislative process of mandatory nonfinancial reporting is still ongoing, and formal conditions favorable to green investments are being created. Goals relating to environmental issues of sustainable development, such as Goals 6, 7, 13, 14, and 15, should be taken into account, especially in industries whose activities cause damage to the natural environment. The EU introduced the principles of the Green Deal.

As we can see, the world has been trying to establish a more sustainable path. Various goals and targets have been set to achieve this, but this process is long and complicated. Halkos and Gkampoura (2021, p. 94) came to interesting research results.

> Their assessments reveal that economy-related targets, such as targets included in Goal 8 (decent work and economic growth), Goal 9 (industry, innovation and infrastructure), and Goal 12 (responsible consumption and production), are close to being achieved, while acceleration is needed in order to achieve targets and goals regarding education (Goal 4), cities and communities' sustainability (Goal 11), and in particular climate change (Goal 13).

In turn, Anderson et al. (2022, p. 1459) conclude that "in particular", efforts toward Goal 5 (*Gender Equality*) and Goal 17 (*Partnerships for the Goals*) can accelerate progress, while Goal 10 (*Reduced Inequalities*) and Goal 16 (*Peace, Justice, and Strong Institutions*) are shown to create potential obstacles. As Montiel et al. (2021) pointed out, the internal investment in the corporate assets described above benefits the company through the positive effects of market development. At the same time, it increases the purchasing power of local stakeholders, especially individual consumers in emerging countries, contributing to the achievement of Goals 1, 5, and 8. Bear in mind that some tasks within sustainable development increase positive effects – knowledge, wealth, or health – and some reduce negative ones – the overuse of natural resources, harm to social cohesion, or overconsumption (Montiel et al., 2021). To create a sustainable development policy and formulate specific actions and strategies, note that there are cause-and-effect relationships between individual SDGs. There is a relationship, for example, between increasing employment and reducing poverty, between reducing poverty, and improving the natural environment. Improvements toward one SDG can have a positive or negative impact on another (Barbier & Burgess, 2019; Kuźniarska, Mania & Jedynak, 2023). This issue will remain crucial for the further implementation of the idea of sustainable development, its social, environmental, and corporate effects, including the role and position of women in further development. The justification for the importance of this problem is the fact that women contribute to the creation of social, environmental, and economic capital (Aracil-Jordá et al., 2023), according to the 3D sustainable development model described by

Mauerhofer (2008). In the model, the environmental dimension and its boundaries are the prerequisite for the existence of the social and economic dimensions. The model also includes social and economic capital. In this way, the three areas indicate the total assets presented by each capital.

Gender indexes for EU countries

Given that one of the SDGs is gender equality, in this part of this Chapter 3 indexes were analysed, that is, Global Gender Gap Index (GGGI), Gender Inequality Index (GII), and Gender Equality Index (GEI).

The first of the indexes is GGGI. It is the longest-standing index, developed in 2006 by the World Economic Forum. It assesses countries on how well they divide their resources and opportunities between their male and female populations, regardless of their overall level of resources and opportunities. Differences in the four key dimensions are analysed, totaling to 14 variables (Table 2.1). To calculate the GGGI, all ratios were truncated at the parity

Table 2.1 Variables used to calculate the Global Gender Gap Index

Subindexes	*Indicators*
Economic participation and opportunity	Ratio of women to men in labor-force participation rates (%)
	Ratio of women to men in wage equality for similar work (1–7 scale in annual Executive Opinion Survey)
	Ratio of estimated female-to-male earned income (PPP, int. $)
	Ratio of women to men among legislators, senior officials and managers (%)
	Ratio of women to men among professional and technical workers (%)
Educational attainment	Ratio of women's literacy rate to men's literacy rate (%)
	Enrolment ratio of women to men in primary-level education (%)
	Enrolment ratio of women to men in secondary-level education (%)
	Enrolment ratio of women to men in tertiary-level education (%)
Health and survival[a]	Sex ratio at birth (%)
	Gap between women's and men's healthy life expectancy (years)
Political empowerment	Ratio of women to men in parliamentary positions (%)
	Ratio of women to men in ministerial positions (%)
	Ratio of women to men in terms of years in executive office (prime minister or president) for the last 50 years (share of tenure years)

Source: Own study based on GGG Report (2023).

[a] Parity 1 is not assumed – there are assumed to be fewer female births than male (944 female for every 1,000 males), and men are assumed to die younger. Provided that women live at least six percent longer than men, parity is assumed. But if it is less than six percent, it counts as a gender gap.

benchmark of 1. Thus, the highest score possible is 1, meaning equal numbers of women and men (except for dimension "health and survival"). In this way, countries are selected as role models for the fair distribution of resources between women and men (GGG Report, 2023). At the same time, the report serves as a catalyst for greater awareness as well as greater exchange between policymakers.

The analysis of the size of GGGI in the European Union shows that in the years 2010–2022 all countries have made progress in eliminating gender differences in the distribution of resources and opportunities – Table 2.2. The most active countries in this respect were Lithuania (increase in the index by 0.087), Estonia (increase by 0.084), and Slovenia (increase by 0.069). The worst performers were Greece (an increase of only 0.001), Denmark (an increase of 0.002), and the Czech Republic (an increase of 0.006).

Throughout the entire period under study, the highest ranking EU countries in terms of gender differences in the distribution of resources and opportunities were two Scandinavian countries, that is, Finland (GGGI value from 0.821 to 0.863) and Sweden (from 0.804 to 0.823). The country that ranked third was usually Ireland (GGGI value from 0.783 to 0.807), although in 2013, it was Denmark (0.803), in 2016 – Slovenia (0.805), in 2020 – Lithuania (0.804), and in 2022 – Germany (0.815). Together, these countries closed about 80% of the gender gap, while the lowest-ranked countries only closed about 70%. And these were most often: Hungary (GGGI value from 0.664 to 0.699), Cyprus (from 0.657 to 0.707), Malta (from 0.664 to 0.713), Greece (from 0.672 to 0.701), Czechia (from 0.674 to 0.711), and Romania (from 0.681 to 0.724).

Although all EU countries have reduced gender differences in the distribution of resources and opportunities, none of them has recorded only increases in the GGGI index in 2010–2022. The largest declines in its level were observed for the Netherlands in 2019 (by as much as 4.1%) and Austria in 2022 (also by 4.1%), as well as for: Denmark in 2014 (by 3.6%), France in 2022 (by 3.5%), Spain in 2011 (by 3.1%), Bulgaria in 2019 (by 2.9%), Belgium in 2014 (by 2.8%), Luxembourg in 2016 (2.8%), and Italy in 2016 (by 2.7%). The greatest progress in terms of equality was made by: France in 2013 (an increase of 5.0%), Spain in 2019 (an increase of 4.9%), Estonia in 2014 and 2022 (an increase of 4.7% and 4.9% respectively), Slovenia in 2014 (an increase of 4.0%), and Bulgaria in 2013 (at 3.5%).

Note that according to the Global Gender Gap Report 2023, it will take exactly 131 years to eliminate the gender gap in the distribution of resources and opportunities (GGG Report, 2023).

The second index – the GII – was introduced in 2010 by the United Nations Development Program (UNDP). It is a composite measure of inequality, which uses a total of 7 variables (Table 2.3) and reflects the unfavorable situation of women in three dimensions: reproductive health, empowerment, and the labor market. The GII shows the loss of potential social development due to the disparity between the achievements of women and men. It ranges from 0 (when men and women perform equally) to 1 (when women perform less well

Table 2.2 Global Gender Gap Index in individual European Union countries in 2010–2022[a]

Country	*2010*	*2011*	*2012*	*2013*	*2014*	*2015*	*2016*	*2017*	*2019*	*2020*	*2021*	*2022*
Average for EU=27	0.720	0.723	0.726	0.733	0.737	0.734	0.736	0.738	0.745	0.753	0.754	0.753
Austria	0.717	0.739	0.744	0.727	0.733	0.716	0.709	0.718	0.744	0.777	0.781	0.740
Belgium	0.753	0.765	0.768	0.781	0.753	0.745	0.739	0.738	0.750	0.789	0.793	0.796
Bulgaria	0.699	0.702	0.710	0.744	0.722	0.726	0.756	0.756	0.727	0.746	0.740	0.715
Croatia	0.701	0.705	0.707	0.708	0.708	0.700	0.711	0.712	0.720	0.733		0.730
Cyprus	0.657	0.673	0.680	0.674	0.671	0.684	0.684	0.684	0.692	0.707	0.696	0.678
Czechia	0.679	0.677	0.677	0.674	0.687	0.690	0.688	0.693	0.706	0.711	0.710	0.685
Denmark	0.778	0.778	0.778	0.803	0.767	0.754	0.776	0.778	0.782	0.768	0.764	0.780
Estonia	0.698	0.698	0.700	0.702	0.749	0.747	0.731	0.734	0.751	0.733	0.733	0.782
Finland	0.838	0.845	0.842	0.845	0.850	0.845	0.823	0.821	0.832	0.861	0.860	0.863
France	0.702	0.698	0.709	0.759	0.761	0.755	0.778	0.779	0.781	0.784	0.791	0.756
Germany	0.759	0.763	0.758	0.778	0.779	0.766	0.778	0.776	0.787	0.796	0.801	0.815
Greece	0.692	0.672	0.678	0.678	0.685	0.680	0.692	0.696	0.701	0.689	0.689	0.693
Hungary	0.664	0.672	0.674	0.676	0.672	0.669	0.670	0.674	0.677	0.688	0.699	0.689
Ireland	0.783	0.784	0.782	0.785	0.807	0.797	0.794	0.796	0.798	0.800	0.804	0.795
Italy	0.680	0.673	0.689	0.697	0.726	0.719	0.692	0.706	0.707	0.721	0.720	0.705
Latvia	0.740	0.757	0.761	0.769	0.752	0.755	0.756	0.758	0.785	0.778	0.771	0.794
Lithuania	0.713	0.719	0.731	0.721	0.740	0.744	0.742	0.749	0.745	0.804	0.799	0.800
Luxembourg	0.722	0.744	0.741	0.733	0.738	0.734	0.706	0.712	0.725	0.726	0.736	0.747
Malta	0.666	0.667	0.676	0.671	0.668	0.664	0.682	0.686	0.693	0.703	0.703	0.713
The Netherlands	0.747	0.766	0.761	0.773	0.776	0.756	0.737	0.747	0.736	0.762	0.767	0.777
Poland	0.704	0.702	0.703	0.705	0.715	0.727	0.728	0.728	0.736	0.713	0.709	0.722
Portugal	0.714	0.707	0.706	0.724	0.731	0.737	0.734	0.732	0.744	0.775	0.766	0.765
Romania	0.681	0.686	0.691	0.694	0.693	0.690	0.708	0.711	0.724	0.700	0.698	0.697
Slovakia	0.680	0.682	0.686	0.681	0.675	0.679	0.694	0.693	0.718	0.712	0.717	0.720
Slovenia	0.704	0.713	0.716	0.744	0.784	0.786	0.805	0.784	0.743	0.741	0.744	0.773
Spain	0.758	0.727	0.727	0.733	0.742	0.738	0.746	0.746	0.795	0.788	0.788	0.791
Sweden	0.804	0.816	0.813	0.817	0.823	0.815	0.816	0.822	0.820	0.823	0.822	0.815

Source: Own study based on GGG Report (2011–2023).

[a] Years of data collected (not years of report publication). No data for 2018.

Table 2.3 Variables used to calculate the Gender Inequality Index

Dimensions	*Indicators and reference population*
Reproductive health	Maternal mortality ratio (deaths per 100,000 live births)
	Adolescent birth rate (births per 1,000 women ages 15–19)
Empowerment	The share of parliamentary seats (% held by women)
	Population with at least secondary education by each sex (% ages 25 and older)
Labor market	Paid work (% ages 15 and older)
	Unpaid work (% ages 15 and older)
	Actively looking for work (% ages 15 and older)

Source: Own study based on UNDP (2023).

compared to men) (UNDP, 2023). GII values are calculated using the association-sensitive inequality measure proposed by Seth (2009). What is important, GII does not allow for high achievements in one dimension to compensate for low achievement in another (UNDP, 2023).

Data published by UNDP as part of annual reports show that in 2010–2021, the average GII value for the European Union was not high, ranging from 0.148 to 0.100 (Table 2.4). At the same time, the EU reduced losses in potential development due to gender inequality by 4.8% over the period considered. Moreover, in the analysed years, there were only year-to-year declines in the GII value. The largest was in 2013, by 0.008.

All EU countries suffer some losses in socio-economic development due to disparities between women and men, as there is no country with perfect equality. In the analysed period, the top EU countries with the smallest losses were two Scandinavian countries: Denmark and Sweden, as well as the Netherlands, for which the GII value ranged from 0.049 to 0.013, 0.052 to 0.023, and 0.052 to 0.025, respectively. Therefore, these countries suffer losses of only approximately 2–5% due to gender inequality. In turn, the ranking was closed by countries such as: Romania (GGI value from 0.358 to 0.277), Hungary (from 0.252 to 0.221) and Malta in 2010–2012 (from 0.264 to 0.162), Latvia in 2013–2016 (from 0.235 to 0.149), and Bulgaria in 2017–2021 (from 0.240 to 0.204).

A decline in GII levels was recorded in all EU countries between 2010 and 2021. Malta had the greatest equal opportunities for women and men (a decrease in the index value by as much as 0.097), as well as Ireland (a decrease by 0.089), Latvia (a decrease by 0.080) and Romania (a decrease by 0.076). The least active in this respect were: Cyprus (decrease in GII value by only 0.007), Hungary (decrease by 0.019), Czechia (decrease by 0.019), Germany (decrease by 0.023), and Slovakia (decrease also by 0.023).

When analysing changes in the GII value year to year, the authors observed that only in Portugal there was no increase. In some years, other countries experienced increased losses in potential development due to gender disproportions (or maintained them at the level from the previous year). This mostly

Table 2.4 Gender Inequality Index in individual European Union countries in 2010–2021

Country	*2010*	*2011*	*2012*	*2013*	*2014*	*2015*	*2016*	*2017*	*2018*	*2019*	*2020*	*2021*
Average for EU=27	0.148	0.141	0.134	0.126	0.125	0.121	0.119	0.112	0.108	0.103	0.100	0.100
Austria	0.111	0.103	0.098	0.086	0.083	0.084	0.082	0.072	0.061	0.054	0.052	0.053
Belgium	0.092	0.090	0.085	0.075	0.068	0.063	0.060	0.057	0.053	0.048	0.048	0.048
Bulgaria	0.240	0.237	0.226	0.213	0.232	0.218	0.216	0.208	0.210	0.205	0.204	0.210
Croatia	0.136	0.133	0.128	0.122	0.119	0.144	0.157	0.130	0.125	0.119	0.095	0.093
Cyprus	0.130	0.137	0.138	0.131	0.117	0.117	0.101	0.105	0.110	0.109	0.104	0.123
Czechia	0.139	0.138	0.142	0.145	0.146	0.139	0.138	0.133	0.129	0.124	0.125	0.120
Denmark	0.049	0.044	0.042	0.039	0.035	0.035	0.034	0.027	0.022	0.016	0.013	0.013
Estonia	0.166	0.179	0.166	0.154	0.163	0.130	0.126	0.106	0.103	0.092	0.095	0.100
Finland	0.070	0.064	0.063	0.061	0.061	0.054	0.048	0.042	0.037	0.031	0.032	0.033
France	0.129	0.126	0.111	0.107	0.103	0.097	0.092	0.073	0.078	0.086	0.084	0.083
Germany	0.096	0.090	0.087	0.078	0.078	0.078	0.085	0.087	0.083	0.079	0.077	0.073
Greece	0.152	0.140	0.124	0.121	0.118	0.122	0.124	0.129	0.127	0.121	0.119	0.119
Hungary	0.240	0.242	0.242	0.250	0.248	0.247	0.252	0.248	0.229	0.227	0.231	0.221
Ireland	0.163	0.140	0.134	0.121	0.115	0.109	0.092	0.086	0.084	0.079	0.073	0.074
Italy	0.123	0.119	0.115	0.086	0.082	0.079	0.075	0.070	0.057	0.054	0.055	0.056
Latvia	0.231	0.227	0.220	0.230	0.235	0.227	0.225	0.204	0.155	0.156	0.149	0.151
Lithuania	0.149	0.153	0.138	0.137	0.135	0.136	0.138	0.133	0.128	0.122	0.107	0.105
Luxembourg	0.109	0.089	0.093	0.072	0.071	0.067	0.063	0.058	0.074	0.062	0.051	0.044
Malta	0.264	0.260	0.244	0.193	0.187	0.190	0.190	0.188	0.184	0.162	0.167	0.167
The Netherlands	0.052	0.048	0.046	0.041	0.038	0.033	0.030	0.029	0.027	0.028	0.027	0.025
Poland	0.171	0.152	0.152	0.150	0.145	0.134	0.132	0.125	0.121	0.111	0.110	0.109
Portugal	0.127	0.120	0.112	0.098	0.091	0.080	0.078	0.077	0.074	0.071	0.069	0.067
Romania	0.358	0.341	0.326	0.314	0.316	0.318	0.320	0.283	0.282	0.278	0.277	0.282
Slovakia	0.203	0.200	0.186	0.186	0.189	0.191	0.192	0.193	0.194	0.194	0.184	0.180
Slovenia	0.128	0.078	0.070	0.070	0.067	0.063	0.057	0.054	0.074	0.070	0.069	0.071
Spain	0.105	0.095	0.089	0.084	0.079	0.074	0.070	0.068	0.062	0.056	0.056	0.057
Sweden	0.052	0.052	0.049	0.048	0.044	0.039	0.038	0.035	0.031	0.024	0.024	0.023

Source: Own study based on Our World in Data (2023).

concerned Croatia in 2015 (increase in the index value by 0.025), Slovenia in 2018 (increase by 0.020), and Bulgaria in 2014 (increase by 0.019). The greatest progress in equal opportunities for men and women was observed in Malta in 2013 (0.051 decrease in GII), Slovenia in 2011 (0.050 decrease), and Latvia in 2018 (0.049 decrease).

Note that the average global GII score in 2021 was 0.465 (UNDP, 2023), while for EU countries, it was only 0.100. This means that the world loses almost half of potential development due to gender disparity, while in the EU, this loss is only 10%. Nevertheless, a 10 percent loss for a region dominated by highly developed countries is still significant.

The last index – the GEI – was developed the latest, in 2013, by the European Institute for Gender Equality (EIGE). It is a tool to measure progress on gender equality in the EU. It provides the opportunity to synthesize complex gender equality issues under a single measure as it consists of six core domains: work, money, knowledge, time, power, and health. Within individual domains, sub-domains were taken into account. These were characterized by 1, 2, or 3 indicators – Table 2.5.

The GEI gives the EU and the Member States a score from 1 to 100. A score of 100 would mean that a country had reached full equality between women and men (EIGE, 2023).

Since the index was developed, its value for the entire European Union has gradually increased. Data for 2010–2022 reveal a total of 7.1 (Table 2.6). The highest GEI values throughout this period concerned: 1) health (from 86.7 to even 88.7 in 2020), and more specifically, access to medical services (from 96.2 to 98.3), and 2) money (from 79.1 to 82.6), and more precisely, the economic situation (from 87.9 to 93.3). The lowest values related to power (only from 41.9 in 2010 to 59.1 in 2021 and 2022), and more precisely, to economic power, from 29.0 to 54.7 (EIGE, 2023).

Among the European Union countries, Sweden stood out in terms of the GEI value in all years (from 79.7 to 83.8) – Table 2.7. Denmark ranked second (from 75.2 to 77.8), and the Netherlands was third in 2010, 2019–2021, and 2022 (from 72.1 to 77.9). In 2012 and 2015, the GEI value was the highest for Finland (from 73.1 to 75.4), and in 2017 and 2018 – for France (from 67.5 to 75.4). The lowest GEI values – approximately one-third lower than those in leading countries – were recorded in: Greece (from 48.6 to 58.0), Hungary (from 50.8 to 57.3), Romania (from 50.8 to 56.1), Slovakia (from 52.4 to 59.2), and Cyprus (from 49.0 to 60.7).

The greatest progress in terms of gender equality in the 2020s was observed in Italy (an index increase of as much as 14.9 points), as well as in: Portugal (increase of 13.8 points), Luxembourg (increase of 13.5 points), Malta (increase of 13.4 points), Austria (increase of 12.5 points), Cyprus (increase of 11.7 points), Bulgaria (increase of 10.1 points), and Spain (increase of 10.0 points). The situation regarding gender equality did not deteriorate in any of the EU countries during the period under study. The smallest increases in the

Table 2.5 Variables used to calculate the Gender Equality Index

Domain	*Sub-domain*	*Indicator and reference population*
Work	Participation	Full-time equivalent employment rate (%, 15+ population)
		Duration of working life (years, 15+ population)
	Segregation and quality of work	Employed people in Education, Human Health, and Social Work activities (%, 15+ employed)
		Ability to take an hour or two off during working hours to take care of personal or family matters (%,15+ workers)
		Career Prospects Index (points, 0–100)
Money	Financial resources	Mean monthly earnings (PPS, working population)
		Mean equivalized net income (PPS, 16+ population)
	Economic situation	Not-at-risk-of-poverty, ≥60% of median income (%,16+ population)
		S20/S80 income quintile share (16+ population)
Knowledge	Attainment and participation	Graduates of tertiary education (%, 15+ population)
		People participating in formal or non-formal education and training (%, 15+ population)
	Segregation	Tertiary students in the fields of education, health and welfare, humanities, and art (tertiary students) (%, 15+ population)
Time	Care activities	People caring for and educating their children or grandchildren, elderly or people with disabilities, every day (%, 18+ population)
		People doing cooking and/or housework, every day (%, 18+ population)
	Social activities	Workers doing sporting, cultural or leisure activities outside of their home, at least daily or several times a week (%, 15+ workers)
		Workers involved in voluntary or charitable activities, at least once a month (%, 15+ workers)
Power	Political	Share of ministers (% W, M)
		Share of members of parliament (% W, M)
		Share of members of regional assemblies (% W, M)
	Economic	Share of members of boards in largest quoted companies, supervisory board or board of directors (% W, M)
		Share of board members of central bank (% W, M)
	Social	Share of board members of research funding organizations (% W, M)
		Share of board members in publicly owned broadcasting organizations (% W, M)
		Share of members of highest decision-making body of the national Olympic sport organizations (% W, M)

(*Continued*)

Table 2.5 (Continued)

Domain	*Sub-domain*	*Indicator and reference population*
Health	Status	Self-perceived health, good or very good (%, 16+ population) Life expectancy in absolute value at birth (years) Healthy life years in absolute value at birth (years)
	Behavior	People who don't smoke and are not involved in harmful drinking (%, 16+ population) People doing physical activities and/or consuming fruits and vegetables (%, 16+ population)
	Access	Population without unmet needs for medical examination (%, 16+ population) People without unmet needs for dental examination (%, 16+ population)

Source: Own study based on EIGE (2023).

Table 2.6 Gender Equality Index in European Union in 2010–2022

Data for the year	*Year of the report*	*GEI (EU=27)*	*Work*	*Money*	*Knowledge*	*Time*	*Power*	*Health*
2010	2013	63.1	69.7	79.1	59.8	65.2	41.9	86.7
2012	2015	64.4	70.2	79.1	61.1	68.1	43.6	86.7
2015	2017	65.7	70.6	80.1	62.4	64.9	48.4	87.1
2017	2019	66.9	71.1	81.1	62.6	64.9	51.6	87.1
2018	2020	67.4	71.4	81.6	62.8	64.9	53.1	87.8
2019	2021	68.0	71.6	82.4	62.7	64.9	55.0	87.8
2020	2022	68.6	71.7	82.6	62.5	64.9	57.2	88.7
2021 and 2022	2023	70.2	73.8	82.6	63.6	68.5	59.1	88.5

Source: Own study based on EIGE (2023).

index were recorded in Finland (by only 1.3 points), Sweden (by 2.1 points), Czechia (by 2.3 points), and Denmark (by 2.6 points).

Note that although there was no decline in the GEI value in any country throughout the study period, declines were identified in several countries in some years. For example, Slovenia experiences declines in 2017–2019 (by 0.1, 0.6, and 0.2 points, respectively), Czechia – in 2015 (by as much as 3.1 points), Sweden – in 2012, 2021, and 2022 (by 0.4 and 1.7 points, respectively), and Lithuania – in 2012 and 2017 (by 0.8 and 1.3 points, respectively).

Given that the GEI identifies areas for improvement and ultimately supports policymakers in developing more effective gender equality measures, this is a much-needed index. The analysis of its value shows that, as Carlien Scheele (EIGE's Director) said:

Table 2.7 Gender Equality Index in individual European Union countries in 2010–2022

Country	*2010*	*2012*	*2015*	*2017*	*2018*	*2019*	*2020*	*2021 and 2022*
Austria	58.7	61.3	63.3	65.3	66.5	68.0	68.8	71.2
Belgium	69.3	70.2	70.5	71.1	71.4	72.7	74.2	76.0
Bulgaria	55.0	56.9	58.0	58.8	59.6	59.9	60.7	65.1
Croatia	52.3	52.6	53.1	55.6	57.9	59.2	60.7	60.7
Cyprus	49.0	50.6	55.1	56.3	56.9	57.0	57.3	60.7
Czechia	55.6	56.7	53.6	55.7	56.2	56.7	57.2	57.9
Denmark	75.2	75.6	76.8	77.5	77.4	77.8	77.8	77.8
Estonia	53.4	53.5	56.7	59.8	60.7	61.6	61.0	60.2
Finland	73.1	74.4	73.0	73.4	74.7	75.3	75.4	74.4
France	67.5	68.9	72.6	74.6	75.1	75.5	75.1	75.7
Germany	62.6	64.9	65.5	66.9	67.5	68.6	68.7	70.8
Greece	48.6	50.1	50.0	51.2	52.2	52.5	53.4	58.0
Hungary	52.4	51.8	50.8	51.9	53.0	53.4	54.2	57.3
Ireland	65.4	67.7	69.5	71.3	72.2	73.1	74.3	73.0
Italy	53.3	56.5	62.1	63.0	63.5	63.8	65.0	68.2
Latvia	55.2	56.2	57.9	59.7	60.8	62.1	61.4	61.5
Lithuania	54.9	54.2	56.8	55.5	56.3	58.4	60.6	64.1
Luxembourg	61.2	65.9	69.0	69.2	70.3	72.4	73.5	74.7
Malta	54.4	57.8	60.1	62.5	63.4	65.0	65.6	67.8
The Netherlands	74.0	74.0	72.9	72.1	74.1	75.9	77.3	77.9
Poland	55.5	56.9	56.8	55.2	55.8	56.6	57.7	61.9
Portugal	53.7	54.4	56.0	59.9	61.3	62.2	62.8	67.4
Romania	50.8	51.2	52.4	54.5	54.4	54.5	53.7	56.1
Slovakia	53.0	52.4	52.4	54.1	55.5	56.0	56.0	59.2
Slovenia	62.7	66.1	68.4	68.3	67.7	67.6	67.5	69.4
Spain	66.4	67.4	68.3	70.1	72.0	73.7	74.6	76.4
Sweden	80.1	79.7	82.6	83.6	83.8	83.9	83.9	82.2

Source: Own study based on EIGE (2023).

> Over the years, the EU has made progress towards gender equality. But we are also aware that it is not enough and gains are fragile. Today, only Sweden with a score above 80 points in the Index is inching closer to gender equality. But Sweden only represents about 2% of the EU population.
>
> (EIGE, 2023)

To sum up, the picture of gender equality in the European Union (and thus the implementation of the fifth SDG) that emerges from the analysis of the values of all three indicators is as follows: the situation of women is the best in the EU's Scandinavian countries (Sweden, Finland, and Denmark). These are the countries that record the least losses in terms of its development on the disproportions between women and men. However, especially in countries such as Hungary and Romania, as well as Greece and Cyprus, there is still much to be done to improve the living conditions and development of women.

EU horizontal policies in light of counteracting inequality and exclusion

The pursuit of balancing inequalities is one of the fundamental rights of the European Union and is reflected in various EU documents: treaties, directives, and strategies. EU's fundamental value is gender equality, as evidenced by, among others, the following provisions: art. 2, art. 3 section 3, and art. 21 of the Treaty on European Union, art. 8 of the Treaty on the Functioning of the European Union (TFEU) and art. 21 and 23 of the Charter of Fundamental Rights of the European Union.

Gender equality is also a universally recognized human right and an element that is essential to well-being, economic growth, prosperity, good governance, peace, and security. The EU highlights this aspect, pointing out the need to step up the promotion of gender-balanced labor market participation, equal working conditions and better work-life balance, as well as better access to affordable care for children and dependents. This means that women and men are assigned the same social value, equal rights and obligations, and are provided with equal access to resources (e.g., money and development opportunities). The principle of equal opportunities is also to guarantee the ability to choose a life path without restrictions resulting from gender stereotypes. There are studies in the literature (Yayla-Kullu & McMurray, 2019; Friedman & Laurison, 2019) that highlight the pay gap between women and men and the "glass ceiling" phenomenon, that is, invisible barriers that hinder women from being promoted above a certain level in the hierarchy, as signs of inequality.

The EU Strategy for Gender Equality 2020–2025 (COM/2020/152, 2020) calls for a Europe based on the equality of men and women. The strategy sets out policy objectives and actions to make significant progress toward gender equality in Europe by 2025. The strategy's goal is a European Union in which all women and girls and all men and boys, in all their diversity, can freely pursue their chosen life path, have equal opportunities for development, and can equally participate in society and be leaders of European society. The main goals of the strategy include (Podgóska-Rykała, 2022):

1. combating gender-based violence,
2. overcoming gender stereotypes,
3. eliminating differences in the treatment of women and men in the labor market,
4. ensuring equal participation in various sectors of the economy,
5. solving the problem of gender pay and pension differences,
6. closing the gender gap in caregiving and achieving gender balance in decision- and policymaking.

The strategy aims to use a two-pronged approach to gender mainstreaming, incorporating targeted actions, with intersectionality as a core principle of implementation. Although the strategy focuses on actions within the EU, it is consistent with EU's external policy on gender equality and women's empowerment.

Note that the new EU Gender Action Plan for 2021–2025 GAP III (SWD 2020, 284, 2020) strives to build a world based on gender equality. This plan also complements the LGBTIQ equality strategy for 2020–2025. It increases the EU's contribution to achieving Goal 5 in all areas of EU internal and external policies and throughout the 2030 Agenda. As the authors of the plan point out, "all people, in all their diversity, should be able to live freely as they choose, to develop socially and economically, and to engage in civic participation and leadership on equal terms" (SDGs, 2019).

It is also worth paying attention to the provisions of the European Charter for Equality between Women and Men in Local Life, adopted in May 2006 by the Council of European Municipalities and Regions. Its signatories can be local government units. Each signatory of the Charter is, first of all, obliged to develop and adopt the so-called Equality Action Plan (Pašuld, 2019). The fundamental principles that constitute the framework for the obligations include the following:

- equality between women and men is a fundamental right.
- based on gender equality, various forms of discrimination and unequal treatment must be taken into account.
- balanced participation of women and men in the decision-making process is a condition for a democratic society.
- elimination of gender-based stereotypes is the foundation for achieving equality between women and men.
- promotion of equality between women and men by integrating gender issues into all activities of local and regional governments.

In addition, the signatories committed to applying the principle of balanced representation in its own decision-making and advisory bodies and in its external nominations. Moreover, they declared their willingness to work with all their public and private partners, as well as with community organizations, to promote greater equality between women and men in all aspects of life.

According to EU regulations, the priority directions of social and economic development, which constitute a general category for the assessment of all public interventions implemented with EU funds, are the so-called horizontal policies. Their implementation is not a goal in itself but is to be an added value to each undertaken project (PE/47/2021/INIT, 2021). Horizontal policies permeate various areas of social, economic, and political life. Currently, the group of EU horizontal policies includes: sustainable development, equal opportunities, and information society.

Gender equality policy is considered important in the implementation of equal opportunity policy. It can be defined as a planned system of long-term actions for gender equality in all areas of social life, at all decision-making levels. Gender equality policy takes into account strategic goals, activities, schedule, resources, and entities responsible for its implementation, as well as set goals and methods of progress verification. UE gender equality policy aims to ensure equal status for women and men by determining the causes of inequalities between the sexes, developing ways to prevent inequalities and creating methods for eliminating existing inequalities (Podgóska-Rykała, 2022).

As stated in the strategic documents, gender equality is not only a matter of diversity and social justice but is also an important condition for sustainable economic growth of the country, which stabilizes employment and protects and strengthens competitiveness. Please note that investing in gender equality policies helps increase the employment rate of women. In turn, it increases the share of women in GDP, as well as tax revenues and long-term fertility rates. Clearly, gender equality policies should be seen as a long-term investment, not a short-term cost.

Meanwhile, in 2022, 56% of people in the EU running single-person households with dependent children were unable to cover unexpected financial expenses (the vast majority of them are assumed to be women). In 2020, single-parent families, especially headed by single mothers, were at higher risk of poverty and social exclusion – 42.1% compared to 29.6% in families with two adults and three or more children (Eurostat, 2021). This is related not only to the feminization of poverty but also to the overrepresentation of women in insecure, low-paid and part-time jobs, their overload with caregiving responsibilities and the pay gap between men and women. The employment gap between men and childless women is 1%, but it increases to 21% for women with a child under 6 years of age, and reaches 37% for women with three children (Burke, 2022).[8] Moreover, in 2021 in the EU-27, 27.9% of unemployed women aged 25–49 indicated that the main reason for not seeking employment was caregiving to children or dependent adults (Eurostat, 2022).

It is also impossible not to mention the inequality in women's health, which is strongly linked to their socio-economic status and geographical region. The social and economic factors that shape women's lives and health at different stages of life must be taken into account (Report – A9-0360/2023, 2023). Therefore, there is no doubt that gender equality policies must be further implemented, as there is still much to be done.

Conclusions

The idea of sustainable development emerged as an antidote to the threats resulting from the dynamic development of the economy of Western countries. These include the depletion of nonrenewable natural resources, environmental pollution, demographic growth, and the increasing disproportion between the prosperity of highly developed countries and the rest of the human population suffering from hunger and malnutrition. In many cases, even ecosystems collapse. The term became popular following the publication of the report of the

UN World Commission on Environment and Development in 1987. However, its origins can be traced back to a 1713 paper of the Saxon official and thinker H.C. von Carlowitz who ventured to apply sustainable principles to forestry economy (Płachciak, 2011). The foundations of sustainable development initiated at that time fit into the modern understanding of this term, in which its goals become important. From the perspective of the position of women revealed in the SDGs, Goal 5 stands out in the context of ensuring equality and women's empowerment, as well as Goals 1 and 3. In turn, Goals 5, 10, 16, and 17 are reflected in horizontal EU policies and in the characteristics of the situation of women in industrial markets. Economic issues, which also appear in Goals 1, 2, 3, and 8, are reflected in the presentation of the labor market. The above-mentioned aspects are discussed in detail in subsequent parts of the monograph. Among others, values of three indexes were analysed, GGGI, GII, and GEI. The authors proved that there is still much room for improvement in the EU in terms of implementing Goal 5, that is, eliminating disproportions between women and men. It was also concluded that gender equality policies should undoubtedly be seen as long-term investments and not as short-term costs.

Notes

1 For more details, see section "Gender indexes for EU countries" in Chapter 2.
2 For more details, see section "EU horizontal policies in light of counteracting inequality and exclusion" in Chapter 2.
3 For selected examples, see Chapter 5.
4 For more details, see section "Statistics on women in the EU" in Chapter 1 and Chapter 3.
5 For more details, see section "Women's education, work, and income" in Chapter 3.
6 For more details, see section "Women in science" in Chapter 5.
7 For more details, see section "Consumption using selected examples" in Chapter 3.
8 For more details, see subsection "Women's education, work, and income" in Chapter 3.

References

Anderson, C. C., Denich, M., Warchold, A., Kropp, J. P. & Pradhan P. (2022). A systems model of SDG target influence on the 2030 Agenda for Sustainable Development. *Sustainability Science, 17*, 1459–1472. https://doi.org/10.1007/s11625-021-01040-8

Aracil-Jordá, J., Clemente-Almendros, J.-A., Jiménez-Zarco, A.-I. & González-González, I. (2023). Improving the social performance of women-led microenterprises: The role of social media marketing actions. *Technological Forecasting and Social Change, 191*(C), 122484. https://doi.org/10.1016/j.techfore.2023.122484

Barbier, E. B. & Burgess, J. C. (2019). Sustainable development goal indicators: Analyzing trade-offs and complementarities. *World Development, 122*, 295–305. https://doi.org/10.1016/j.worlddev.2019.05.026

Belova, G. & Ivanova, A. (2022). EU institutions: Revisiting gender balance and women's empowerment. *Laws, 12*(3). https://doi.org/10.3390/laws12010003

Bowen, H. (1953). *The social responsibilities of businessman*. New York: Harper.

Burke, H. (2022). *Living and working conditions in Europe 2021*. Eurofound. Luxembourg: Publications Office of the European Union.

Carroll, A. B. (2016). Carroll's pyramid of CSR: Taking another look. *International Journal of Corporate Social Responsibility*, *1*(3). https://doi.org/10.1186/s40991-016-0004-6

Cassotta, S. & Sidortsov, R. (2019). Sustainable cybersecurity? Rethinking approaches to protecting energy infrastructure in the European High North. *Energy Research & Social Science*, *51*, 129–133. https://doi.org/10.1016/j.erss.2019.01.003

Chen, J., Hu, X., Razi, U. & Rexhepi, G. (2022). The sustainable potential of efficient air-transportation industry and green innovation in realising environmental sustainability in G7 countries. *Economic Research-Ekonomska Istrazivanja*, *35*(1), 3814–3835. https://doi.org/10.1080/1331677X.2021.2004190

COM/2020/152. (2020). *Communication from the Commission to the European Parliament*. The Council, the European Economic and Social Committee and the Committee of the Regions a Union of Equality: Gender Equality Strategy 2020–2025. Retrieved from: https://eur-lex.europa.eu/legal-content/EN/TXT/?uri=CELEX%3A52020DC0152

Davidson, J. P. L. & Kemp, L. (2024). Climate catastrophe: The value of envisioning the worst-case scenarios of climate change. *WIREs Climate Change*, *15*(2). https://doi.org/10.1002/wcc.871

Desogus, M., & Karthikeyan, S. I. (2024). The effect of reducing wages of remote workers on society. A preliminary assessment. *PSL Quarterly Review*, *76*(307), 373–392. https://doi.org/10.13133/2037-3643/18063

Ditlev-Simonsen, C. D. (2022). Economic theories and sustainable development. In *A guide to sustainable corporate responsibility*. Cham: Palgrave Macmillan. https://doi.org/10.1007/978-3-030-88203-7_3

Duflo, E. (2012). Women empowerment and economic development. *Journal of Economic Literature*, *50*(4), 1051–1079.

Eden, L. & Wagstaff, M. F. (2021). Evidence-based policymaking and the wicked problem of SDG 5 Gender Equality. *Journal of International Business Policy*, *4(1)*, 28–57.

EIGE. (2023). *Gender equality index*. European Institute for Gender Equality. Retrieved from: https://eige.europa.eu/gender-equality-index/2022

Eurostat. (2021). *1 in 4 children in the EU at risk of poverty or social exclusion*. Retrieved from: https://ec.europa.eu/eurostat/web/products-eurostat-news/-/ddn-20211028-1

Eurostat. (2022). *More women than men outside the labour force*. Retrieved from: https://ec.europa.eu/eurostat/web/products-eurostat-news/-/ddn-20220622-1

Fischer, M., Foord, D., Frecè, J., Hillebrand, K., Kissling-Näf, I., Meili, R., Peskova, M., Risi, D., Schmidpeter, R. & Stucki, T. (2023). The concept of sustainable development. In *Sustainable business. SpringerBriefs in business*. Cham: Springer. 17–27. https://doi.org/10.1007/978-3-031-25397-3_2

Friederich, S. & Symons, J. (2023) Operationalising sustainability? Why sustainability fails as an investment criterion for safeguarding the future. *Global Policy*, *14*, 61–71. https://doi.org/10.1111/1758-5899.13160

Friedman, S. & Laurison, D. (2019). *Class ceiling: Why it pays to be privileged*. University of Bristol: Policy Press. https://doi.org/10.2307/j.ctv5zftbj

GGG Report. (2011–2023). *The global gender gap report*. Geneva: World Economic Forum.

GGG Report. (2023). *The global gender gap report*. Geneva: World Economic Forum.

Gupta, V. K., Turban, D. B., Wasti, S. A., Sikdar, A. (2009). The role of gender stereotypes in perceptions of entrepreneurs and intentions to become an entrepreneur. *Entrepreneurship Theory and Practice*, *33*(2), 397–417. https://doi.org/10.1111/j.1540-6520.2009.00296.x

Halkos, G. & Gkampoura, E. C. (2021). Where do we stand on the 17 Sustainable Development Goals? An overview on progress. *Economic Analysis and Policy*, *70*, 94–122. https://doi.org/10.1016/j.eap.2021.02.001

Hariram, N. P., Mekha, K. B., Suganthan, V. & Sudhakar, K. (2023). Sustainalism: An integrated socio-economic-environmental model to address sustainable development and sustainability. *Sustainability*, *15*(3), 10682. https://doi.org/10.3390/su151310682

Heras-Saizarbitoria, I., Urbieta, L. & Boiral, O. (2022). Organizations' engagement with sustainable development goals: From cherry-picking to SDG-washing? *Corporate Social Responsibility and Environmental Management*, *29*(2), 316–328. https://doi.org/10.1002/csr.2202

ILO. (2023). *Global Wage Report 2022-23. The impact of COVID-19 and inflation on wages and purchasing power*. Retrieved from: https://www.ilo.org/digitalguides/en-gb/story/globalwagereport2022-23#home

Isakova, A. & Luna, F. (2021). Gender equality and inclusive growth. *IMF Working Papers*, *2021*(059), A001. https://doi.org/10.5089/9781513571164.001.A001

Kioupi, V. & Voulvoulis, N. (2019). Education for sustainable development: A systemic framework for connecting the SDGs to educational outcomes. *Sustainability*, *11*(21), 6104. https://doi.org/10.3390/su11216104

Korontzis, T. C. (2013). Corporate social responsibility: Impact of corporation on our lives. *European Scientific Journal*, *9*(22), 301–308. https://doi.org/10.2139/ssrn.4882748

Księżak, P. & Fischbach, B. (2018). Triple bottom line: The pillars of CSR. *Journal of Corporate Responsibility and Leadership*, *4*(95). https://doi.org/10.12775/JCRL.2017.018

Kuźniarska, A, Mania, K. & Jedynak, M. (Eds.). (2023). *Organizing sustainable development*. New York: Routledge. https://doi.org/10.4324/9781003379409

Kwapisz, A. & Hechavarría, D. M. (2018). Women don't ask: An investigation of start-up financing and gender. *Venture Capital*, *20*(2), 159–190. https://doi.org/10.1080/13691066.2017.1345119

Matuszczak, A. (2011). Koncepcja zrównoważonego rolnictwa w obszarze ekonomicznym, środowiskowym i społecznym [The concept of sustainable agriculture in the economic, environmental and social areas]. In A. Grzelak & K. Pająk (Eds.), *Nowe trendy w metodologii nauk ekonomicznych i możliwości ich wykorzystania w procesie kształcenia akademickiego*, tom 2. Poznań: Wyd. Uniwersytetu Ekonomicznego w Poznaniu.

Mauerhofer, V. (2008). 3-D Sustainability: An approach for priority setting in situation of conflicting interests towards a sustainable development. *Ecological Economics*, *64*, 496–506. https://doi.org/10.1016/j.ecolecon.2007.09.011

Mensah, J. & Ricart Casadevall, S. (2019). Sustainable development: Meaning, history, principles, pillars, and implications for human action: Literature review. *Cogent Social Science*, *5*(1). https://doi.org/10.1080/23311886.2019.1653531

Montiel, I., Cuervo-Cazurra, A., Park, J., Antolín-López, R. & Husted, B. W. (2021). Implementing the United Nations' Sustainable Development Goals in international business. *Journal of International Business Studies*, *52*(5), 999–1030. https://doi.org/10.1057/s41267-021-00445-y

Niemczyk, A., Gródek-Szostak, Z., Adler, D., Niewiadomski, M. & Benková, E. (2023). Green entrepreneurship: Knowledge and perception of students and professionals from Poland and Slovakia. *Sustainability*, *16*(1):273, 1–24. https://doi.org/10.3390/su16010273

Ochoa-Dąderska, R., Ochoa-Dąderska, G., Sánchez García, J., Callarisa-Fiol, L., Navikiene, Z., Demirci, M., Niemczyk, A., Gródek-Szostak, Z., Gasińska-Bańka, K. & Ochoa Siguencia, L., (2024). *Digital inclusion to improve people's lives and promote sustainable development: Workshop III*. Częstochowa: Instytut Badań i Innowacji w Edukacji. https://doi.org/10.5281/zenodo.10676614

Opoku, A., (Ed.). (2024). *The Elgar companion to the built environment and the sustainable development goals*. Elgar Companions to the Sustainable Development Goals series, Copyright Edward Elgar Publishing. https://doi.org/10.4337/9781035300037

Opoku, A., Ekung, S., Kugblenu, G. & Mushtaha, E. (2024). Education for sustainable development, the built environment, and the sustainable development goals. In A. Opoku (Ed.), *The Elgar companion to the built environment and the sustainable development goals*. Cheltenham, UK: Edward Elgar Publishing. https://doi.org/10.4337/9781035300037.00019

Opoku, A., Frimpong, E. T., Ekung, S., & Etokakpan, R. (2024). Gender equality in the built environment towards the 2030 agenda for sustainable development. In A. Opoku (Ed.), *The Elgar companion to the built environment and the sustainable development goals*. Cheltenham, UK: Edward Elgar Publishing. https://doi.org/10.4337/9781035300037.00018

Our World in Data. (2023). *Gender Inequality Index, 2021*. Retrieved from: https://ourworldindata.org/grapher/gender-inequality-index-from-the-human-development-report

Our World in Data Team. (2023). SDG Tracker: Measuring progress towards the Sustainable Development Goals, Published online at OurWorldInData.org. Retrieved from: https://ourworldindata.org/sdgs

Oxfam. (2024). *Why the majority of the world's poor are women*. Retrieved from: https://www.oxfam.org/en/why-majority-worlds-poor-are-women

Pašuld, S. (2019). The European charter for equality of women and men in local life as a tool for increasing the representation of women in the representative bodies of local and regional self-government. *EU and Comparative Law Issues and Challenges Series, 3*, 422–455. https://doi.org/10.25234/eclic/9010

PE/47/2021/INIT. (2021). Regulation (EU) 2021/1060 of the European Parliament and of the Council of 24 June 2021 laying down common provisions on the European Regional Development Fund, the European Social Fund Plus, the Cohesion Fund, the Just Transition Fund and the European Maritime, Fisheries and Aquaculture Fund and financial rules for those and for the Asylum, Migration and Integration Fund, the Internal Security Fund and the Instrument for Financial Support for Border Management and Visa Policy. Retrieved from: https://eur-lex.europa.eu/eli/reg/2021/1060/oj

Pelsa, I. & Balina, S. (2022). Development of economic theory – from theories of economic growth and economic development to the paradigm of sustainable development. *Dubrovnik International Economic Meeting*, *7*(1), 91–101. https://doi.org/10.17818/DIEM/2022/1.10

Peters, B. (2023). The historical perspective. In *Sustainability through participation?* Leiden: Brill Nijhoff. https://doi.org/10.1163/9789004509382_003

Peters, B. & Lohse, E. J. (Eds.). (2023), *Sustainability through participation? Perspectives from national, European and international law series*. Legal Aspects of Sustainable Development, 27. Leiden Boston: Brill Nijhoff. https://doi.org/10.1163/9789004509382_019

Płachciak, A. (2011). Geneza idei rozwoju regionalnego, [The origin of sustainable development idea]. *Ekonomia*, *5*(17), 231–248.

Podgóska-Rykała, J. (2022). *Polityka równości płci na szczeblu samorządowym [Gender equality policy at the local government level]*. Opinie i komentarze FRFL, Centrum Ekspertyzy Lokalnej, 2. Warszawa: Fundacja Rozwoju Demokracji Lokalnej im. Jerzego Regulskiego.

Porter, M. E. & Kramer, M. R. (2006). Strategy and society: The link between competitive advantage and corporate social responsibility. *Harvard Business Review December*, *84*(12), 78–92, 163.

Porter, M. E. & Kramer, M. R. (2011). Creating share value. *Harvard Business Review*, *89*(1–2), 62–77.

Report – A9-0360/2023. (2023). *Report on reducing inequalities and promoting social inclusion in times of crisis for children and their families*. Strasbourg: Committee on Employment and Social Affairs, European Parliament 2019–2024.

Roh, H. & Kim, E. (2016). The business case for gender diversity: Examining the role of human resource management investments. *Human Resource Management*, *55*(3), 519–534. https://doi.org/10.1002/hrm.21736

Romanowski, R. & Wieja, M. (2021) Business model as an innovation. In R. Romanowski (Ed.), *Sustainable development: Innovations in business* (pp. 11–26). Poznań: Poznan University of Economics and Business. https://doi.org/10.18559/978-83-8211-084-5

Sala, S., Ciuffo, B. & Nijkamp, P. (2015). A systemic framework for sustainability assessment. *Ecological Economics*, *119*, 314–325. https://doi.org/10.1016/j.ecolecon.2015.09.015

SDGS. (2019). *Goals 5 Achieve gender equality and empower all women and girls*. Retrieved from: https://sdgs.un.org/goals/goal5

Seth, S. (2009). *Inequality, interactions, and human development*. OPHI Working Paper 23. University of Oxford. https://doi.org/10.1080/19452820903048878

Siegel, J., Pyun, L. & Cheon, B. Y. (2019). Multinational firms, labor market discrimination, and the capture of outsider's advantage by exploiting the social divide. *Administrative Science Quarterly*, *64*(2), 370–397. https://doi.org/10.1177/0001839218769634

Sikora, A. (2021). European Green Deal – legal and financial challenges of the climate change. *ERA Forum*, *21*, 681–697. https://doi.org/10.1007/s12027-020-00637-3

SWD 2020, 284. (2020). *Objectives and indicators to frame the implementation of the Gender Action Plan III (2021–25)*. Retrieved from: https://eur-lex.europa.eu/legal-content/EN/TXT/?uri=CELEX%3A52020SC0284

The Sustainable Development Goals Report. (2023). *Special edition. Towards a rescue plan for people and planet*. New York: United Nations.

UNDP. (2023). *Gender Inequality Index (GII)*. United Nations Development Programme. Retrieved from: https://hdr.undp.org/data-center/thematic-composite-indices/gender-inequality-index#/indicies/GII

United Nations. (2015). *The 17 goals*. Retrieved from: https://sdgs.un.org/goals

Van der Waal, J. W. & Thijssens, T. (2020). Corporate involvement in sustainable development goals: Exploring the territory. *Journal of Cleaner Production*, *252*, 119625. https://doi.org/10.1016/j.jclepro.2019.119625

Wagner, J. (2007). What a difference a Y makes-female and male nascent entrepreneurs in Germany. *Small Business Economics*, *28*, 1–21. https://doi.org/10.1007/s11187-005-0259-x

Woetzel, J., Madgavkar, A., Ellingrud, K., Labaye, E., Devillard, S., Kutcher, E., Manyika, J., Dobbs, R. & Krishnan, M. (2015). *How advancing women's equality can add $12 trillion to global growth*. McKinsey & Company. Retrieved from: https://www.mckinsey.com/featured-insights/employment-and-growth/how-advancing-womens-equality-can-add-12-trillion-to-global-growth

Yayla-Kullu, H. M. & McMurray, L. (2019). The pay equity dilemma women face around the world. In H. Yang & R. Qiu (Eds.), *Advances in service science. INFORMS-CSS 2018*. Springer Proceedings in Business and Economics. Cham: Springer. https://doi.org/10.1007/978-3-030-04726-9_13

3 Living conditions of women in the European Union

Women's education, work, and income

Education, labor, and income constitute a triad that significantly determines the level and conditions of life for the population. Each of these elements not only influences consumption needs and the means of satisfying them but also impacts each other. Education translates into occupation, as higher education typically opens the door to better-paid and more prestigious professions. Work, in turn, is the sphere of life where individuals utilize their education, knowledge, skills, and experience to earn income and fulfill other non-economic needs, such as self-realization. Income is a fundamental factor in determining the standard of living. It proportionally affects the degree of satisfaction of needs; as income increases, the standard of living improves, and vice versa (Grzega, 2012).

Given the aforementioned triad, it is pertinent to commence the analysis of the socio-professional and economic situation of women with a focus on education. The data presented in Figure 3.1 indicates that the percentage of women in the EU with higher education increased between 2010 and 2022. In 2010, one in four women in the EU had attained tertiary education. By 2022, this figure had reached 37% of the total female population. In contrast, the percentage of women with only primary education, completed or not, decreased. In 2010, this percentage was 29%, but by 2022, it had decreased to 20%. The smallest change observed between 2020 and 2022 was in the percentage of women with secondary education, which decreased by 3 pp.

This positive picture of European women's education is further elucidated through a comparison with men. According to Eurostat data, by 2022, 31% of men had attained tertiary education (at least a bachelor's or engineer's degree), which is 6 pp less than women. Men were more likely than women to have completed secondary education (by 4 pp) and primary education (by 1.5 pp).

The prevalence of women who achieve higher levels of education is observed in almost all member states, with the largest gender disparities in education found in the Baltic states, followed by Ireland, Sweden, and Luxembourg. Germany stands out as the only country where a higher percentage of men

DOI: 10.4324/9781003477532-3

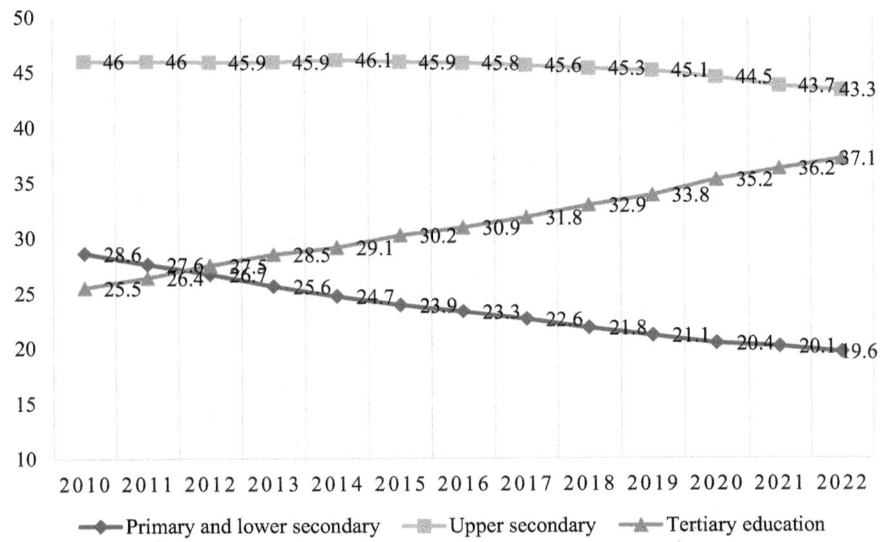

Figure 3.1 Women by educational attainment level in the European Union in 2010–2022.

Source: (Eurostat, 2024t).

than of women have tertiary education (by 4 pp). In Austria, the percentages of men and women with tertiary education are very similar (Eurostat, 2024t).

In 2022, the highest share of women with tertiary education was in Ireland (57%) and Sweden (56%), while the lowest shares were in Romania (22%) and Italy (23.5%). The highest share of women with secondary education was observed in the Czech Republic (64%) and Romania (59%), whereas the lowest shares were in Spain (23%) and Portugal (28%). On the contrary, Portugal (35.5%) and Italy (34%) had the highest proportions of women with primary education, while Lithuania had the lowest (4%), followed by the Czech Republic, Latvia, and Poland (6% each) – Table 3.1.

An important group of measures describing the socio-occupational situation of women, particularly their position in the labor market, are the employment and unemployment rates.

The data in Figure 3.2 indicate that the status of women in the European labor market evolved between 2010 and 2022. Specifically, the female employment rate increased by 7.5 pp, while the unemployment rate decreased by 3.7 pp. The employment rate for women showed an almost continuous increase throughout the study period, with the exception of a decrease in 2020, which was quickly offset in the following two years. In 2010, the difference in employment rates between women and men was 12.8 pp (with men's employment rate at 72.2%), and by 2022, this gap had narrowed to 10.2 pp (with men's employment rate at 77.6%) (Eurostat, 2024e).

Table 3.1 Women in the European Union (EU=27) – social and economic characteristics in 2022 (in %)

Geo/Subject	*Women by educational attainment level*			*Employment rate of women aged 18–64 years*						*Unemployment rate of women aged 15–74 years*
	Primary and lower secondary	*Upper secondary*	*Tertiary education*	*Total women*	*Without children*	*With 1 child*	*With 2 children*	*With 3 or more children*	*Part-time employment*	
EU (27)	19.6	43.3	37.1	67.4	66.4	69.6	72.2	56.7	28.2	6.5
Austria	16.2	48.4	35.4	72.5	70.2	77.4	80.3	61.9	50.7	4.5
Belgium	16.6	33.2	50.2	66.1	63.1	69.4	77.2	55.8	38.0	5.3
Bulgaria	15.8	48.2	36.0	70.0	69.8	73.2	72.4	41.1	2.0	4.1
Croatia	13.1	57.2	29.7	63.2	59.6	66.7	71.1	67.4	6.0	7.9
Cyprus	13.3	34.7	52.0	70.7	69.6	70.3	76.5	66.5	11.9	7.7
Czechia	6.3	63.9	29.8	71.7	75.7	67.1	68.2	54.8	11.4	2.8
Denmark	15.5	35.5	49.0	77.0	73.4	81.5	84.5	81.6	32.4	4.5
Estonia	7.0	39.5	53.5	78.7	78.6	80.6	80.4	69.7	18.2	5.1
Finland	8.4	41.6	49.9	76.9	75.5	80.6	82.6	72.5	20.8	4.6
France	16.6	38.7	44.7	69.4	67.4	73.7	77.9	56.0	24.9	6.4
Germany	16.7	53.0	30.3	75.8	77.1	76.4	75.4	55.0	47.4	2.9
Greece	18.4	44.4	37.1	54.6	51.7	57.2	61.5	59.6	12.9	16.4
Hungary	13.7	52.4	33.9	73.3	72.2	77.9	77.7	56.7	6.0	3.5
Ireland	10.1	32.8	57.2	71.8	72.5	74.0	71.0	65.3	29.4	4.6
Italy	34.3	42.2	23.5	53.5	52.4	56.4	56.4	39.9	31.7	9.4
Latvia	6.1	45.0	48.9	73.9	73.8	73.9	74.0	75.2	10.2	5.6
Lithuania	3.6	42.3	54.1	76.8	75.6	79.7	80.5	65.8	7.3	5.5
Luxembourg	17.8	28.6	53.6	69.2	64.9	74.1	81.3	65.5	30.1	4.7
Malta	32.0	34.1	33.9	73.2	72.8	75.7	75.5	55.1	17.8	2.6

The Netherlands	17.9	36.4	45.7	78.7	76.4	82.0	85.6	75.9	60.6	3.8
Poland	6.1	53.5	40.4	63.1	60.2	68.4	68.1	54.7	7.6	2.9
Portugal	35.5	27.8	36.7	72.8	69.0	77.3	84.4	63.8	8.7	6.7
Romania	19.5	58.9	21.6	57.2	56.6	62.1	58.1	36.1	2.8	5.1
Slovakia	6.9	58.5	34.6	70.7	70.2	73.2	74.5	50.9	4.4	6.4
Slovenia	9.2	42.5	48.3	72.5	66.8	78.8	83.3	81.5	12.1	4.3
Spain	32.6	22.7	44.7	62.4	60.8	63.5	70.7	51.8	22.4	14.8
Sweden	10.4	33.4	56.3	79.6	75.2	84.0	87.4	83.4	27.0	8.0

Source: Eurostat (2024t, 2024e, 2024n, 2024z).

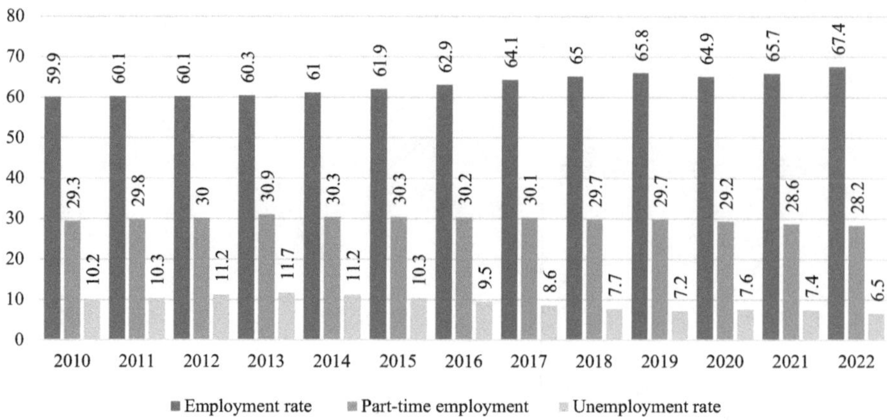

Figure 3.2 Employment and unemployment rates of women in the EU in 2010–2022.

Source: Eurostat (2024e, 2024n, 2024z).

Considering the employment rates of women in the EU in relation to the number of children they have, it is evident that the gender gap in employment widens with the number of children (Eurostat, 2024e). In 2022, for women without children, the employment rate was 66%, compared to 74% for men, a difference of 8 pp. For individuals with one child, the employment rate difference between men (82%) and women (70%) was 12 pp. This gap widened to 17 pp for those with two children, with 72% of women employed compared to 89% of men. The disparity peaked at 27 pp for those with three or more children, where the female employment rate was 57% compared to 84% for men. This pattern is observed in the vast majority of member states, with the largest differences found in Italy (43 pp), the Czech Republic (36 pp), and Romania (35 pp).

Although the female unemployment rate declined overall from 2010 to 2022, it experienced increases over four years within the review period. The first slight increase occurred in 2011, followed by two more in 2012 and 2013, and the last in 2020. In 2010, the unemployment rates for women and men were similar (both around 10%), but by 2022, the difference had shifted to the disadvantage of women by 0.6 pp (with men's unemployment rate at 5.9%).

In 2022, the unemployment rate in the EU was 6.5% for women and 5.9% for men. In 14 member countries, the unemployment rate was higher for women, while in 12 countries, it was higher for men. In Poland, the unemployment rates were the same for both genders. The largest disparities in unemployment rates, to the detriment of women, were observed in Greece (7 pp) and Spain (3.5 pp) (Eurostat, 2024z).

The data in Figure 3.2 also reveal a minimal change in the proportion of women working part-time between 2010 and 2022, with a slight decline of 1.1 pp. This indicator fluctuated only slightly each year. Throughout the period, there were significant gender differences in part-time employment. In 2010, 29% of women and only 7% of men worked part-time. By 2022, this gap had narrowed by 2 pp, with 8% of men working part-time.

Furthermore, in 2022, more than a quarter of women (28%) worked part-time, compared to 8% of men. Part-time work is an important aspect of balancing work and family life but remains unevenly distributed between genders. The extent of part-time employment varies significantly between countries (Table 3.1). The highest percentages of women working part-time were in the Netherlands (61%) and Austria (51%), with corresponding figures for men at 20% in the Netherlands and 11% in Austria. On the contrary, the lowest percentages of part-time work for both women and men were observed in Bulgaria, where only 2% of both genders worked part-time (Eurostat, 2024n).

Differences in the employment situation of women compared to men are also evident in the area of managerial employment.[1] The data in Figure 3.3 show that in 2022, 35% of the managers in the EU were women. In particular, the situation has improved by only 1.8 pp during the period 2010–2022. This indicates that men have been and continue to be more likely to occupy higher

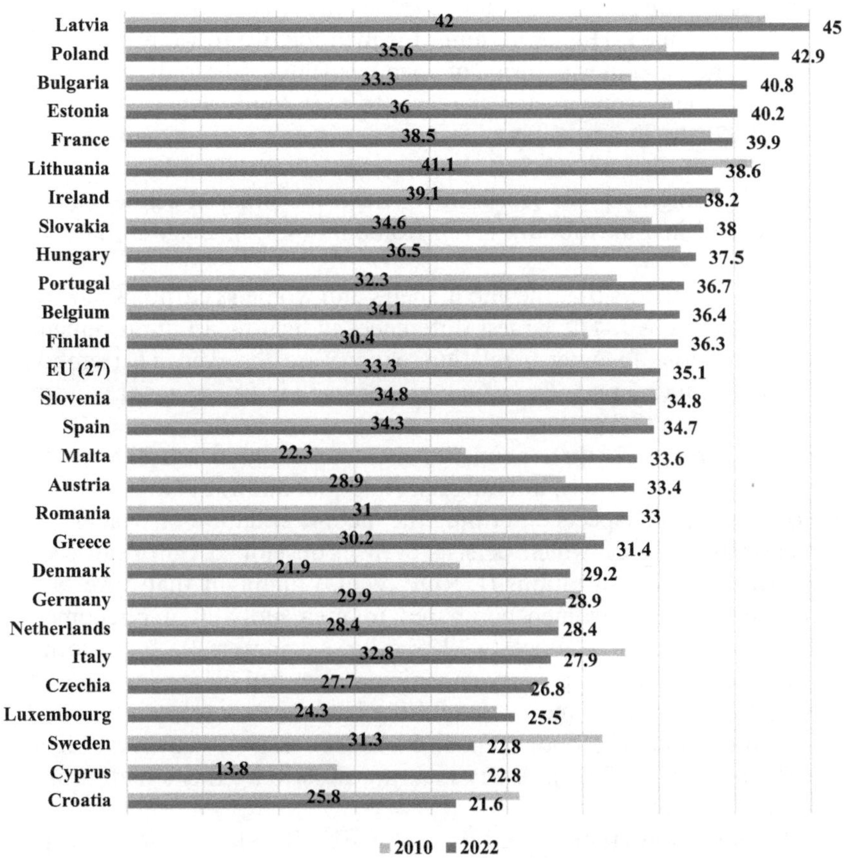

Figure 3.3 Women employed as managers in the EU in 2010 and 2022 (% of all managers).

Source: Eurostat (2024d).

positions at work than women. In 2022, no country had a share of women in managerial positions that exceeded 50%. The highest percentages of female managers were recorded in Latvia, followed by Poland. In contrast, the smallest percentages of female managers were found in Croatia, Cyprus, and Sweden. Over the analysed period, Croatia and Sweden saw a deterioration in the situation of women in managerial roles, whereas Cyprus noted an improvement.

So why are women, who are statistically better educated than men, far less likely to hold managerial positions? The answer is neither simple nor clear-cut; there are likely many contributing factors, including lack of time, domestic workload, gender stereotypes related to the traditional division of roles within the family, difficulties and barriers due to prejudice, lack of access to support, lack of self-confidence, and others (Galsanjigmed & Sekiguchi, 2023). Any of these reasons can hinder women's ability to advance professionally and improve their income situation.

The data in Figure 3.4 shows that in 2022, women in the EU earned on average 13% less than men. Higher earnings for men relative to women's earnings are found in the absolute majority of member states. The only exception is Luxembourg, where women earn similarly to men (and even 1% more than them). In 2022, the largest differences between men's and women's earnings were recorded in Estonia (21%), Austria, the Czech Republic, Germany, Slovakia, and Hungary (18% each). In contrast, the smallest gender earnings gaps were found in Luxembourg (1%), Romania (4.5%), Belgium, and Italy (5% each).

Figure 3.4 also shows that the gap in men's and women's earnings narrowed over the period studied. The largest differences indicating an improvement in the income situation of women in relation to men were observed in Luxembourg (10 pp.) and Spain (7.5 pp.). The situation worsened in five member countries, the most in Slovenia (7.3 pp.) and Croatia (6.8 pp.), the least in Latvia (1.6 pp.). Between 2010 and 2022, three countries showed no significant differences in gender wage spreads, namely, in Hungary, Bulgaria, and Lithuania.

One of the critical aspects describing the income situation of women is the phenomenon of poverty, which persists even in developed European economies. International organizations (UNDP, WFO) highlight that poverty disproportionately affects women compared to men globally, a phenomenon termed the "feminization of poverty" (Kubecka, Koziorzemska & Nowotniak, 2019). The feminization of poverty encompasses several dimensions: a higher percentage of women than men among those in poverty, a worse situation for poor women compared to poor men, and a higher risk of women falling into poverty (Firlit-Fesnak, 2015). A key measure describing this situation is the at-risk-of-poverty rate.

Eurostat data shows that in 2022, 16.5% of EU citizens were at risk of poverty. Women are more likely to be at risk of poverty than men and this risk increases with age (Eurostat, 2024a). In 2022, 17.3% of women in the EU were

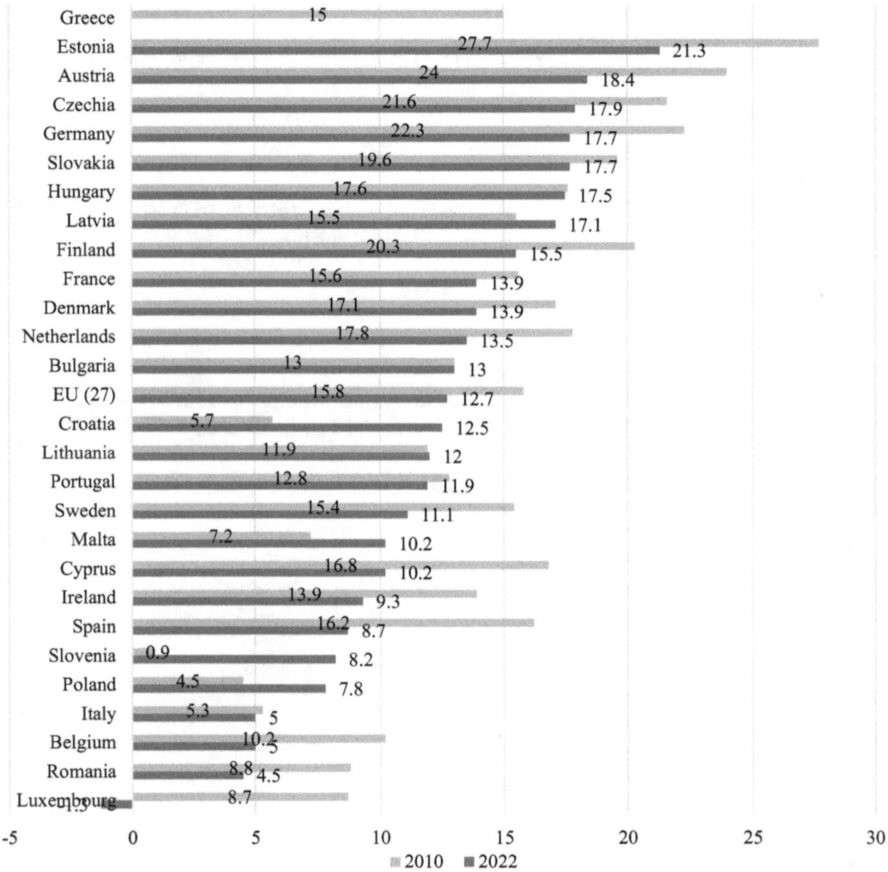

Figure 3.4 Difference between the average gross hourly earnings of male and female employees as % of male gross earnings in 2010 and 2022.

Source: Eurostat (2024l).

at risk of poverty, 1.7 pp higher than men. In 2010, this gender gap was slightly smaller, 1.4 pp. Several factors contribute to the poorer situation of women relative to men, including a lower employment rate among women, a higher prevalence of part-time employment, overrepresentation in lower-paid industries with limited career opportunities or slow earnings growth, a greater likelihood of precarious employment, earlier retirement, and a heavier burden of household and family responsibilities (EIGE, 2017).

The data in Table 3.2 indicates that between 2010 and 2022, the risk of poverty among women increased in 14 EU member states, most notably in Estonia (by 8.4 pp), followed by Latvia (4.8 pp), Luxembourg (4.4 pp), and the Netherlands (4.2 pp). In the remaining EU countries, the risk of poverty among women decreased, with six countries showing changes equal to or less

Table 3.2 At-risk-of-poverty rate of women in European Union in 2020–2022 (% share of total women)

Geo/year	*2010*	*2012*	*2014*	*2016*	*2018*	*2020*	*2022*
EU-27	17.1	17.6	17.7	18.2	17.5	17.5	17.3
Austria	15.8	15.3	14.9	14.6	15.2	14.3	15.2
Belgium	15.2	15.9	15.9	16.6	17.1	14.4	13.5
Bulgaria	22.3	22.8	22.6	24.1	23.4	25.8	25.8
Croatia	21.4	21.3	20.1	20.4	20.4	19.6	20.0
Cyprus	17.2	16.4	15.6	17.2	15.9	15.3	15.1
Czechia	10.0	10.5	10.5	10.8	11.4	11.7	12.2
Denmark	13.4	11.9	11.8	11.9	12.8	12.1	12.4
Estonia	16.2	18.1	23.3	24.0	24.2	22.3	24.6
Finland	13.8	13.6	13.3	11.6	12.3	12.1	13.3
France	13.9	14.6	14.1	14.4	13.3	14.8	16.5
Germany	16.4	17.2	17.4	17.8	16.8	16.8	15.4
Greece	20.9	23.6	22.0	21.2	18.5	17.8	19.4
Hungary	12.0	14.0	14.5	14.5	13.6	12.1	12.6
Ireland	15.8	16.5	17.0	17.5	16.3	14.6	14.3
Italy	20.0	20.8	20.5	21.4	21.2	21.1	21.7
Latvia	20.4	19.1	22.5	23.9	25.8	23.7	25.2
Lithuania	20.0	19.0	20.3	23.1	24.9	23.1	23.6
Luxembourg	14.4	15.6	16.6	16.6	18.0	17.7	18.8
Malta	16.2	15.8	16.0	16.5	18.1	18.3	17.8
The Netherlands	10.8	10.6	11.9	12.7	13.5	13.7	15.0
Poland	17.7	17.1	16.8	17.4	15.0	15.7	14.1
Portugal	18.4	18.2	20.0	19.6	17.9	16.7	16.8
Romania	22.1	22.8	24.9	25.7	24.5	24.6	21.7
Slovakia	12.2	13.3	12.6	12.8	12.3	11.7	13.9
Slovenia	14.1	14.6	15.2	15.2	14.0	13.1	12.6
Spain	21.3	20.9	22.1	22.1	22.2	21.7	21.1
Sweden	15.6	16.1	16.4	17.3	17.7	17.2	16.7

Source: Eurostat (2024a).

than 1 percentage point. The largest decreases in the risk of poverty among women were recorded in Poland (by 3.6 pp) and Cyprus (by 2.1 pp).

It should be noted that although the overall risk of poverty among women in the EU has remained relatively stable over several years, there are significant spatial differences. In 2022, women in Bulgaria, Estonia, Latvia, Lithuania, Romania, and Italy were the most at risk of poverty, while those in the Czech Republic, Denmark, Slovenia, and Hungary were the least at risk. In 2010, the highest risk was observed in Bulgaria and Romania, while the lowest was in the Czech Republic. The gap between the most and least at-risk-of-poverty women in the EU widened from 12.3 pp in 2010 to 13.6 pp in 2022.

Summarizing it should be noted that the general situation of women in the EU gradually improved between 2010 and 2022. In all EU countries, women have had equal and full access to education and training opportunities, enabling them to pursue ambitious career goals. Despite these advances, women still face significant constraints in their professional and social lives. Compared to men, they more frequently encounter higher unemployment rates, unequal pay, insufficient representation in top management positions, and a greater risk of falling into poverty.

Consumption using selected examples

Consumption, defined as the process of satisfying human needs through the use of material goods and services, is a crucial component of the population's living conditions and an indicator of the actual standard of living (Szulce & Walkowiak-Markiewicz, 2017). To identify the living conditions of women in the EU, this study utilizes indicators related to the frequency of consumption of selected foodstuffs and information services. These indicators provide a robust basis for understanding and assessing the degree of satisfaction with nutritional, health, and information needs, as well as the personal living conditions of women in different regions.

Health, constituting an intrinsic prerequisite for human fulfilment, physical vigor, cognitive acuity, and overall welfare, is contingent upon a multitude of interconnected factors, among which lifestyle, and notably nutrition therein, assumes paramount significance. Rational dietary habits stand as a cornerstone in health-centric preventative measures. The examination of women's dietary habits within the European Union will be conducted by employing two distinct categories of food items for analysis, namely, those deemed "healthy" and "unhealthy". Given the inherent complexity in categorizing products based on their nutritional merits and demerits, considering both quantity and quality, this segment of the investigation will examine the prevalence of consumption pertaining to products endorsed or unequivocally discouraged by physiologists and other health experts. The former category will encompass fruits and vegetables, while the latter will encompass sugar-sweetened soft drinks, alcoholic beverages, and tobacco products. Additionally, within the section that evaluates the adequacy of information requirements, an index will be adopted that indicates the frequency of internet usage.

Considering that regular consumption of fruits and vegetables constitutes a vital component of a balanced and healthful dietary regimen, it is pertinent to commence with an examination of the statistics from 2019 within the EU. In that year, 62% of women participated in consuming at least one serving of fruit daily, while among men, the corresponding figure was 49%. Similarly, the ingestion of at least one serving of vegetables per day was reported by 56% of women, as opposed to 47% of men during the same period (Eurostat, 2024h). Notably, an increase of 1.6 pp (pp) in the frequency of fruit consumption was discernible among women across the EU during the study timeframe. In terms of specific countries, the highest rates of fruit consumption among female residents were recorded in Spain (73%), Italy (72%), and Portugal (70.5%), while the lowest rates were noted in Romania (28%), Latvia (41%), and Luxembourg (44%). Over the period spanning from 2014 to 2019, 11 EU nations witnessed an enhancement in the frequency index of fruit consumption, with Ireland exhibiting the most substantial increase (by 10.8 pp), followed by Germany (10.3 pp) and Bulgaria (6.6 pp). Conversely, 13 countries experienced a decline in the frequency of daily fruit intake, with Luxembourg demonstrating the most pronounced decrease (by 11.6 pp), followed by Denmark (8.6 pp), and Greece (6.7 pp). Notably, negligible differences in consumption frequency, equal to or less than 0.5 pp, were observed in Croatia, Malta, and Sweden. Regarding vegetable consumption, a 2.8 pp increase in frequency among women in the EU-27 was documented during the specified period. Although this increment may not be substantial, it does signify a positive trend. In 2019, the highest rates of vegetable consumption among female residents were recorded in Belgium (82%), Ireland (74%), and France (69%), while the lowest rates were observed in Romania (19%), Malta (34%), and the Netherlands (37.5%). Over the period from 2014 to 2019, eight EU countries noted an improvement in the frequency index of vegetable consumption, with Ireland exhibiting the most significant enhancement (15 pp), followed by Germany (14 pp), and Bulgaria (9 pp). Conversely, thirteen countries experienced a decline in the frequency of daily vegetable intake, with Luxembourg showing the most considerable decrease (16 pp), followed by Portugal (14.5 pp), and Romania (12 pp). In six EU countries, differences in consumption frequency were marginal, equal to or less than 1 pp, namely, Austria, Belgium, the Czech Republic, Denmark, Lithuania, and Sweden (Table 3.3).

Figure 3.5 illustrates the daily consumption of fresh and chilled fruits by women in the EU for the years 2017 and 2022. A discernible positive trend emerges from the data, indicating an increase of 2.8 pp in the consumption of fruit once a day across the EU-27 by 2022. Noteworthy variations in consumption patterns were observed among member states, with Slovenia (57%), Cyprus (53.5%), and Italy (51%) recording the highest rates, and Bulgaria (28%), Romania, and Luxembourg (29% each) registering the lowest. While the changes observed between 2017 and 2022 align with those noted between 2014 and 2019, it is essential to acknowledge that the data from these two periods are not directly comparable due to variations in the indicators utilized in the respective surveys.

Table 3.3 Frequency of consumption of selected products by women in the European Union (EU = 27) in %

Subject/geo	*Fruit*		*Vegetables*		*Sugar-sweetened soft drinks*	*Alcohol*		*Tobacco products*	
	At least once a day					*Every week*		*Daily*	
	2014	*2019*	*2014*	*2019*	*2019*	*2014*	*2019*	*2014*	*2019*
EU-27	60.6	62.2	53.6	56.4	6.7	20.2	22.2	16.2	15.8
Austria	66.0	58.5	54.4	54.4	5.0	21.6	25.7	22.5	18.1
Belgium	59.6	61.4	82.7	81.8	16.3	31.5	35.7	16.3	12.4
Bulgaria	38.2	44.6	40.2	49.4	9.0	11.4	15.0	21.2	21.7
Croatia	62.2	62.1	65.3	63.5	8.8	8.4	11.6	21.3	19.8
Cyprus	62.4	64.1	54.9	50.9	6.0	8.6	9.2	14.9	13.9
Czechia	56.0	54.0	48.1	48.8	8.8	24.4	24.5	16.1	16.5
Denmark	61.8	53.2	53.4	54.1	6.2	35.8	35.3	12.8	12.6
Estonia	59.6	55.5	57.6	50.9	1.2	9.7	12.7	15.9	14.1
Finland	53.8	55.3	53.3	59.5	2.0	29.2		11.1	8.5
France	61.5	64.5	64.1	68.8	7.7		28.3	19.7	16.3
Germany	55.5	65.8	42.0	55.7	7.9	33.3	26.8	14.3	19.6
Greece	58.9	52.2	67.1	58.9	2.8	16.4	16.1	21.8	19.6
Hungary	64.8	60.7	50.1	49.0	9.4	8.3	10.7	21.0	22.6
Ireland	58.7	69.5	59.0	74.1	7.4	38.1	35.4	14.1	13.4
Italy	74.2	72.4	66.1	67.4	4.2	16.7	22.2	13.8	13.5
Latvia	45.0	40.6	46.2	43.0	1.6	7.9	6.3	14.9	12.5
Lithuania	52.8	54.1	58.3	58.2	1.5	5.3	6.3	9.5	10.0
Luxembourg	55.8	44.2	62.1	46.5	4.5	35.2	37.2	12.7	9.9
Malta	62.1	61.6	45.4	34.0	10.4	20.9	21.2	17.4	17.7
The Netherlands	47.1	49.7	34.5	37.5			40.5	17.0	13.6
Poland	63.9	60.8	59.6	55.5	8.7	8.6	7.9	17.7	15.4

(*Continued*)

Table 3.3 (Continued)

Subject/geo	*Fruit*		*Vegetables*		*Sugar-sweetened soft drinks*	*Alcohol*		*Tobacco products*	
	At least once a day					*Every week*		*Daily*	
	2014	*2019*	*2014*	*2019*	*2019*	*2014*	*2019*	*2014*	*2019*
Portugal	74.8	70.5	60.9	46.4	6.8	13.9	16.9	11.7	9.2
Romania	31.8	27.6	31.4	19.4	2.4	5.1	6.9	8.5	8.0
Slovakia	54.1	60.1	49.9	51.6	6.5	7.6	8.9	16.1	15.8
Slovenia	68.5	63.6	66.2	63.4	6.0	16.9	15.3	16.2	15.9
Spain	71.7	72.8	49.6	52.7	5.0	17.6	19.5	19.1	16.9
Sweden	55.7	55.6	61.9	61.3	6.7	34.4	33.9	10.6	7.4

Source: Eurostat (2024h, 2024g, 2024f, 2024v).

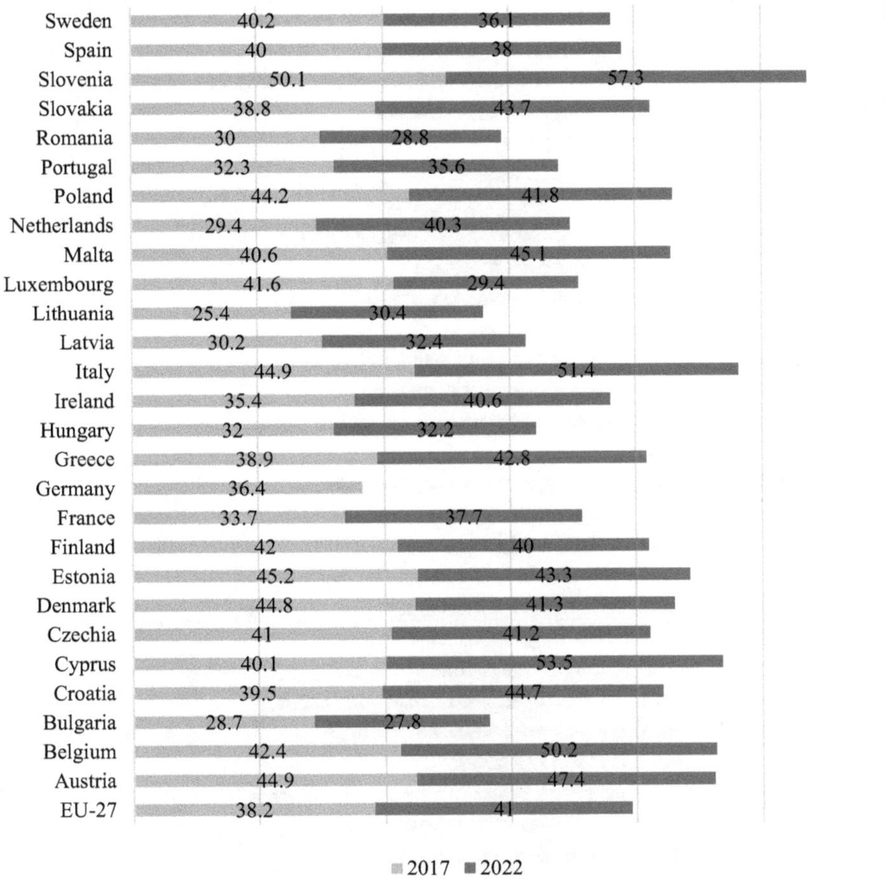

Figure 3.5 Women eating fresh or chilled fruit once a day in 2017 and 2022 (%).

Source: Eurostat (2024o).

Figure 3.6 depicts the daily consumption of fresh or chilled vegetables, excluding potatoes and other tubers, in the years 2017 and 2022. The data reveals a notable uptick in vegetable consumption among women in the EU-27, with an increase of 1.4 pp documented during this interval. By 2022, the countries exhibiting the highest values of this indicator were Belgium (72%), Slovenia (61%), and the Netherlands (60%), whereas Hungary (26%), Romania (27%), and Lithuania (32%) recorded the lowest rates of consumption.

Shifting focus to health behaviors manifested through the consumption of deleterious substances, it is imperative to underscore that alcohol ranks among the most prevalent psychoactive agents globally. Despite its pervasive availability and societal acceptance, alcohol is distinctively more hazardous and addictive compared to substances like nicotine and caffeine. In reality, its consumption is associated with a considerably higher mortality rate among

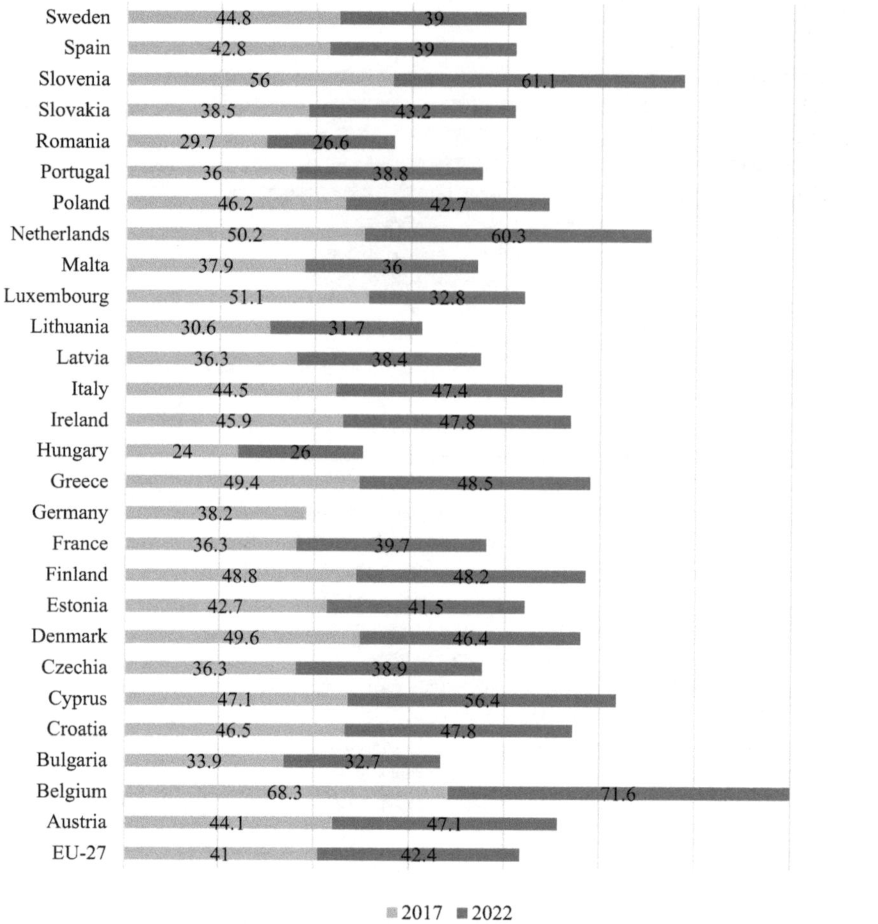

Figure 3.6 Women eating fresh or chilled vegetables other than potatoes and other tubers once a day in 2017 and 2022 (%).

Source: Eurostat (2024o).

alcohol consumers. According to Eurostat data spanning from 2014 to 2019, the frequency of alcohol consumption among women in the EU-27 was notably elevated and exhibited an ascending trajectory. Specifically, in 2019, 22.2% of women reported consuming alcohol at least once a week, representing a 2 pp increase from 2014. In contrast, the prevalence of weekly alcohol consumption among men was substantially higher, with 37.4% acknowledging such habits in 2019. Nonetheless, the escalation in alcohol consumption among men from 2014 to 2019 was comparatively lower, standing at 1.1 pp (Eurostat, 2024f). In 2019, the highest prevalence of alcohol consumption among female residents was reported in the Netherlands (40.5%), Luxembourg (37%), Belgium, and Ireland (36% each), whereas the lowest rates were observed among female residents of Latvia and Lithuania (6% each), Romania (7%), and Poland (8%). Over the period from 2014 to 2019, a cohort of 12 EU countries witnessed an uptick in the frequency of alcohol consumption among women, with Italy recording the most substantial increase (5.5 pp), followed by Austria and Belgium (4 pp each). Conversely, only four EU countries experienced a decrease in alcohol consumption frequency, notably Germany (by 6.5 pp), Ireland (2.7), Latvia, and Slovenia (2 pp each). Eight countries displayed differences of less than 1 percentage point, while three lacked sufficient data for comparative analysis – Table 3.3.

The consumption of tobacco, known to be detrimental to health, witnessed a marginal improvement, with a decrease of 0.4 pp observed among women in the EU-27 overall. In 2019, 15.8% of women reported daily consumption of tobacco products, as opposed to 24.3% of men. By comparison, in 2014, daily tobacco consumption was reported by 16.2% of female EU residents and 25% of men (Eurostat, 2024v). Notably, in 2019, the highest prevalence of daily tobacco consumption among female residents was reported in Hungary (23%), Bulgaria (22%), followed by Croatia, Germany, and Greece (20% each), while the lowest rates were declared by Swedish (7%), Romanian (8%), Finnish (8.5%), and Portuguese (9%) women. Analysis spanning from 2015 to 2019 revealed that eleven EU countries exhibited minimal changes in the frequency of tobacco consumption within a range of equal to or less than 1 percentage point. However, two EU countries experienced a notable increase in declared daily consumption of tobacco products, namely Germany (up by 5 pp) and Hungary (up by 2 pp). Conversely, the remaining 14 countries observed a decrease in the value of the frequency index during the analysed period. Notably, Austria and Belgium recorded the most significant declines (4 pp each), followed by France and the Netherlands (3 pp each) – Table 3.3.

The final component in evaluating the consumption habits of European women pertains to the frequency of sugar-sweetened soft drink consumption. While Eurostat data is available solely for 2019, it reveals that 6.7% of women and 11.7% of men in the EU indulge in such beverages at least once a day (Eurostat, 2024g). Among women, the most prevalent consumption of sweetened soft drinks is reported in Belgium (16.3%) and Malta (10.4%), whereas the least common consumption is observed in the Baltic states (ranging from 1.2% to 1.6%), Finland (2%), Romania (2.4%), and Greece (2.8%) – Table 3.3.

In summarizing the dietary habits of European women as reflected in the frequency of consumption of selected healthy and unhealthy products between 2014 and 2019, it becomes apparent that both positive and negative changes occurred in their consumption patterns. These shifts were contingent upon the country under analysis and the specific type of product. However, considering all the analysed indicators of consumption frequency, notably the prevalence of fruit and vegetable consumption juxtaposed with the lesser occurrence of alcohol, tobacco products, and sweetened beverages, the most favorable situation in 2019 was observed in Italy and Portugal, while the least favorable was noted in Romania.

Access to the internet serves as a crucial determinant of the living standards of a population, encompassing various facets such as employment opportunities, educational resources, information databases, entertainment outlets, social interactions, and access to diverse e-services. In recent years, particularly since the onset of the COVID-19 pandemic in 2020, previously gradual advancements in digitizing select aspects of consumer activities now propelled by revolutionary momentum. In the contemporary landscape, a lack of internet access translates to exclusion from numerous vital domains of consumer life. Therefore, the final component of the analysis pertaining to women's consumption within the EU focuses on the frequency of online service utilization among women aged 16–74 years old.

Eurostat data reveals that nearly nine out of ten women in the EU-27 accessed the internet at least once a week in 2022. Notably, the percentages of men and women utilizing internet services have converged closely, with 88% of women and 89% of men in the EU-27 reported to have accessed the internet in 2022 (Eurostat, 2024m). Table 3.4 illustrates that between 2020 and 2022, the frequency rate of internet usage surged by 29 pp.

However, the rate of change varied across the countries under analysis. The most significant strides in internet usage were observed among women in Romania (51 pp), Greece (45 pp), and Cyprus (42.5 pp), while comparatively lesser progress was noted in the Netherlands (8 pp), Sweden (9 pp), and Denmark (12 pp). It is essential to recognize that individual EU countries commenced from different starting points concerning internet usage frequency, hence, the observed changes may not entirely reflect the current status of internet access within the analysed scope. In 2022, the nations with the highest frequency of internet usage among women were Denmark (96.5%), Sweden (96%), and Finland (95%), while the least frequent users were Bulgarians (78%), Croats (79%), Greeks (81%), Italians, and Portuguese (82% each).

Health and life satisfaction for women

Another facet contributing to the portrayal of women's living conditions pertains to health. Health embodies one of the paramount values in human life and, in accordance with the definition furnished by the World Health Organization (WHO), denotes a state of complete physical, mental, and social well-being, rather than merely the absence of disease or disability (WHO, 2024). In evaluating the extent to which the populace's health needs are met, researchers may opt for various metrics, including objective or subjective indicators. In investigating the health status of women and their overall contentment, this study employs subjective measures, which capture their sentiments concerning the fulfilment of health-related needs as articulated by themselves.

The data presented in Figure 3.7 reveals that in 2022, within the European Union (EU), more than 65% of women aged 16 and above reported their health as either good or very good. However, the proportion of women holding positive health perceptions was slightly lower compared to their male

Table 3.4 Frequency of internet use of women in the European Union in 2010–2022 – once a week (aged 16–74 in % of all women)

Geo/year	*2010*	*2012*	*2014*	*2016*	*2018*	*2020*	*2022*
EU-27	59.10	65.06	70.07	75.71	80.47	85.08	88.02
Austria	64.69	70.44	72.75	77.73	83.54	83.99	89.26
Belgium	70.26	75.26	81.43	82.42	85.36	89.44	92.68
Bulgaria	41.20	49.50	52.64	57.40	62.40	67.82	78.04
Croatia	42.03	50.71	62.57	66.99	70.85	73.96	78.64
Cyprus	47.90	54.82	63.76	72.53	83.75	90.85	90.41
Czechia	55.02	66.12	72.94	77.49	83.14	85.78	88.74
Denmark	84.80	87.61	92.05	94.89	95.10	96.48	96.53
Estonia	71.09	73.98	81.46	84.82	86.96	88.29	90.56
Finland	81.15	87.21	87.78	91.22	92.73	95.49	95.21
France	71.01	76.82	78.33	81.54	85.03		90.62
Germany	69.92	74.29	79.04	84.88	88.95	91.78	88.56
Greece	36.34	48.16	56.51	63.68	68.43	74.29	81.23
Hungary	57.59	67.58	72.82	77.40	73.91	84.32	88.78
Ireland	64.38	73:76	77.35	80.48	80.03	91.04	90.84
Italy	41.72	47.32	55.15	63.69	69.61	74.44	81.64
Latvia	61.74	69.12	71.34	76.08	81.48	87.73	90.93
Lithuania	57.47	63.74	68.97	72.31	78.43	83.24	87.44
Luxembourg	80.96	85.92	91.38	94.76	91.78	95.77	93.91
Malta	55.47	63.51	69.15	76.50	80.10	86.56	90.74
The Netherlands	85.66	88.58	89.84	91.61	93.66	92.78	93.68
Poland	52.85	57.87	62.38	69.48	74.34	81.08	85.00
Portugal	41.93	51.09	56.98	66.45	69.75	74.90	82.46
Romania	32.52	41.81	45.51	54.04	67.36	74.62	83.49
Slovakia	69.89	71.44	76.09	76.71	77.96	88.20	88.51
Slovenia	62.41	62.05	68.20	72.37	76.80	84.63	87.29
Spain	54.41	61.08	69.01	74.57	82.04	91.39	92.83
Sweden	87.59	88.86	89.00	90.81	92.32	95.30	96.37

Source: Eurostat (2024m).

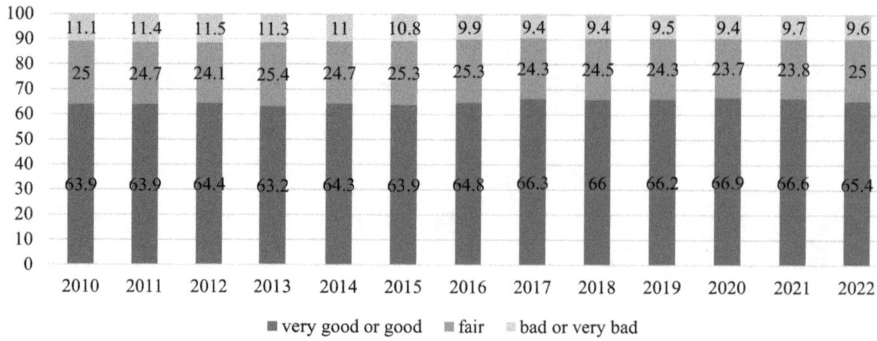

Figure 3.7 Self-perceived health of women in 2010–2022 (in % of total women).

Source: Eurostat (2024u).

counterparts, with 70% of men expressing similar sentiments. Among the EU member states, the highest proportions of women aged 16 and over who appraised their health as good or very good were observed in Ireland (80%), Cyprus (77%), and Greece (75%). Conversely, at the opposite end of the spectrum, the EU member states with the lowest percentages of women rating their health as very good or good were Lithuania (44%), Latvia (46%), and Portugal (47%). Notably, across all EU member states, men exhibited a greater tendency than women to assess their health as very good or good. The most significant disparities in health status between genders were documented in Latvia and Lithuania (10 pp each), followed by Romania (9 pp). Conversely, the most negligible gender gap in self-assessed health status was observed in Ireland (0.2 pp) (Eurostat, 2024u).

Examining the evolution of women's health assessments over the scrutinized period, it becomes evident that between 2020 and 2022, there was a marginal uptick of 1.5 pp in the proportion of women across the European Union (EU) who rated their health as very good or good. Notably, 17 out of the 27 EU countries witnessed an amelioration in the health assessments of women aged 16 and above. The most substantial positive shifts were discernible in Croatia (12 pp increase), Hungary (9 pp), and Malta and Slovenia (8 pp each). Conversely, 10 countries experienced a decrement in the aforementioned metric, signaling a deterioration in the perceived health status of women. The most notable declines in ratings were registered in Sweden (11.5 pp), followed by the Netherlands and Denmark (7 pp each).

The data depicted in Table 3.5 delineates that between 2010 and 2022, the enhancement in perceptions of health as good or very good among women in the EU-27 coincided with a reduction in ratings indicative of poor and very poor health, diminishing by 1.5 pp. In 2022, 1 out of every 10 women appraised their health as bad or very bad. In contrast, one in four European women evaluated it as average. Remarkably, the proportions of average ratings remained consistent across the extremities of the analysis period, standing at 25%.

Table 3.5 Share of women aged 16 years or over with very good or good self-perceived health in 2010–2022

Geo/year	*2010*	*2012*	*2014*	*2016*	*2018*	*2020*	*2022*
EU-27	63.9	64.4	64.3	64.8	66.0	66.9	65.4
Austria	67.2	68.4	67.2	68.5	70.3	73.3	68.6
Belgium	70.8	72.2	72.8	71.2	72.5	73.3	72.5
Bulgaria	62.3	62.6	62.5	61.9	62.8	62.7	64.6
Croatia	48.3	45.6	55.5	56.0	58.2	61.2	60.6
Cyprus	72.2	75.6	76.2	78.0	76.4	76.3	76.6
Czechia	60.0	58.4	58.8	59.0	60.7	62.3	65.4
Denmark	69.3	70.0	70.5	70.2	67.9	69.8	62.7
Estonia	50.8	50.6	49.9	50.6	49.7	56.2	55.9
Finland	66.7	66.0	69.1	68.7	67.1	69.2	62.7
France	64.9	65.9	65.6	64.5	65.5	66.8	63.2
Germany	64.1	63.8	63.5	63.5	64.3	62.4	62.5
Greece	73.3	72.1	71.0	71.4	74.2	76.9	75.1
Hungary	51.4	53.1	53.4	56.2	57.5	58.8	60.7
Ireland	82.2	82.7	82.1	83.1	84.4	83.1	79.9
Italy	62.9	64.7	64.5	67.7	70.5		70.6
Latvia	43.6	43.0	42.0	42.8	42.9	45.7	45.6
Lithuania	47.1	40.4	40.4	40.0	41.1	41.1	44.3
Luxembourg	73.9	72.4	71.0	66.7	66.4	72.5	73.0
Malta	65.5	70.7	73.1	71.4	72.4	73.4	73.7
The Netherlands	75.9	72.1	74.2	73.2	73.1	75.6	68.9
Poland	54.7	54.3	55.2	55.5	56.8	59.1	59.1
Portugal	44.1	42.7	41.9	43.3	44.7	47.3	46.6
Romania	63.5	63.0	64.0	65.3	65.7	68.9	69.2
Slovakia	59.2	60.7	61.1	63.0	62.8	61.6	63.2
Slovenia	56.3	59.7	61.5	60.9	61.6	64.4	64.5
Spain	68.4	71.5	69.2	69.8	70.7	70.3	67.6
Sweden	76.1	77.5	76.0	72.4	73.6	73.3	64.6

Source: Eurostat (2024u).

Health ratings exhibited more pronounced differences observed between countries (Figures 3.8 and 3.9). In 2010, women in Ireland reported the highest health ratings, followed by those in Sweden and the Netherlands, whereas women in Latvia, Lithuania, and Portugal rated their health the lowest. By 2022, Irish women continued to report the highest health ratings, but women from Cyprus and Greece moved into the second and third positions, respectively. Despite these shifts, the countries with the lowest health ratings remained unchanged; women in Latvia, Lithuania, and Portugal continued to rate their health the lowest compared to other women in the EU.

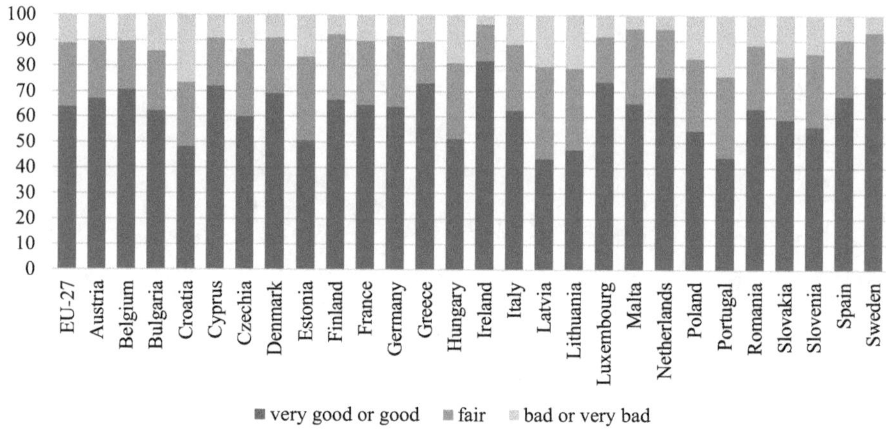

Figure 3.8 Self-perceived health of women in 2010 (in % of total women).

Source: Eurostat (2024u).

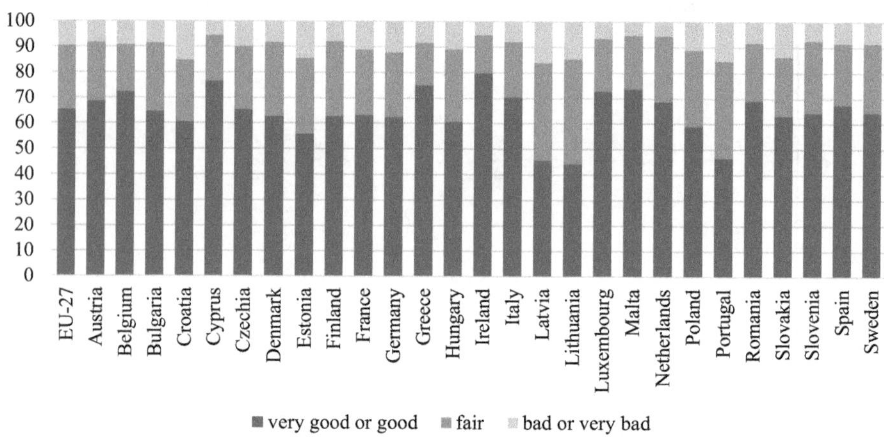

Figure 3.9 Self-perceived health of women in 2022 (in % of total women).

Source: Eurostat (2024u).

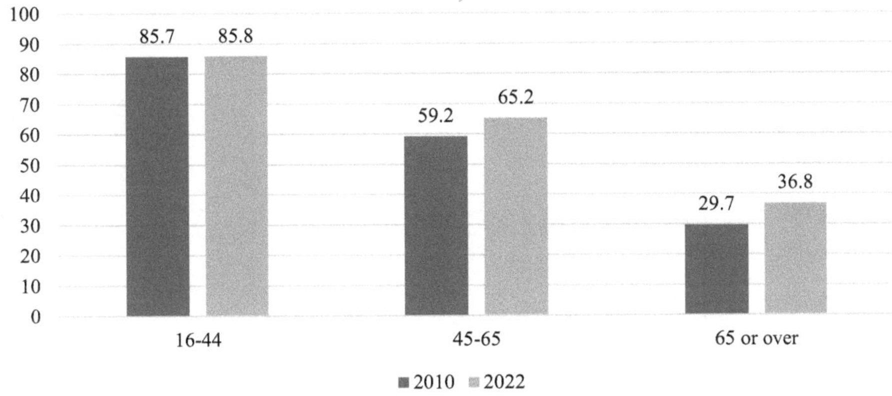

Figure 3.10 Share of women with very good or good self-perceived health by age in 2010 and 2022.

Source: Eurostat (2024u).

People's perceptions of their health are influenced by a myriad of factors, including socioeconomic, occupational, cultural, and environmental conditions, among others. Generally, however, the perception of good health declines with age among women.

Figure 3.10 illustrates that in both 2010 and 2022, the percentage of women reporting good or very good health decreased with age. Nearly 9 out of 10 women aged 16–44 believed they were in good or very good health. This proportion was 60% among women aged 45–65 in 2010, increasing to 65% in 2022. Among women aged 65 and older, the share was 30% in 2010 and 37% in 2022. Importantly, this trend was consistent across all member states.

Although gender disparities in health perception are evident, women and men exhibit nearly equal levels of life satisfaction. On average, in the EU, women aged 16 and older rated their life satisfaction in 2022 at 7.1 on a scale from 0 (very dissatisfied) to 10 (very satisfied). Men reported the same average satisfaction rating (Eurostat, 2024c). In most member states, the ratings were equal or nearly equal between genders (Table 3.6). In 18 of the 27 EU countries, women's overall life satisfaction was rated higher than or equal to the EU average. The highest ratings were observed in Austria (7.9), followed by Finland, Poland, and Romania (7.7 each), while the lowest ratings were in Bulgaria (5.6), Germany (6.5), and Greece (6.7). According to Eurostat data on overall life satisfaction in the EU, women were less satisfied with their lives in both 2021 and 2022 than in 2018. This decline likely reflects the impact of the COVID-19 pandemic on people's lives. The EU average life satisfaction rating decreased by 0.2 points, from 7.3 in 2018 to 7.1 in 2021. Despite this slight decline, the index remained relatively high, surpassing the 2013 average of 7.0. In 2022, overall life satisfaction among women declined in seven countries compared to 2013. A general trend emerged, showing that women's life

Table 3.6 Overall satisfaction of life of women in the UE in 2013, 2018, and 2022 (16 years or over)

Geo/year	*2013*	*2018*	*2022*	*Geo/year*	*2013*	*2018*	*2022*
EU-27	7.0	7.3	7.1	Ireland	7.4	8.1	7.4
Austria	7.8	8.0	7.9	Italy	6.7	7.1	7.2
Belgium	7.6	7.6	7.6	Latvia	6.5	6.7	6.8
Bulgaria	4.8	5.4	5.6	Lithuania	6.7	6.4	7.1
Croatia	6.3	6.3	6.8	Luxembourg	7.5	7.6	7.2
Cyprus	6.2	7.1	7.2	Malta	7.1	7.5	7.4
Czechia	6.9	7.4	7.4	The Netherlands	7.8	7.7	7.6
Denmark	8.0	7.8	7.5	Poland	7.3	7.8	7.7
Estonia	6.5	7.0	7.2	Portugal	6.2	6.7	7.0
Finland	8.0	8.1	7.7	Romania	7.1	7.3	7.7
France	7.1	7.3	7.0	Slovakia	7.0	7.1	7.0
Germany	7.3	7.4	6.5	Slovenia	7.0	7.3	7.5
Greece	6.2	6.4	6.7	Spain	6.9	7.3	7.1
Hungary	6.1	6.5	6.9	Sweden	7.9	7.8	7.4

Source: Eurostat (2024c).

satisfaction decreased in member states with previously higher levels of satisfaction, while it increased in states with lower satisfaction levels. The largest decline was observed in Germany (−0.8 points), followed by Denmark and Sweden, both of which saw a decrease of 0.5 points, resulting in satisfaction levels of 7.5 and 7.4, respectively. Conversely, women's overall life satisfaction increased in 17 member states between 2013 and 2022, with the most significant increase in Cyprus (by 1.0 point to 7.2), followed by Hungary and Portugal (both up by 0.8 points to 6.9 and 7.0, respectively).

Data on selected elements of the satisfaction assessment presented in Table 3.7 show that in 2018, women in the EU-27 rated their satisfaction with personal relationships highest at 7.8 points and their satisfaction with their financial situation lowest at 6.0 points. The other two categories, satisfaction with work and satisfaction with use of time, each scored 6.9 points. In particular, there was an improvement in the ratings in all these areas from previous years, with the highest increase observed in satisfaction with the financial situation and the lowest in satisfaction with work and use of time.

Regarding satisfaction with their financial situation in 2018, the highest scores were reported by residents of Finland (7.7), Sweden (7.6), and Denmark (7.5), while the lowest ratings came from Bulgaria (2.9), followed by Croatia (4.1) and Lithuania (4.2). Between 2013 and 2018, the most significant increase in ratings was among women in Ireland, with an improvement of 1.5 points. In terms of job satisfaction, the highest ratings in 2018 were given by residents of Finland and Ireland (8.2 each), and Sweden (7.9). In contrast, the lowest ratings were reported in Bulgaria (4.8), Greece (5.4), and Romania (6.0). The most significant decrease in job satisfaction ratings was observed between 2013 and 2018 in Denmark, with a drop of 0.9 points to 7.5. For time use satisfaction in 2018, the highest ratings were observed in Finland (8.3), Sweden (7.8), and Austria (7.6), while the lowest ratings were in Greece (5.1), Bulgaria (5.3), and Hungary and Lithuania (6.0 each). Again, Denmark saw the largest decline in this area between 2013 and 2018, with a decrease of 0.7 points to 7.7. Regarding satisfaction with personal relationships in 2018, the highest ratings were in Malta and Sweden (8.8 each), followed by Austria and Finland (8.6 each), and Cyprus and Ireland (8.5 each). The lowest ratings were in Bulgaria (5.8), followed by Croatia, Greece, and Romania (7.0 each). The most significant positive change between 2013 and 2018 was among Bulgarian women, whose satisfaction rating with personal relationships increased by 1 point, reaching 5.8.

Generally, women's life satisfaction increases with higher levels of education and decreases with age (Figure 3.11). This indicates that the higher a woman's educational attainment, the more satisfied she tends to be with her life; conversely, older women tend to feel less satisfied. However, this trend does not hold uniformly across all member states (Eurostat, 2024b). In 2022 and 2013, women with higher education consistently rated their overall life satisfaction at 7.5 points. For women with secondary education, the rating also remained unchanged at 7.1 points. On the contrary, for women with primary education,

Table 3.7 Average satisfaction rating of women in the EU in various areas in 2013 and 2018 (16 years or over)

Geolyear	*Satisfaction with the financial situation*		*Job satisfaction*		*Satisfaction with use of time*		*Satisfaction with personal relationships*	
	2013	*2018*	*2013*	*2018*	*2013*	*2018*	*2013*	*2018*
EU-27	5.5	6.0	6.8	6.9	6.8	6.9	7.6	7.8
Austria	6.4	6.7	7.7	7.7	7.5	7.6	8.6	8.6
Belgium	6.4	6.4	7.4	7.4	7.1	7.2	7.5	7.8
Bulgaria	2.7	2.9	4.7	4.8	5.4	5.3	4.8	5.8
Croatia	3.8	4.1	5.7	6.1	6.3	6.3	6.6	7.0
Cyprus	5.1	5.7	7.1	6.8	6.8	6.9	7.9	8.5
Czechia	5.1	5.5	6.5	6.2	7.1	7.2	8.0	8.1
Denmark	7.8	7.5	8.4	7.5	8.4	7.7	9.0	8.4
Estonia	5.1	5.7	7.0	7.1	6.9	7.5	7.4	7.7
Finland	7.4	7.7	8.1	8.2	8.2	8.3	8.4	8.6
France	6.0	6.2	7.0	7.1	7.3	7.2	7.8	7.9
Germany	5.8	6.3	6.7	7.1	6.8	6.9	7.8	7.8
Greece	4.0	4.6	5.4	5.4	6.0	5.1	6.7	7.0
Hungary	4.4	4.6	6.4	6.2	6.2	6.0	7.4	7.3
Ireland	5.3	6.8	7.6	8.2	7.2	7.8	8.6	8.5
Italy	5.3	5.8	6.6	6.7	6.4	6.5	7.2	7.3
Latvia	4.4	4.6	6.7	6.6	7.0	6.9	7.8	7.6
Lithuania	5.3	4.2	6.4	6.6	6.7	6.0	7.9	7.4
Luxembourg	6.5	6.6	7.7	7.0	7.3	7.1	8.0	7.8
Malta	5.6	6.4	7.2	7.6	6.7	6.9	8.4	8.8
The Netherlands	7.3	7.1	7.7	7.7	7.7	7.3	8.3	8.1
Poland	5.1	5.4	6.9	6.7	7.3	7.3	7.9	7.8
Portugal	4.2	4.7	7.1	6.9	6.5	6.4	7.8	8.1
Romania	5.5	5.8	6.0	6.0	6.5	6.3	7.3	7.0
Slovakia	4.8	4.9	6.0	6.1	7.5	7.1	7.7	8.1
Slovenia	4.5	5.2	7.3	6.7	6.7	7.3	8.4	8.4
Spain	5.4	5.6	6.8	6.9	6.7	6.9	7.7	8.2
Sweden	7.5	7.6	8.0	7.9	7.9	7.8	8.5	8.8

Source: Eurostat (2024c).

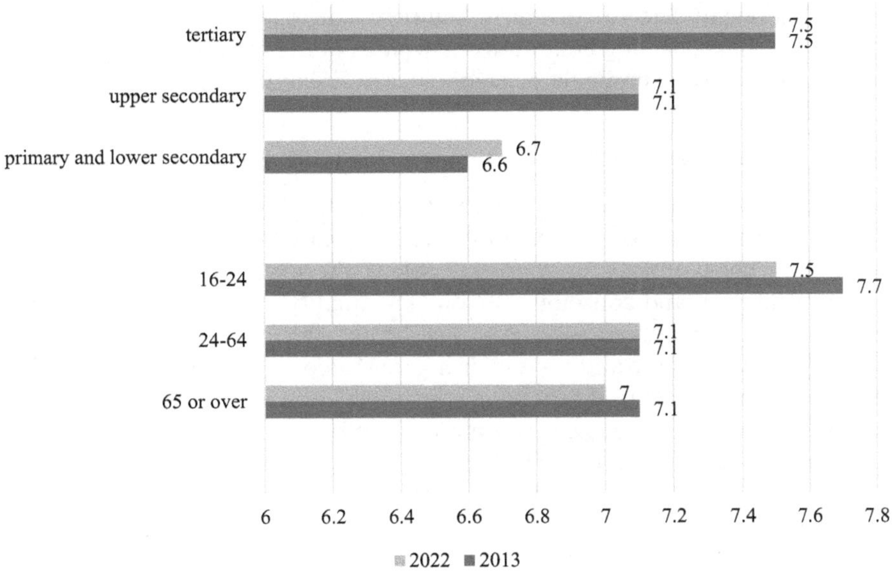

Figure 3.11 Overall satisfaction with life of women in the UE by age and educational attainment level in 2013 and 2022.

Source: Eurostat (2024c).

the satisfaction rating increased slightly by 0.1 points, reaching 6.7 points in 2022. When examining life satisfaction by age within the EU-27 in 2022, the youngest generation (aged 16–24) reported a satisfaction level of 7.5 points. Women aged 24–64 years rated their life satisfaction at 7.1 points and women over 65 years rated theirs at 7 points. Compared to 2013, life satisfaction declined among the youngest (16–24) and oldest (over 65) age groups, with a more significant decrease observed in the youngest cohort. On the contrary, the life satisfaction scores of women aged 24–64 remained stable over the same period.

In conclusion, assessing the living conditions of women in the EU requires a multifaceted problem. Education, occupation, income, consumption patterns, and subjective assessments of health and life satisfaction represent only a fraction of the elements required to paint a comprehensive picture of women's living conditions in the EU. While many EU member states have made strides in addressing the analysed issues, indicating an overall improvement in the living conditions of contemporary women and offering promising prospects for future generations, challenges persist. These include the gender pay gap, limited access to leadership roles for women, unsustainable consumption patterns, and health disparities relative to men. Moreover, it is crucial to recognize that the living conditions of women across the EU exhibit significant spatial disparities, largely influenced by the socioeconomic development of individual countries. Varying resource allocations and development potentials among nations underscore divergent abilities to meet residents' needs. It is for this reason that the living conditions of women in the countries that make up the Union, including immediate neighbors, are different.

Leisure time of women of the 21st century and how it is used

Technical and socioeconomic progress, as well as the development of medicine and new forms of work organization, have increased the amount of leisure time. These days, it plays an important role in the sustainable life of a world citizen: a modern and conscious person. The quality of work, education and professional development, everyday well-being, and health depends on the quantity of leisure time and ways of using it. Moreover, the forms and content of leisure time can help discover new attitudes, priorities, and values introduced into everyday life. Leisure time is therefore an important element of standard and quality of life. Modern society is called leisure society and is accompanied by the development of a broad leisure industry sector (Niemczyk et al., 2023).

Despite active policies for gender equality in EU countries, men have more leisure time than women (Kolpashnikova et al., 2018, Barca, 2018). After all, women are the ones who experience motherhood, care for children, and take care of the home, striving to provide their family and themselves with adequate living conditions, rest, and development. The results of the Harmonized European Time Use Survey (HETUS) for the years 2008–2015 show that in all 15 EU countries covered by the study, women are much more involved in household and family care, that is, unpaid work done for their household, than men. The women of Italy and Romania spend the most time on this activity (over 5 hours a day), and the women of the Netherlands (less than 3.5 hours) and Finland (3 h and 41 min), spend the least time on this activity, as well as the women in Germany (3 h and 50 min) and Luxembourg (3 h and 54 min) – Figure 3.12.

The difference between women and men in the time spent on household and family care is greatest in Italy (2 h and 47 min more for women than for men) and Romania (2 h and 17 min). Furthermore, it is quite high in Greece (2 h and 21 min) and Spain (2 h), and the lowest – in the Netherlands (1 h and 2 min) and Finland (1 h and 9 min).

In addition to unpaid domestic work, women are professionally active, which is a common phenomenon in many countries around the world, as mentioned earlier (see section "Women's education, work, and income"). As a consequence, women often struggle with a deficit of leisure time and, thus, many of them cannot afford to participate in leisure time activities.

When analysing the issue of nonparticipation in leisure activities by EU residents, it should be noted that this problem currently affects over 13% of women. Although this percentage is gradually decreasing, still approximately 2 pp more women than men cannot afford to engage in leisure activities on a regular basis – Figure 3.13. What makes the authors optimistic is the fact that

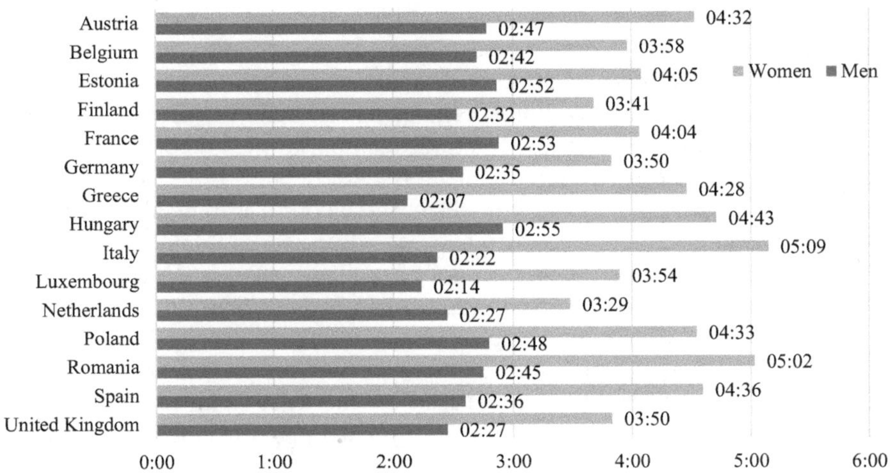

Figure 3.12 Participation time per day in household and family care (in hh:mm) in selected UE countries in 2008–2015 (by gender).

Source: Eurostat (2019).

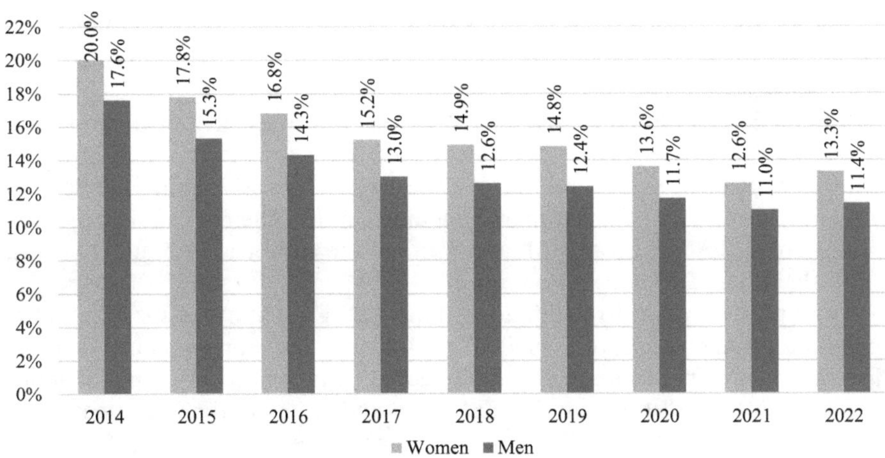

Figure 3.13 Percentage of women and men from European Union who cannot afford to regularly participate in a leisure activity in 2014–2022.

Source: Eurostat (2024s).

this difference decreased in the analysed period by 1/5, that is, 0.5 pp (and if 2015 and 2016 are adopted as a basis, even by 0.6 pp). However, almost every eighth woman from the EU still does not participate in leisure activities, whereas in the group of men, it is every ninth person.

The EU country where the highest percentage of people cannot afford regular leisure activities is Romania. Here, the problem affects every second woman (and every second man) on average. Ranking next are: Hungary, Bulgaria, Lithuania, and Greece, where the percentage of people who do not engage in leisure activity is around 20–30% (both among women and men). The countries whose citizens can afford most regular leisure activities are Luxembourg and the Scandinavian countries (Finland, Denmark, and Sweden), as well as Croatia and the Czech Republic. During the study period, the percentage of women participating in leisure activities in these countries ranged from 89.9% to 97.2%, depending on the country and year (Eurostat, 2024s).

The largest percentage of women not participating in leisure activities versus men occurs in the following EU countries: Latvia (1.6 pp – 6.2 pp, depending on the year), Lithuania (1.7 pp – 5.9 pp), Hungary (2.6 pp – 4.3 pp), but also France (2.9 pp – 5.0 pp) and Ireland (1.5 pp – 5.2 pp). On the other hand, the following countries are characterized by the least significant difference: Cyprus (−0,6 pp – 2.3 pp), Croatia (−0.3 pp – 0.9 pp), Luxembourg (0.6 pp – 2.0 pp), Italy (0.2 pp – 1.3 pp), and Finland (0.1 pp – 1.6 pp). It is also worth mentioning that in the period under study, that is, in the years 2014–2022, the greatest progress in reducing the percentage of women not engaging in leisure activity was observed in the following: Romania (by 24.0 pp), Bulgaria (by 21.2 pp), Lithuania (by 17.4 pp), Hungary (by 16.3 pp), and Malta (by 15.2 pp). In turn, in countries such as Denmark, Greece, Sweden, Finland, and Luxembourg, the percentage of women who cannot afford regular leisure activities increased during the analysed period by 3.7 pp, 3.2 pp, 2.1 pp, 0.5 pp, and 0.5, respectively (Eurostat, 2024s).

Women living in Finland spend most time of day in leisure, social, and associative life (5 h and 43 min). German women rank second (5 h and 36 min), followed by the Dutch (5 h and 22 min), the Greek (5 h and 15 min), the Belgian (5 h and 13 min), and the Estonian (5 h and 1 min). The ranking is closed by women from Romania (only 4 h and 1 min), Luxembourg (4 h and 11 min), and Italy (4 h and 29 min) – Figure 3.14.

An important point to highlight is that in all EU countries surveyed, men spend more time on leisure, social, and associative life than women. The most significant difference is observable in Greece (1 h and 1 min), Belgium (58 min), Italy (52 min), and Romania (51 min). Men and women's time devoted to leisure, social, and associative life is most similar in the Netherlands (25 minutes more for men) and Germany (31 minutes).

Gender is related not only to the amount of leisure time but also to leisure activities and patterns. Both women and men can use their free time by choosing active or passive recreation (more: Niemczyk et al., 2023). In general terms, forms of leisure time management are divided into: physical, cultural, sport, artistic, social, and travel activity.

When it comes to physical activity, the available Eurostat data show that on average every third woman in the EU does not engage in it at all (Figure 3.15). In the men's group, this percentage is 3.5 pp lower. Only every 20th European woman works out outside working time at least twice a day, and every seventh

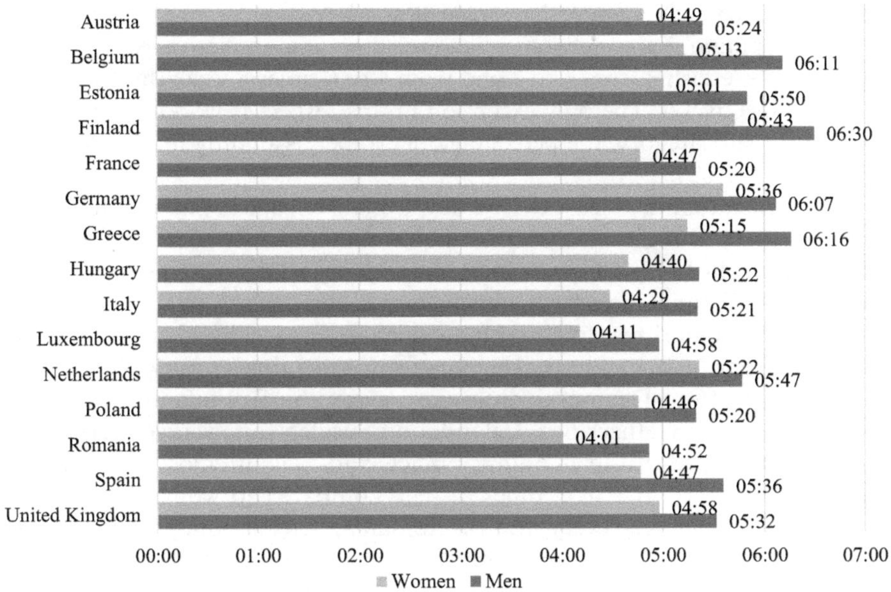

Figure 3.14 Participation time per day in leisure, social and associative life (in hh:mm) in selected UE countries in 2008–2015 (by gender).

Source: Eurostat (2024w).

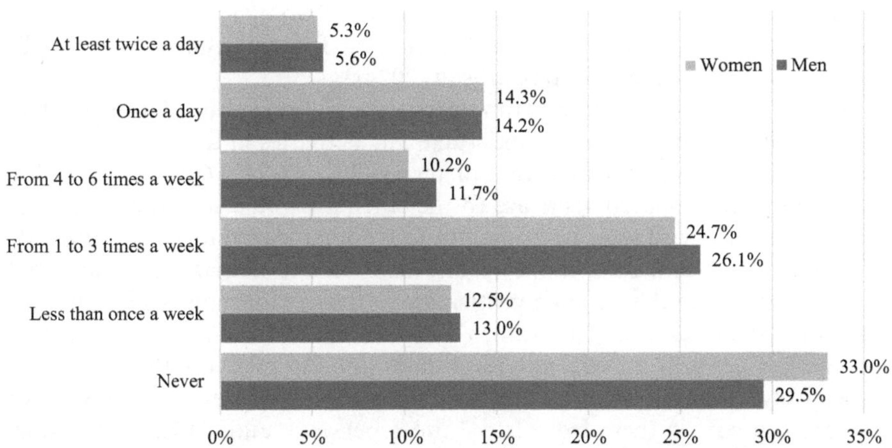

Figure 3.15 Percentage of women and men from European Union performing physical activity outside working time in a typical week in 2022 (by frequency).

Source: Eurostat (2024r).

woman – once a day. Note that, regardless of frequency, the percentage of people working out among women is lower than among men, especially when it comes to exercising from 1 to 3 and from 4 to 6 times a week (by 1.4 pp and 1.5 pp, respectively). The only exception in this respect is working out once a day. In this subcategory, the percentage of women is slightly higher than that of men (by 0.1 pp).

Most often, that is, at least twice a day, women engage in physical activity in Estonia (every fourth on average), the Netherlands, Sweden and Finland (almost every fifth), and Greece (on average every sixth). Female residents of Slovenia and Estonia most frequently engage in this type of activity once a day (on average one in three) followed by women in Greece, Sweden, and Cyprus (on average one in four). Physical activity from 4 to 6 times a week is most typical of women from Denmark (on average every third), Finland (on average every fourth), the Netherlands, Ireland, and Sweden (on average every fifth). Women from Austria, Luxembourg, France, and Belgium most often declare physical activity from 1 to 3 times a week compared to women from other countries (on average, every third). Romania, Luxembourg, Poland, and Slovakia have the highest percentage of women working out less than once a week (24.5%, 21.3%, 20.5%, and 20.1%, respectively). Slovenia, Ireland, and Estonia close the ranking (5.6%, 5.8%, and 6.0%, respectively). The least active in terms of exercise are women from Bulgaria and Croatia. Approximately 60% of them do not engage in physical activities. Only 0.7% and 1.0%, respectively, engage in them at least twice a day, 5.6% and 7.9% – once a day, 3.4% and 4.4% – from 4 to 6 times a week, 9.4% and 16.2% – from 1 to 3 times a week. Note also that in almost all EU countries (except Denmark, Ireland, Slovenia, Lithuania, and Latvia) the percentage of women who do not practice physical activity is higher than that of men – especially in Bulgaria, where the difference is as much as 8.9 pp (Eurostat, 2024r).

Another form of using leisure time is to participate in culture. Unfortunately, most European women do not undertake any activities in this area. However, their share is still greater than that of men – 86% vs 74% (Figure 3.16). The most frequently declared visits are to the cinema (from 1 to 3 times per year 24% of women spend their free time this way and at least 4 times a year 8% do so). Visiting cultural sites ranks second as a leisure activity (22% and 9%, respectively). Note that women participate in live performances slightly more often than men – 21% of EU women go to the theater, concert or ballet from 1 to 3 times per year and 6% at least 4 times (among men it is 18% and 5.5%, respectively). However, women are less interested in sports events – only 8% of women take part in them from 1 to 3 times per year, and 6% at least 4 times (among men it is 14% and 12%, respectively).

Women from Denmark, Luxembourg, and the Netherlands attend the cinema the most often – on average every second woman. In turn, up to 87.0% of Bulgarian, 85.9% of Romanian, 85.5% of Latvian, and 80.4% of Cypriot women did not go to the cinema at all in 2022. Also in terms of participation in live performances, women from Luxembourg (50.3%), Denmark (47.6%),

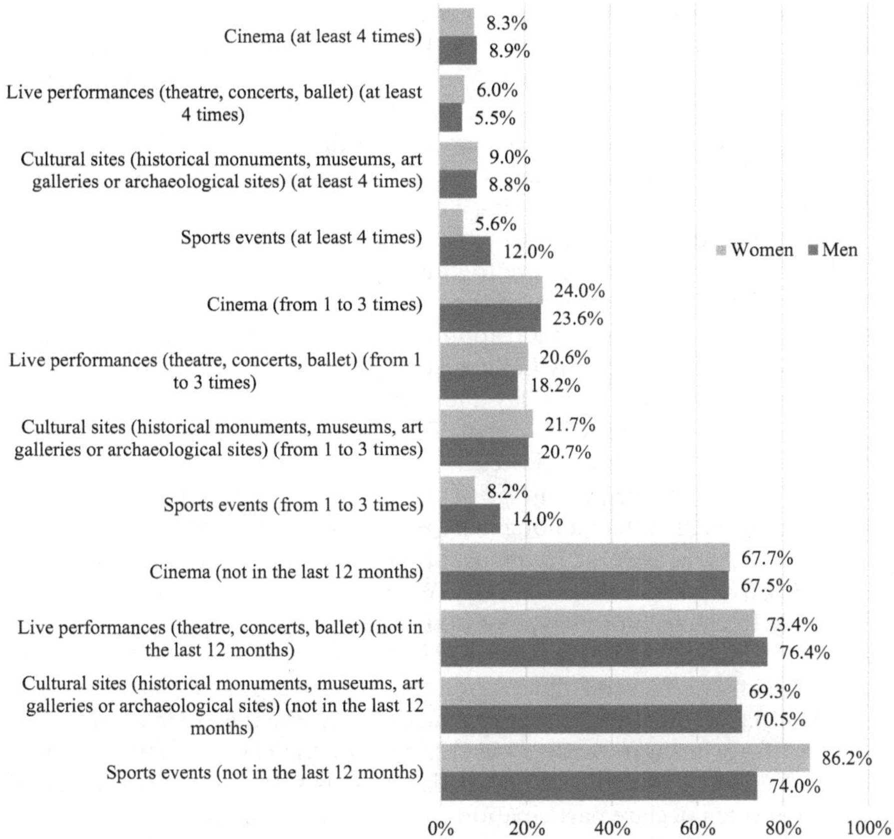

Figure 3.16 Percentage of women and men from European Union participating in the different cultural or sport activities in 2022 (by frequency).

Source: Eurostat (2024j).

and the Netherlands (43.6%) are the most active, and women from Romania (10.8%), Bulgaria (13.2%), Slovakia (16.8%), and Italy (18.9%) are the least active. Visiting cultural sites is also most preferred by female residents of Luxembourg (63.2%), Denmark (55.1%), and the Netherlands (46.1%), but also Finland (44.1%) and the Czech Republic (44.1%). However, up to 87.7% of women from Bulgaria, 86.3% from Romania, and 85.1% from Cyprus did not undertake such cultural activity at all in 2022. In terms of participation in sporting events, women from the Netherlands (32.8%), Luxembourg (30.8%), and Ireland (29.9%) take the lead, and the ranking is again closed by Romanian (2.7%), Bulgarian (3.8%), and Cypriot women (7.0%) (Eurostat, 2024j).

The greatest participatory advantage of women over men is observed in live performances, in the Czech Republic and Finland (from 1 to 3 times per year – by 7.8 pp and by 6.8 pp, respectively) and Estonia (at least 4 times per year – by 3.1 pp).

Also in terms of visiting monuments from 1 to 3 times per year, Czech women stand out, as they undertake this activity 4.3 pp more often than men. In turn, a much higher percentage of women go to the cinema 1 to 3 times per year than men in Ireland (by 3.5 pp). Worth emphasizing is that only women from the Czech Republic participate in sports events more often than men (by 1.3 pp at least 4 times per year). In other countries, men dominate, especially in Slovakia, Croatia, Greece, Cyprus, and Ireland (Eurostat, 2024j).

Another way to spend one's free time is artistic activities, that is, pursuits in visual arts (drawing, painting, photography, sculpting, etc.), literary arts (fiction, drama, poetry, and prose), and performing arts (dance, music, and theater). According to Eurostat data, approximately two-thirds of EU women do not engage in such leisure activities at all (Figure 3.17). Only 1 in 20 Europeans practice artistic activities every day and once a month, 1 in 14 several times a month, and 1 in 17 at least once a year. The most popular frequency in artistic activities is every week, as indicated by every tenth woman from the EU. It should be noted that the percentage of people engaging in artistic activities is higher among women than among men, regardless of frequency.

Artistic activities are practiced most often, that is, every day, by residents of Finland (21.6%) and Denmark (13.2%). Women from Finland (26.4%) are also more likely to engage in this type of activity every week, followed by women from the Netherlands (25.3%), Austria (21.5%), and Ireland (20.0%). Engaging in artistic activities several times a month is most typical for women from Slovakia (15.0%), Austria (13.1%) and again from Finland (13.9%), and once a month – for women from Slovakia (12.1%), Austria (11.5%), and Lithuania (10.0%). European women from countries such as Denmark, Lithuania, and Spain most often declare participation in artistic activities at least once a year compared to women from other countries – 16.3%, 12.8%, and 10.0%, respectively. Women from Italy, Croatia, and Romania are the least active in terms of engaging in artistic activities – more than 80% of them did not pursue them at all in 2022. Note that the greatest advantage of women over men in artistic

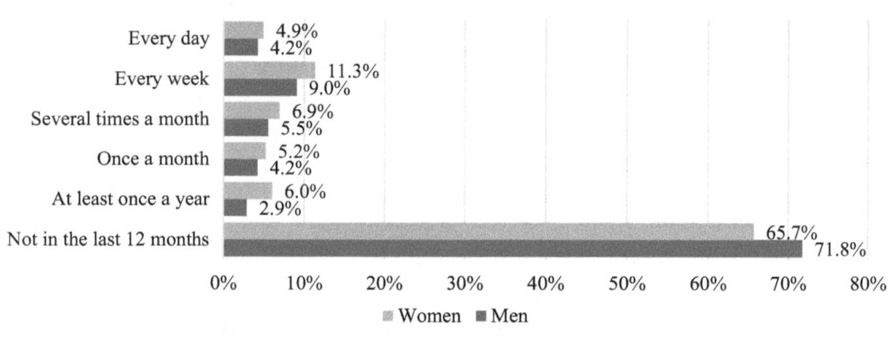

Figure 3.17 Percentage of women and men from European Union participating in the artistic activities in 2022 (by frequency).

Source: Eurostat (2024k).

activity participation is observable in Finland (every day by 12.2 pp and every week by 8.3 pp) and Lithuania (by 12.2 pp at least once a year). In turn, Italian women outnumber Italian men (by 2.8 pp) in terms of not engaging in artistic activities at all (Eurostat, 2024k).

Social gatherings are an important leisure activity. In their research, Banach and Orlińska (2013, p. 101) showed that women value this way of spending their free time more than men. Men, on the other hand, devote more time to themselves. This is due to the nature of women and men. Women are usually more open, talkative, and sociable, while men are more introverted and shy.

When analysing the social relationships of EU residents, it should be stated that they meet with family and relatives more often than with friends. Fourteen percent of women indicate family contacts every day, and 37% every week, while meetings with friends – 11% and 36%, respectively (Figure 3.18). In turn, every fourth woman meets with friends several times a month, and every fifth woman meets with her family several times a month. More European women also declare that they meet with friends less often than with family, once a month – 14% and 13%, respectively, and not at all – 6% and 3%, respectively. Note that in more frequent contact with family and less frequent contact with friends, women dominate over men and vice versa. The greatest percentage advantage of women over men is observable in weekly and daily meetings with family – by 2.9 pp and 2.2 pp, respectively.

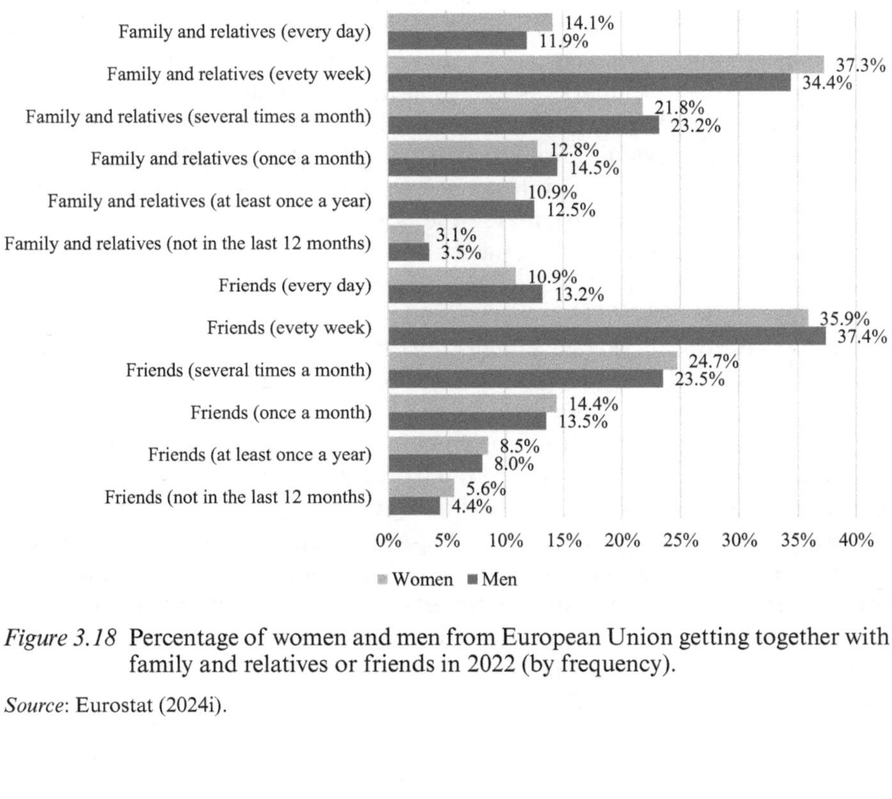

Figure 3.18 Percentage of women and men from European Union getting together with family and relatives or friends in 2022 (by frequency).

Source: Eurostat (2024i).

In terms of family contacts, Cyprus and Bulgaria are the leading EU countries – almost every second woman from these countries meets her family every day. Bulgarian women (28.7%), as well as Greek and Croatian women (27.1% and 26.6%, respectively), also declare the most frequent contacts with friends. Every week, people from Belgium and Italy (every second person) contact their family the most, and those from Belgium (53.1%) and Cyprus (48.2%) contact their friends the most. Poland, Denmark, and Lithuania lead in terms of the percentage of women meeting family and relatives several times a month (37.1%, 33.4%, and 31.6%, respectively). Poland, Denmark, and Romania also dominate due to contacts with friends several times a month (35.9%, 32.4%, and 34.0% respectively). When it comes to meeting with family once a month, women from Latvia, Estonia, and Sweden prevail (every fifth does so) and also women from Latvia, Estonia, and Sweden. Every fourth of them meets with their family at least once a year. In turn, in terms of women's contacts with friends once a month, Sweden (20.3%) and Estonia (20.1%) are the leaders, and at least once a year, Lithuania (19.6%), Estonia (16.3%), and Poland (12.9%). Women from Estonia and Latvia did not contact their family even once in 2022, although this percentage is not very high – 6.4% and 5.3%, respectively. The situation is slightly different in the case of women's lack of contact with friends. Here, once again, women from Latvia and Estonia stand out, as well as Maltese, but their percentage is much higher – 22.1%, 15.5%, and 16.0%, respectively (Eurostat, 2024i).

Note that Denmark and Slovakia are the leaders in terms of the percentage of women over men in family contacts, where the difference is 6.9 pp in every weekly meetings and 4.1 pp in everyday meetings, respectively. In turn, in Slovenia and again Denmark, as well as in Malta, women dominate over men in terms of relatively rare meetings with friends, by 6.3 pp in once a month contacts, 6.0 pp in several times a month contacts, and 5.5 pp in the case of no contact in the last 12 months. It should also be emphasized that as the frequency of family contacts decreases, the number of countries where the percentage of men is greater than the percentage of women increases. The opposite situation occurs when it comes to meeting with friends (Eurostat, 2024i).

Another important way to spend free time is tourism. In 2012–2019, the number of European women taking tourist trips increased and only in two years (2013 and 2016), it was slightly lower than the year before (by 0.78% and 0.82%, respectively) – Figure 3.19. In total, in 2012, almost 116 million EU residents participated in tourism, and in 2019, it was almost 125 million, that is, almost 8% more. In 2020, due to the COVID-19 pandemic, the number of European female tourists decreased by more than 1/5, but in 2021, it increased by 8.16%, and in 2022 by another 10.72%. As a result, in the last year analysed, the number of female tourists from the EU was only 5.5% lower than in the pre-pandemic year of 2019 and amounted to almost 118 million. Note that in all the years under study, the number of women travelers was greater than the number of men. The largest advantage was recorded in 2014 (by 7.76%), and the smallest in 2016 (by 1.02%).

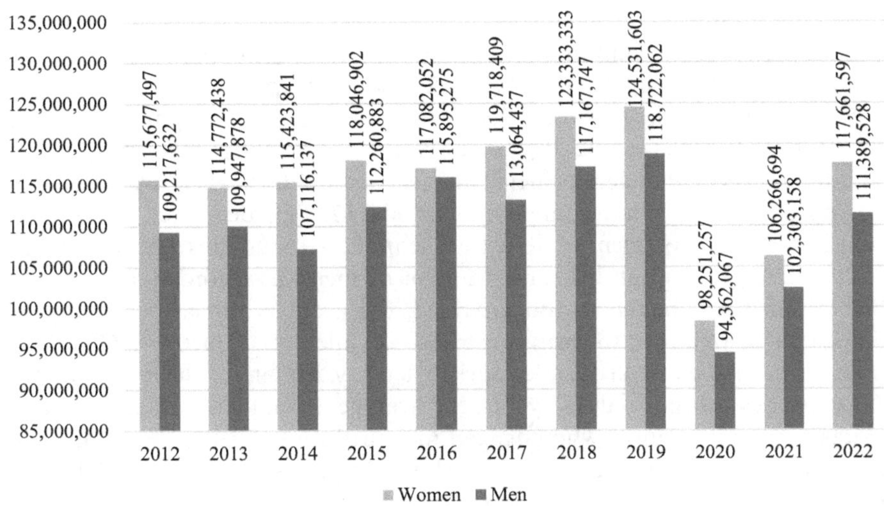

Figure 3.19 Number of women and men from European Union participating in tourism for personal purposes in 2012–2022.

Source: Eurostat (2024p).

It is common knowledge that the most active tourist nation in Europe is Germany (Seweryn, 2011). This is confirmed by Eurostat data on the number of women travelers – in the years under study, on average, over 26.3 million female residents of this country went on a tourist trip each year. France is second, with an average of almost 20.2 million women. By 2017, the United Kingdom ranked third (over 17.6 million), and Spain and Italy follow with almost half as many women travelers (an average of approximately 12.4 million and 10.6 million, respectively). However, which comes as no surprise, the ranking among EU countries is closed by territorially small countries, that is, Malta (an average of 105,000 women), Luxembourg, and Cyprus (an average of over 194,000 and almost 242,000, respectively). Moreover, in the period under question, it is noteworthy that there is a successive annual increase in the number of women traveling from Ireland (in total by over one-fifth) and Luxembourg (in total by almost one-third, of course, apart from the pandemic year of 2020). A positive dynamics indicator from 2022 to 2012 was also recorded in countries such as: Malta (by as much as 63.77%), Bulgaria (by 44.71%), Spain (by 29.39%), Belgium (by 27.36%), Poland (by 15.56%), Latvia (by 14.09%), Romania (by 11.55%), Greece (by 10.84%), the Netherlands (by 8.18%), Slovakia (by 7.06%), Slovenia (by 6.80%), Austria (by 6.15%), France (by 4.39%), and Hungary (by 1.23%) (Eurostat, 2024p).

It should be emphasized that in most EU countries, the number of women travelers is greater than that of men. The opposite situation is observed in Romania, and in recent years also in Sweden and Malta. In the period under study, the greatest advantage of women over men was recorded in France (over 15.8 million), Germany (over 7.5 million), Spain (almost 6.2 million), and Poland (over 5.8 million). In turn, in Romania, there were almost 1.4 million more men traveling than women (Eurostat, 2024p).

Upon analysing the percentage of EU female residents engaging in tourism, different conclusions can be drawn than in the case of the number of travelers. Although this percentage was increasing (except for 2013, when it decreased by 0.42 pp and 2020, when the pandemic caused a 12.98 pp decrease), it was lower than in the group of men in almost all years under study (except for 2014) – Figure 3.20. The largest difference in favor of men was recorded in 2016 – by 2.08 pp. In total, in the period analysed, the average annual percentage of women participating in tourism was 59.94%, while that of men was 60.80%.

In terms of the rate of female tourism activity, Finland is the leader among EU countries. In the analysed years, the average annual percentage of female residents of this country who engaged in tourism was 86.48%. Ranking next are women from the Netherlands (83.75%), followed by Luxembourg (79.60%), almost equal to Sweden (79.10%). At the bottom of the list are Romania (only 24.00%) and Bulgaria (26.85%). It should be emphasized that since 2014, there has been an increase in the percentage of women traveling from Poland, since 2015 – from Belgium, Portugal, and Slovakia, and since 2016 – from Croatia, Hungary, Malta, and Austria. It is also impossible not to note that in the EU only one country, Ireland, had a higher percentage of female travelers than male travelers throughout the entire period under study. The opposite situation occurred in two countries, namely, Italy and Romania, where men were more active in tourism than women throughout the study period (Eurostat, 2024p).

Finally, note that the beginning of the 21st century brought a change in the approach to professional life and time outside of work. As a result of the increase in employees' expectations toward the work environment and their employers, time outside work was appreciated, which is part of the concept of work-life balance, to improve the level and quality of people's lives. This is a priority element in many strategic activities of the EU, which results from the

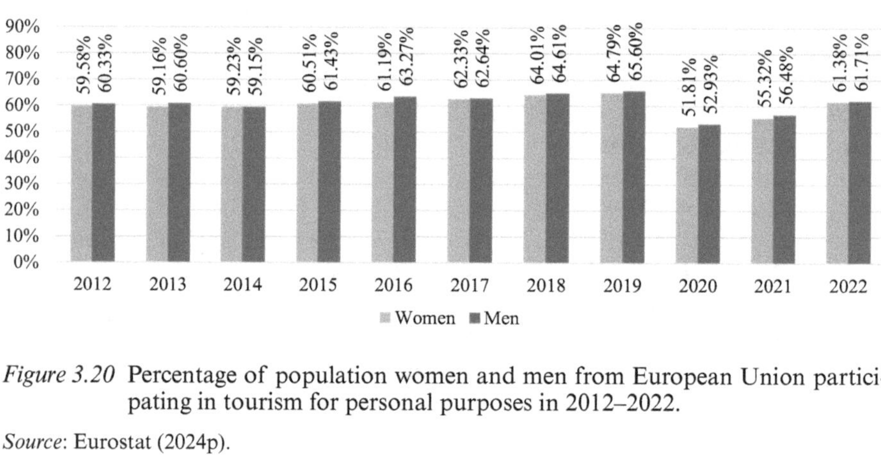

Figure 3.20 Percentage of population women and men from European Union participating in tourism for personal purposes in 2012–2022.

Source: Eurostat (2024p).

large differences in the level and quality of life in EU countries and their individual regions (Pomarańska, 2020, p. 28).

Work–life balance is a reaction to the extension and intensification of working time and the fad for, or necessity of workaholism that follows the new phase of development of postmodern capitalism in highly developed countries (Jung, 2003, p. 17). Therefore, the attitudes of both the employee and the employer are important, as their actions may facilitate or hinder maintaining a balance between professional work and private life. What seems important is the perception of these two spheres as complementary and not opposed or disconnected. This means adopting a holistic concept and treating career as an integral part of life, and not as a separate, obligatory activity. This does not mean, however, that private life should be lived at work and professional life in the personal sphere. On the contrary, in work–life balance, it is important to clearly separate private and professional life and not to exceed the established boundaries.

Professionally active women struggling with a deficit of free time could find some recommendations for themselves on the concept of work–life balance. However, a support network is crucial and can take many forms. In business, it most often comes down to effective human capital management. In their private lives, partners can help each other focus on what is important, plan their time to live a healthy life, and make informed choices about work, home management, and leisure time activities.

Conclusions

The data analysis conducted has shown the diversified situation of women in the EU-27, both related to time and spatial, in terms of employment, income, consumption, and life satisfaction. Most EU member states have made progress on the issues analysed, indicating a general improvement in the conditions in which modern women live. However, it is important to keep in mind that there are still challenges in terms of gender wage inequality, limited access to leadership and management positions for women, inappropriate consumption patterns or inferior health ratings relative to men. The highlighted areas define women's functioning in their leisure time and determine its quantity and quality. It is common knowledge that women spend more time than men on household and family chores, which results in limitations in the amount of their leisure time. They spend their money especially on contacts with family and relatives, participation in culture, and tourism. However, they meet with friends, engage in physical activity, or take part in sports events less often. Research has shown that Finland, the Netherlands, and Luxembourg stand out among the EU countries, where women spend the least time on household chores and therefore can afford to engage in leisure activities. In turn, Romanian and Bulgarian women have the least amount of leisure time; therefore, they participate in leisure activities less often. In essence, the heterogeneous landscape of living conditions among EU countries underscores the importance of targeted policies and initiatives aimed at addressing disparities and fostering equitable opportunities for women across the region. By acknowledging and addressing these complex dynamics, policymakers can work towards creating a more inclusive and prosperous future for all women in the European Union.

Note

1 More about women's entrepreneurship in Chapter 4.

References

Banach, M. & Orlińska, M. (2013). Formy aktywności wolnoczasowej ludzi starszych [Forms of free-time activities of the elderly]. In M. Banach & T. W. Gierat (Eds.), *Formy spędzania czasu wolnego* [*Forms of leisure activities*] (75–106). Kraków: Scriptum.

Barca, F. (2018). *Women still work more and enjoy less free time*. Retrieved from http://www.voxeurop.eu/en/2018/international-women-s-day-5121855

EIGE. (2017). *Ubóstwo a płeć w cyklu życia człowieka* [Poverty and gender in the human life cycle]. Retrieved from https://eige.europa.eu/sites/default/files/documents/ti_pubpdf_mh0616074pln_pdfweb_20171204165148.pdf

Eurostat. (2019). *How do women and men use their time – statistics*. Retrieved from https://ec.europa.eu/eurostat/statistics-explained/index.php?title=How_do_women_and_men_use_their_time_-_statistics&oldid=463738

Eurostat. (2024a). *At-risk-of-poverty rate by sex*. Retrieved from https://ec.europa.eu/eurostat/databrowser/view/tessi010/default/table?lang=en

Eurostat. (2024b). *Average life satisfaction in the EU rated 7.1 out of 10*. Retrieved from https://ec.europa.eu/eurostat/en/web/products-eurostat-news/w/ddn-20240115-1

Eurostat. (2024c). *Average rating of satisfaction by domain, sex, age and educational attainment level*. Retrieved from https://ec.europa.eu/eurostat/databrowser/view/ilc_pw01__custom_10271875/default/table?lang=en&page=time:2023

Eurostat. (2024d). *Employment by sex, age, professional status and occupation (1 000)*. Retrieved from https://ec.europa.eu/eurostat/databrowser/view/LFSA_EGAIS__custom_5271507/bookmark/table?lang=en&bookmarkId=9a0280db-fa89-4452-9aaf-0ca61f44817d

Eurostat. (2024e). *Employment rate of adults by sex, age groups, educational attainment level, number of children and age of youngest child (%)*. Retrieved from https://ec.europa.eu/eurostat/databrowser/view/LFST_HHEREDCH__custom_3724312/bookmark/table?lang=en&bookmarkId=49c7a2c7-2a9a-41ab-817b-d4c27c46b5ed

Eurostat. (2024f). *Frequency of alcohol consumption by sex*. Retrieved from https://ec.europa.eu/eurostat/databrowser/view/HLTH_EHIS_AL1E__custom_9936611/default/table?lang=en

Eurostat. (2024g). *Frequency of drinking sugar-sweetened soft drinks by sex*. Retrieved from https://ec.europa.eu/eurostat/databrowser/view/hlth_ehis_fv7e/default/table?lang=en

Eurostat. (2024h). *Frequency of fruit and vegetables consumption by sex*. Retrieved from https://ec.europa.eu/eurostat/databrowser/view/hlth_ehis_fv1c__custom_9934562/default/table?lang=en&page=time:2014

Eurostat. (2024i). *Frequency of getting together with family and relatives or friends by sex, age and educational attainment level*. Retrieved from: https://ec.europa.eu/eurostat/databrowser/view/ilc_scp09__custom_10839434/default/table?lang=en

Eurostat. (2024j). *Frequency of participation in cultural or sport activities in the last 12 months by sex, age, educational attainment level and activity type*. Retrieved from https://ec.europa.eu/eurostat/databrowser/view/ilc_scp03__custom_10767216/default/table?lang=en

Eurostat. (2024k). *Frequency of practicing of artistic activities by sex, age and educational attainment level.* Retrieved from https://ec.europa.eu/eurostat/databrowser/view/ilc_scp07__custom_10794538/default/table?lang=en

Eurostat. (2024l). *Gender pay gap in unadjusted form by NACE Rev. 2 activity – structure of earnings survey methodology.* Retrieved from https://ec.europa.eu/eurostat/databrowser/view/EARN_GR_GPGR2__custom_1294276/bookmark/table?lang=en&bookmarkId=cd12b396-055c-4e4a-83f9-eed77c521952

Eurostat. (2024m). *Individuals – frequency of internet use.* Retrieved from https://ec.europa.eu/eurostat/databrowser/view/ISOC_CI_IFP_FU__custom_9939240/default/table?lang=en&page=time:2023

Eurostat. (2024n). *Percentage of part-time employment of adults by sex, age groups, number of children and age of youngest child.* Retrieved from https://ec.europa.eu/eurostat/databrowser/view/LFST_HHPTECHI__custom_3724335/bookmark/table?lang=en&bookmarkId=787ada5b-3caa-4b86-8b88-452a9dbc1261

Eurostat. (2024o). *Persons eating fruit, vegetables or salad by sex.* Retrieved from https://ec.europa.eu/eurostat/databrowser/view/ilc_hch11__custom_9935640/default/table?lang=en

Eurostat. (2024p). *Persons participating in tourism for personal purposes by sex.* Retrieved from https://ec.europa.eu/eurostat/databrowser/view/tour_dem_tosex__custom_10859184/default/table?lang=en

Eurostat. (2024r). *Persons performing physical activity outside working time by frequency in a typical week, educational attainment level, sex and age.* Retrieved from https://ec.europa.eu/eurostat/databrowser/view/ilc_hch07b__custom_10739978/default/table?lang=en

Eurostat. (2024s). *Persons who cannot afford to regularly participate in a leisure activity by age, sex and income group.* Retrieved from https://ec.europa.eu/eurostat/databrowser/view/ilc_mdes11a__custom_10735885/default/table?lang=en

Eurostat. (2024t). *Population by educational attainment level, sex and age (%).* Retrieved from https://ec.europa.eu/eurostat/databrowser/view/EDAT_LFS_9903__custom_1290134/bookmark/table?lang=en&bookmarkId=1e41534c-23a1-48a7-a6b3-cd69444d3001

Eurostat. (2024u). *Self-perceived health by sex, age and labour status.* Retrieved from https://ec.europa.eu/eurostat/databrowser/view/HLTH_SILC_01__custom_3560082/bookmark/table?lang=en&bookmarkId=b3a88ffa-33a9-469b-b4a0-e87548e6653e

Eurostat. (2024v). *Smoking of tobacco products by sex.* Retrieved from https://ec.europa.eu/eurostat/databrowser/view/hlth_ehis_sk1e/default/table?lang=en&category=hlth.hlth_det.hlth_smok

Eurostat. (2024w). *Time spent, participation time and participation rate in the main activity by sex and age group.* Retrieved from https://ec.europa.eu/eurostat/databrowser/view/tus_00age__custom_10886604/default/table?lang=en&page=time:2010

Eurostat. (2024z). *Unemployment by sex and age – annual data.* Retrieved from https://ec.europa.eu/eurostat/databrowser/view/UNE_RT_A__custom_1291586/bookmark/table?lang=en&bookmarkId=c670f035-12bf-4638-8160-12df52ed4f75

Firlit-Fesnak, G. (2015). *Bieda i płeć. Sfery podziału kreujące ubóstwo kobiet w krajach Unii Europejskiej* [*Poverty and gender. Spheres of division creating female poverty in European Union countries*]. Warszawa: Oficyna Wydawnicza ASPRA-JR.

Galsanjigmed, E., & Sekiguchi, T. (2023). Challenges women experience in leadership careers: An integrative review. *Merits*, *3*(2), 1–24. https://doi.org/10.3390/merits3020021

Grzega, U. (2012). *Poziom życia ludności w Polsce – determinanty i zróżnicowania* [*The standard of living of the population in Poland – determinants and variations*]. Katowice: UE w Katowicach.

Jung, B. (2003). Work-life balance: Wracamy do punktu wyjścia? (debata nad czasem wolnym z lat siedemdziesiątych XX wieku) [Work-life balance: Are we back to square one? (1970s debate on leisure time)]. *Zarządzanie Zasobami Ludzkimi*, *2*, 17–29. GICID: 01.3001.0015.0862.

Kolpashnikova, K. (2018). American househusbands: New time use evidence of gender display, 2003–2016. *Social Indicators Research*, *140*(3), 1259–1277. https://doi.org/10.1007/s11205-017-1813-z
Kubecka, A., Koziorzemska, M. & Nowotniak J. (2019). *Oblicza ubóstwa kobiet w Polsce* [Faces of women's poverty in Poland]. *Women and Business*, *1–4*, 10–20. https://doi.org10.33119/KiB.2019.1-4.2
Niemczyk, A., Szalonka, K., Gardocka-Jałowiec, A., Nowak, W., Seweryn, R. & Gródek-Szostak, Z. (2023). *The silver economy an ageing society in the European Union*. Routledge. https://doi.org/10.4324/9781003377313
Pomarańska, R. (2020). Harmonia życia zawodowego i czasu wolnego w życiu kobiet w Polsce w perspektywie andragogicznej [Harmony of professional life and free time in the lives of women in Poland in the andragogical perspective]. *Edukacja dorosłych*, *82(2)*, 27–46. https://doi.org/10.12775/ED.2020.012
Seweryn, R. (2011). Tourism of Polish seniors against the background of selected Western European countries. *Zeszyty Naukowe Uniwersytetu Szczecińskiego*, *660*, 627–641.
Szulce, H., & Walkowiak-Markiewicz, K. (2017). Poziom i rozkład dochodów oraz ich konsekwencje dla konsumpcji – na przykładzie wybranych krajów europejskich [The level and distribution of income and their consequences for consumption - using selected European countries as examples]. *Unia Europejska.pl*, *1(242)*, 26–33.
WHO. (2024). Constitution. Retrieved from https://www.who.int/about/accountability/governance/constitution

4 Female entrepreneurship

Forms of professional activity of women

Female entrepreneurs are increasingly recognized as the latest drivers of social inclusion and sustainable industrial development, as well as rising stars of developing country economies (Thaddeus et al., 2022). In 2012, they were recognized by the World Economic Forum as "the way forward". Despite this, female entrepreneurs struggle to take their rightful place in economic life. More women are setting up their businesses around the world, but they still run fewer businesses than men and do so in less profitable markets: those that grow more slowly and are more likely to fail (UNIDO, 2014). The impact of women entrepreneurs on economic growth is undeniable: they help create jobs, reduce poverty, and sustain economic growth. Therefore, it is essential to empower women and support them to become entrepreneurs (Zeidan & Bahrami, 2020). Female entrepreneurship should be properly modeled, based on industry characteristics and knowledge, to adapt to changing trends and opportunities in domestic and global markets.

In addition, there is evidence (Kemp, Wong & Berry, 2020) that women do not choose entrepreneurship as their career path as often as men and that entrepreneurship is generally considered a masculine career path (Bruni, Gherardi & Poggio, 2004). The main points of the typology are presented in Table 4.1.

Researchers tend to associate these phenomena with social pressures caused by gender stereotypes (understood as widespread and established beliefs about a specific group of people, things, and phenomena), as well as cultural specificities (Burkhardt, Nguyen & Poincelot, 2020).

A gender perspective in entrepreneurship research has highlighted differences between male and female entrepreneurs, with particular emphasis on motivational factors for starting a business (Bourgain & Chaudat, 2015). Therefore, women entrepreneurs appear to be motivated by economic factors and often take up entrepreneurship for self-development (Verheul, Van Stel & Thurik, 2006).

However, there are significant differences between starting a business by men and women. For example, Berger and Kuckertz (2016) concluded that

DOI: 10.4324/9781003477532-4

Table 4.1 Typology of profiles of female entrepreneurs

No.	*Type*	*Incentives*
1.	Aimless	Young women who pursuit entrepreneurship due to unemployment.
2.	Success-oriented	Young women who perceive entrepreneurial activity as a long-term strategy.
3.	Strongly success-oriented	Women who perceive entrepreneurship as an opportunity for self-realization or as a means to overcome the phenomenon of the "glass ceiling".
4.	Dualists	Women who seek flexibility for work–life balance.
5.	Return workers	Women who left their jobs to fulfill family duties and are still motivated to self-fulfillment outside their families.
6.	Traditionalists	Women who have a strong family entrepreneurial background.
7.	Radicals	Women who initiate introducing more pro-female tendencies in society.

Source: Bruni, Gherardi, and Poggio (2004).

women provide greater diversity in business processes, leading to higher quality entrepreneurship (Vershinina et al., 2019). However, women are often considered less growth-oriented entrepreneurs and generating lower value-added than men (Marlow, Carter & Shaw, 2008). Although women-owned businesses are linked to public service (Hanson, 2008), such enterprises are still considered underpowered, limited, and less concentrated (Ahl & Marlow, 2012).

Based on an extensive review of the literature on women and entrepreneurs, Castiblanco (2013) emphasized that gender is a moderating element of entrepreneurialism. This is because the characteristics of self-employed women and men are determined by cultural factors (assumed roles, differentiated socialization) and social factors (institutional support, expectations). Certainly, individual factors also matter, since both the abilities and skills of men and women ultimately determine and characterize their projects. In a similar tone, Álvarez, Rebollo, and Rodríguez (2013) emphasize that when women face a task, they encounter a number of obstacles, both individual and social, which are generally specific and different from the barriers and opportunities that men face. Blocking factors include mainly external factors, such as difficulties in maintaining work–life balance. On the other hand, among facilitators, individual issues stand out, as some skills and abilities are primarily developed by women as part of management practice, such as a sense of responsibility or versatility. These qualities are subsequently transferred to the vision and management of the business, adding value. Then they were transferred to the vision and management of the business as added values.

As research shows, in addition to social factors, the lack of female entrepreneurs is also influenced by personal factors. Traditionally, women are family caregivers, significantly affecting their willingness to work overtime and travel for business (Kuschel & Lepeley, 2016). Research also emphasizes that women are not risk-takers by nature, which is a key characteristic of entrepreneurs (Manzanera-Román & Brändle, 2016). Moreover, female perfectionism is identified as a factor causing women's self-doubt.

Different faces of female entrepreneurship

Gender gaps in self-employment have narrowed over the last decade in 21 EU Member States (Figure 4.1). The average gender gap for self-employed workers in the EU has remained stable over the last decade, with a slight decrease in 2021–2022. The decrease is mainly due to two factors. First, the reopening of the economy after the COVID-19 pandemic has led to a faster recovery among self-employed women compared to self-employed men, as lockdown measures have disproportionately affected sectors where self-employed women are overrepresented.

The long-term decline in self-employment is greater among men than among women. The self-employment rate among women dropped from 10% in 2013 to 9.4% in 2022 (i.e., a decrease of 3.6%), while among men it dropped from 18.4% to 16.2% over a decade. In the EU in 2014–2018, the most frequently given reason for women to abandon a business was the lack of profitability (Figure 4.2).

Almost 30% of women declared this factor, which is approximately the same percentage as in the case of men (GEM, 2019). The second most frequently mentioned reason was personal (20.2%), which was less frequently indicated by men (15.7%). Moreover, there were minor differences in the motivations behind men and women, both positive (e.g., the possibility of selling the company,

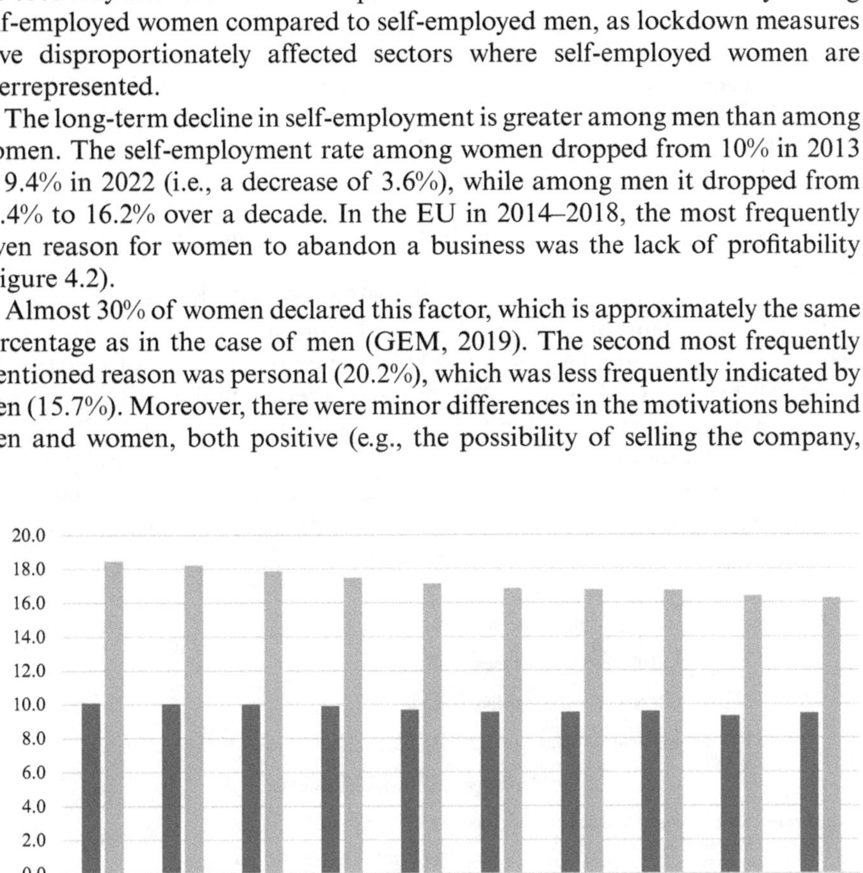

	2013	2014	2015	2016	2017	2018	2019	2020	2021	2022
■ Women	10.0	10.0	9.9	9.9	9.6	9.5	9.5	9.5	9.3	9.4
■ Men	18.4	18.2	17.9	17.5	17.1	16.8	16.7	16.7	16.4	16.2

■ Women ■ Men

Figure 4.1 The gender gap in self-employment in the EU in 2013–2022 (%).

Source: Own study based on the OECD (2023a).

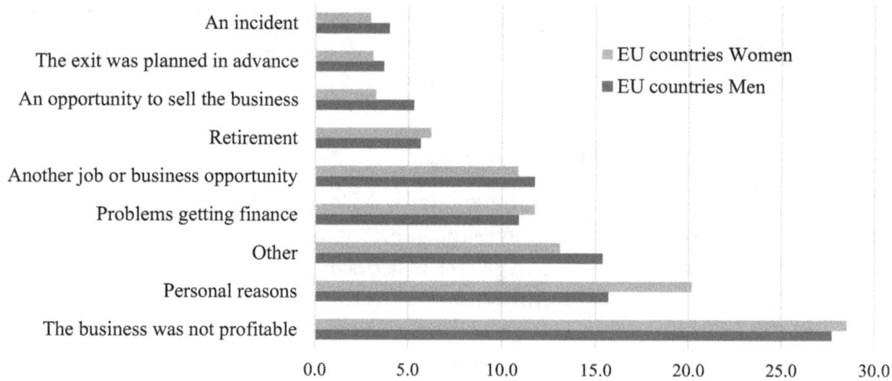

Figure 4.2 Percentage of entrepreneurs (18–64 years old) that exited in the past 12 months, 2014–2018.

Source: Global Entrepreneurship Monitor (2019).

retirement) and negative (e.g., problems with obtaining financial resources, another job or business opportunity).

Upon analysing the professions of the self-employed, the authors observed that more than half of women in 2018 (Figure 4.3) worked as specialists (28.3%) or service and sales workers (27.0%) compared to 29.3% of men (18.2% as specialists and 11.1% as service and sales workers). On the contrary, women worked in crafts much less often than men (3.6% vs. 21.8%).

When observing the share of self-employed women in total employment, it can be concluded that in all EU member states in 2022, women engaged in this type of activity less often than men (Figure 4.4). The self-employment rates

Figure 4.3 Distribution of self-employed people aged 15–64, 2018.

Source: Own study based on Eurostat.

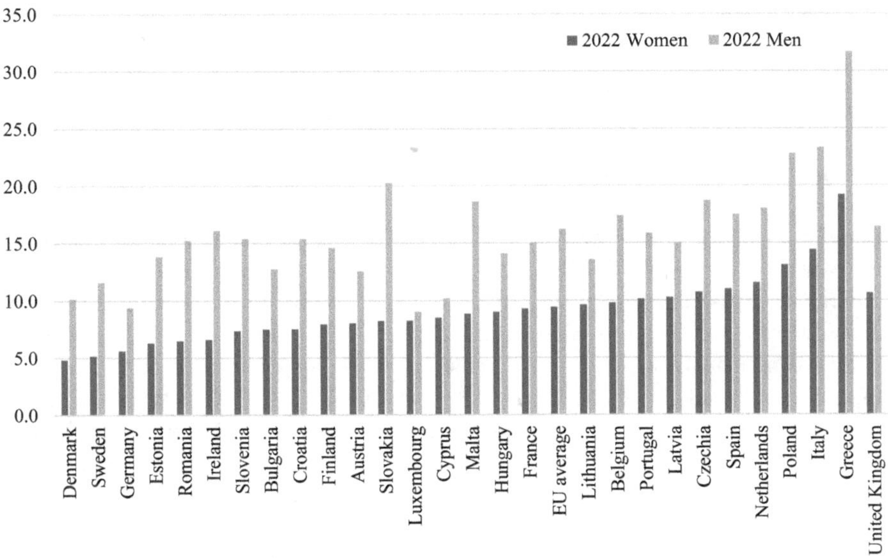

Figure 4.4 Self-employment as a percentage of employment (15–64 years old) in 2022.

Source: Eurostat (2023).

among women were highest in Greece (19%), Italy (14%), and Poland (13%), and in these countries the rates were also high for men.

On the other hand, women's self-employment rates tended to be lower in countries such as Denmark (5%), Sweden (5%), and Germany (6%). Countries with low rates of self-employment for men and women tend to have strong social protection systems that limit the need to start a business out of necessity. They also have social attitudes that favor working in employment (OECD, 2023b). In 2022, in nine EU member states, women were more than twice as likely to be self-employed as men. These countries are: Croatia (2.0 times), Slovenia (2.1 times), Malta (2.1 times), Denmark (2.1 times), Estonia (2.2 times), Sweden (2.3 times), Romania (2.4 times), Ireland (2.5 times), and Slovakia (2.5 times). Note that in 2022, the gender gap was the smallest in Luxembourg, where self-employment among men was only 1.1 times higher than among women (OECD 2023b).

Entrepreneurship is conditioned by many factors, and some of them have been pointed out. One that left a particular mark in this regard was the COVID-19 pandemic, which clearly exposed gender inequalities in entrepreneurialism. Growing evidence shows that women entrepreneurs have experienced disproportionate negative impacts of the pandemic compared to men, including higher rates of business closures and greater loss of income (OECD, 2021). The OECD and World Bank (2020) Future of Business Survey found that between January and May 2020, women-owned businesses were more likely to close than men-owned businesses (26% vs. 20%). This gender gap in business closure rates narrowed as the pandemic continued, but increased again in 2021. In July 2021, the same study found that 25% of women-owned businesses reported closing compared to 17% of men-owned businesses (META, 2022). These gender differences related to the pandemic can be largely explained by sectoral effects. More women entrepreneurs operated in the sectors most affected by the crisis (e.g., personal services, accommodation and food services, arts and entertainment, and retail). However, several other factors also played a role. First, there is evidence to suggest that women entrepreneurs were more likely than men to take on more household responsibilities during the crisis. Therefore, the time they could dedicate to their business was limited. In the OECD and World Bank Survey (2020), approximately a quarter of all women business leaders reported spending six or more hours a day on unpaid household chores between May and October 2020. On the other hand, the ratio for men who were business-minded was just 11%. Research conducted during the first six months of the pandemic found that women entrepreneurs had difficulty accessing pandemic-related entrepreneur support programs. This was often because their businesses did not meet revenue thresholds or because the programs were targeted at sectors where women are underrepresented (OECD, 2021). However, an OECD study conducted in July 2021 showed that women-owned enterprises were as likely as those men-owned to report that they had access to support systems (META, 2022). This indicates that access to support systems has improved over time.

In conclusion, women still face greater challenges and greater barriers to entrepreneurship and self-employment than men. In addition, these barriers are often interconnected and mutually reinforced. These include negative social and cultural attitudes toward women's and men's entrepreneurship, institutional barriers that hinder women to run a business (e.g., family policy and tax policy), political frameworks that discourage women from entrepreneurship, and market flaws (e.g., biases in financial markets, ineffective policies and programs, and information asymmetries).

Entrepreneurship of immigrant women in the EU

During the last three decades, researchers have dedicated themselves to gaining deeper insights into women and their roles, both direct and indirect, in fostering entrepreneurship and driving economic growth (Tiwari & Goel, 2020; Sarihasan et al., 2023). Immigrant women's entrepreneurship is shaped by the dual effects of gender and ethnic diversity (Levent, Masurel & Nijkamp, 2003). The sociocultural environment directly affects women's entrepreneurial activity. For example, values such as tolerance, cooperation, and cultural affinity can help women succeed (Anggadwita et al., 2017).

Historically, immigrant entrepreneurship has been linked to economic challenges. Immigrants often choose self-employment as a source of livelihood due to limited opportunities in the labor market. There are studies that confirm this perspective (Barrett, Jones & McEvoy, 1996). On the other hand, OECD studies (2011) note that some immigrants choose self-employment to avoid low-paid jobs and discrimination at work. The gender inequality among self-employed is also visible among immigrants, regardless of their place of birth (Figure 4.5).

Although self-employment rates among immigrants have remained stable over the last decade, the convergence in self-employment rates between immigrants and non-immigrants has been greater for women than for men. This is particularly true for immigrants born in another EU member state. These shares converged in 2021 and remained almost unchanged in 2022 (approximately 11%). Among women born in a non-EU country, the percentage of self-employed immigrants is decreasing, around 9%. However, the gender gap among self-employed workers was smaller among immigrants and non-immigrants. The smallest difference between the sexes occurred among immigrants from non-EU countries and amounted to almost 6 pp in 2022. On the other hand, while the gender gap among self-employed immigrants born in another EU Member State was slightly higher and amounted to 7 pp. The largest gender gap amounted to almost 8 pp in 2022.

Russia's aggression on Ukraine has caused a historic and massive wave of refugees. Starting in February 2022, over several weeks, more than 150,000 people daily fled Ukraine. By the end of March 2023, 4.7 million Ukrainians had signed up for temporary protection programs in the EU (OECD, 2022).

Many countries have either directly introduced measures to support Ukrainian refugees in entrepreneurship or indirectly supported organizations implementing entrepreneurship programs. Examples include business incubators such as Garage48 in Estonia, which, in cooperation with the Estonian Refugee Council, run a regular program "Women's Empowerment in Estonia for Ukrainian Refugee Women" (Garage48, 2023). There are also many other

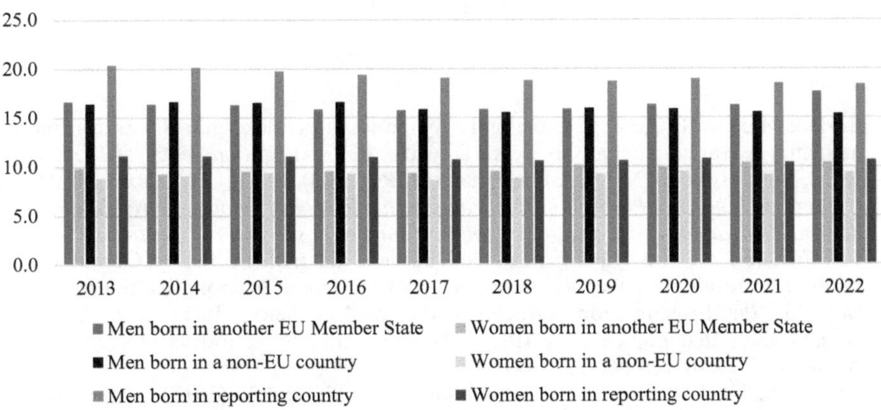

Figure 4.5 Self-employment of immigrant women (15–64 years) as a percentage of employment in the EU by place of birth.

Source: Own study-based Eurostat (2023).

foundations and social enterprises that offer entrepreneurship training to Ukrainian refugees in Estonia (OECD, 2023b). Other examples include bilingual entrepreneurship training programs offered by Local Enterprise Offices in Ireland. In 2023, in Fingal (Ireland), 80 Ukrainian refugees were enrolled in the "Start your business" program (Fingal County Council, 2023). Other countries, such as Poland, have adjusted some regulations to allow Ukrainian refugees to start certain types of businesses. In March 2022, in Poland, regulations on establishing a business were adjusted to allow Ukrainian refugees to start certain types of business activities, including self-employment and limited partnerships (Poland, 2022).

Conclusions

In summary, one of the most important trends in inclusive entrepreneurship is the increase – both absolute and relative – of immigrant entrepreneurship. There is also growing recognition of the contribution of immigrant entrepreneurs to innovation and job creation, although policies are slow to adapt to the changing context. This requires greater investment in supporting high-potential immigrant entrepreneurs, including greater use of outreach and incentives to attract them.

Women are not only potential beneficiaries of efforts to achieve the ambitious Sustainable Development Goals (SDGs) by 2030. They are also active participants in the process. The role of women-owned enterprises has attracted the attention of national governments, especially international development organizations such as the UN, the World Bank, and the OECD, which are increasingly investing in building women's entrepreneurial capacity. Such efforts also express the belief that investing in women's entrepreneurial capacity will increase their empowerment and reduce gender inequality, which is a key precursor to any sustainable development.

References

Ahl, H. & Marlow S. (2012). Exploring the dynamics of gender, feminism and entrepreneurship: Advancing debate to escape a dead end? *Organization*, *19*(5), 543–562.

Álvarez, M. J., Rebollo, M. A. & Rodríguez, M. R. (2013). In M. C. Cardona Moltó, E. Chiner Sanz, A. Giner Gomis (Eds.), *Factores facilitadores y bloqueadores del emprendimiento femenino: orientar para el emprendimiento desde una perspectiva de género.* Investigación e Innovación Educativaal Servicio de Instituciones y Comunidades Globales, Plurales y Diversas. Actas del XVI Congreso Nacional/II Internacional Modelos de Investigación Educativa de la Asociación Interuniversitaria de Investigación Pedagógica (AIDIPE). 427–435. https://www.uv.es/aidipe/congresos/Actas_XVI_Congreso.pdf

Anggadwita, G., Luturlean, B. S., Ramadani, V. & Ratten, V. (2017). Socio-cultural environments and emerging economy entrepreneurship women entrepreneurs in Indonesia. *Journal of Entrepreneurship in Emerging Economies*, *9*(1), 85–96, Emerald Group Publishing Ltd.

Barrett, G., Jones T. & McEvoy D. (1996). Ethnic minority business: Theoretical discourse in Britain and North America. *Urban Studies*, *3*, 4–5. https://doi.org/10.1080/00420989650011825

Berger, E. S. C. & Kuckertz, A. (2016). Female entrepreneurship in startup ecosystems worldwide. *Journal of Business Research*, *69*(11), 5163–5168. https://doi.org/10.1016/j.jbusres.2016.04.098

Bourgain, M. & Chaudat, P. (2015). Vie professionnelle et maternité: Représentations comparées de jeunes entrepreneures et cadres en TPE et PME en croissance. *Revue de l'Entrepreneuriat*, *14*(2), 83–108.

Bruni, A., Gherardi, S. & Poggio, B. (2004). Entrepreneur reality, gender and the study of women entrepreneurs. *Journal of Organizational Change Management*, *17*(3), 256–268.

Burkhardt, K., Nguyen, P. & Poincelot, E. (2020). Agents of change: Women in top management and corporate environmental performance. *Corporate Social Responsibility and Environmental Management*, *27*(4), 1591–1604. https://doi.org/10.1002/csr.1907

Castiblanco, S. E. (2013). La construcción de la categoría de emprendimiento femenino Revista Facultad de Ciencias Económicas. *Investigación y Reflexión*, *XXI*(2), 53–66.

Eurostat. (2023). *Employment and unemployment (LFS) database*. https://ec.europa.eu/eurostat/web/lfs/database

Fingal County Council. (2023). *Budding Ukrainian entrepreneurs complete business start-up programme*. https://www.fingal.ie/news/budding-ukrainian-entrepreneurs-complete-business-start-programme

Garage48. (2023). *Empowering women Estonia*. Retrieved from https://entrepreneur.pagulasabi.ee/empowering-women-estonia-2022

Global Entrepreneurship Monitor (GEM). (2019). *Special tabulations of the GEM survey* 2014–2018. https://doi.org/10.1787/3ed84801-en

Hanson, S. (2008). Changing places through women's entrepreneurship. *Economic Geography*, *85*(3), 245–267.

Kemp, P. E. J., Wong, B. & Berry, M. G. (2020). Female performance and participation in computer science: A national picture ACM. *Transactions on Computing Education*, *20*(1), 1–28. https://doi.org/10.1145/3366016

Kuschel, K. & Lepeley, M. T. (2016). Women start-ups in technology: Literature review and research agenda to improve participation. *International Journal of Entrepreneurship and Small Business*, *27*(2/3), 333. https://doi.org/10.1504/IJESB.2016.073995

Levent, T. B., Masurel, E. & Nijkamp, P. (2003). Diversity in entrepreneurship: Ethnic and female roles in urban economic life. *International Journal of Social Economics*, *30*(11–12), 1131–1161, V.U. University, Amsterdam.

Manzanera-Román, S. & Brändle, G. (2016). Abilities and skills as factors explaining the differences in women entrepreneurship. *Suma Negocios*, *7*(15), 38–46. https://doi.org/10.1016/j.sumneg

Marlow, S., Carter, S. & Shaw, E. (2008). Constructing female entrepreneurship policy in the UK: Is the US a relevant benchmark? *Environment and Planning. C, Government & Policy*, *26*(2), 335–351. https://doi.org/10.1068/c0732r

META. (2022). *Global State of Small Business: A look at the continuing recovery in 2022, with insights on women-led and minority-led SMBs*. Retrieved from https://dataforgood.facebook.com/dfg/resources/March-2022-Global-State-of-Small-Business-Report

OECD. (2011). *International migration outlook 2011*. Paris: OECD Publishing. https://doi.org/10.1787/migr_outlook-2011-en

OECD. (2021). *The missing entrepreneurs 2021: Policies for inclusive entrepreneurship and self-employment*. Paris: European Commission, OECD Publishing. https://doi.org/10.1787/71b7a9bb-en

OECD. (2022). *The potential contribution of Ukrainian refugees to the labour force in European host countries*. Retrieved from https://www.oecd.org/ukraine-hub/policy-responses/the-potential-contribution-of-ukrainian-refugees-to-the-labour-force-in-european-host-countries-e88a6a55/

OECD. (2023a). *The missing entrepreneurs 2023: Policies for inclusive entrepreneurship and self-employment*. Paris: European Commission, OECD Publishing. https://doi.org/10.1787/230efc78-en

OECD. (2023b). *Inclusive entrepreneurship policies: Country assessment notes*. Retrieved from https://www.oecd.org/cfe/smes/inclusive-entrepreneurship-policies-country-assessment-notes.htm

OECD, World Bank. (2020). *The future of business survey*. Retrieved from https://dataforgood.fb.com/global-state-of-smb

Poland. (2022). *How a citizen of Ukraine can set up a company in Poland*. Retrieved from https://www.biznes.gov.pl/pl/portal/001466

Sarihasan I., Novotny Á., Meyer N. & Máté D. (2023). Female immigrant entrepreneurship: A contextual approach. *International Journal of Entrepreneurship and Small Business*, *51*(3), 342–363, Inderscience Enterprises Ltd.

Thaddeus, K. J., Bih, D., Nebong, N. M., Ngong, C. A., Mongo, E. A., Akume, A. D. & Onwumere, J. U. J. (2022). Female labour force participation rate and economic growth in sub-Saharan Africa: A liability or an asset? *Journal of Business and Socio-economic Development*, *2*(1), 34–48. https://doi.org/10.1108/JBSED-09-2021-0118

Tiwari, N. & Goel, G. (2020). Empirical analysis of women entrepreneurs and their success perception. *International Journal of Entrepreneurship and Small Business*, *39*(4), 530–547, Inderscience Enterprises Ltd.

UNIDO. (2014). *Empowering women: Fostering entrepreneurship*. Vienna, Austria: United Nations Industrial Development Organization (UNIDO). https://www.unido.org/gender

Verheul, I., Van Stel, A. & Thurik, R. (2006). Explaining female and male entrepreneurship at the country level. *Entrepreneurship & Regional Development*, *18*(2), 151–183. https://doi.org/10.1080/08985620500532053

Vershinina, N., Rodgers, P., Tarba, S., Khan, Z. & Stokes, P. (2019). Gaining legitimacy through proactive stakeholder management: The experiences of high-tech women entrepreneurs in Russia. *Journal of Business Research*, (February 2018). https://doi.org/10.1016/j.jbusres.2018.12.063

Zeidan, D. & Bahrami D. (2020). Women entrepreneurship in GCC: A framework to address challenges and promote participation in a regional context. *International Journal of Business and Social Science*, *2*(14), 100–107.

5 Women in selected industry markets in the European Union

Women in science

Science is the discipline where women's position is visible, although not on a staggering scale. The first to be mentioned are the women who were awarded the Nobel Prize. In the years 1901–2023, 64 of them received this award, and one was a double laureate. The one woman honored twice was Marie Sklodowska-Curie (the first woman awarded), who received the Nobel Prize in 1903 in physics and in 1911 – in chemistry (Nobel Prize, 2023). Note that in the years 1901–2023, 965 individual winners were awarded, among whom the share of women was only 6.1%. Nineteen Nobel Prizes were awarded to women for peace, 17 for literature, 13 for science or medicine, 8 for chemistry, 5 for physics, and 3 for economics.

The position of women in science is related to a phenomenon described in the literature on the subject as the Matilda effect. It is a phenomenon that women's accomplishments tend to be co-opted, outright stolen, or overshadowed by those of male peers. This phenomenon was named in 1993 by Margaret W. Rossiter, after Matilda Joslyn Gage, who both experienced and publicized this phenomenon in the late 19th century (Rossiter, 1993).

Female "victims" of the Matilda effect include Cecilia Payne-Gaposchkin, who discovered that the main component of stars is hydrogen (Perkowitz, 2022). Although her views, as a woman, were rejected, they gained recognition thanks to a man, and this happened after joint publications in co-authorship with her husband. In 1925, Cecilia Payne became the first woman to receive a Ph.D. in astronomy from Radcliffe College. In 1938 Cecilia Payne-Gaposchkin received her astronomer title and became the first woman professor of astronomy at Harvard University. An Austrian nuclear physicist, Lisa Meitner, was the first to describe the splitting of the atomic nucleus, but all credits in this field were attributed to Otto Hahn, a Nobel Prize winner from 1944 (Nanal, 2017). In turn, Candace Pert, a neurobiologist, made a discovery that became the foundation for further research on brain biochemistry. For this discovery, her promoter received the Lasker Prize (a scientific award for research in medicine).

DOI: 10.4324/9781003477532-5

Despite the passage of time, the phenomenon described by Pert is still relevant, which is also emphasized by contemporary publications. For example, Rajkó et al. (2023) drew attention to the aspect of communication/dissemination of the views of scientists. They conducted their research for the years 2010–2019. In their findings, the authors classified publications according to two indicators: (1) publication in the Scopus journal index, or (2) classification as a publication in a communications journal. They proved that among the most prolific authors dealing with communication, women scientists are still significantly underrepresented in all 11 regions analysed (the United States, the United Kingdom, France, Spain, Germany and Italy, Russia, Poland, Hungary, Romania, and Ukraine). Moreover, the analysis of views and the number of citations showed that the works of women scientists are systematically reviewed more frequently, and at the same time much less frequently cited than the works of men. Consequently, it has been proven that gender inequality is still widespread in the scientific field.

Feeley and Yang (2022) observed a bias in the citation of author's works depending on gender. They verified the Matilda effect in 8 communication magazines for 10 years of publication (2002–2006, 2012–2016). Mixed results were found in 3,324 articles, and 2 out of 8 examined journals showing the Matilda effect. In a subset of six journals, men were more likely than women to cite their own work.

Following this trend is the research team of Wang et al. (2021), who also examined scientists' citations in 14 communication journals in the years 1995–2018. Their observations show that works with women, as the first and last authors, attract fewer citations than works with men. This imbalance results largely from the practice of citing men, and, according to the authors, it is slowly decreasing over time. The structure of the network of male coauthors that they establish partially explains the observed overcitation of men by other men. In their conclusion, Wang et al. (2021) find that citations are an important form of social capital. They have a significant impact on academic careers, with men being overcited and women being undercited in works across disciplines, including communications.

The Matilda effect revealed in the science world was also noticed in the next publication. Fiorentin, Pereira, and Suárez (2022) address the presence of gender bias in public funding for science and technology (R&D), known as the Matilda effect in STEM disciplines (science, technology, engineering, and mathematics) in Argentina. Admittedly, the subject is beyond the spatial scope of the study of this publication, but it enriches the topic. The empirical analysis conducted by the authors is based on the program of scientific and technological research projects (in Spanish: PICT) for the years 2003–2015. It showed that women scientists are less likely to receive a grant when first applying for it (by 6.2 pp) compared to men. Even for post-first submissions that have not previously received a grant, women scientists are less likely to receive it (by 3.8 pp). However, the probability of receiving another grant[1] is the same for both male and female researchers. The article stated that women in STEM struggle with inconvenience in the process of obtaining public funds to finance their research projects. Only those who overcome the initial barriers and obtain the first grant will be able to increase their chances of winning further. These results suggest the need for policies to reduce the initial gender gap in access to public grants for women researchers in STEM.

The emerging faces of the Matilda effect helped to recognize statistics related to women in science and the evolution of the role of women in this area.

The first woman to study at the university – in Utrecht (1636) – was Anna Maria van Schurman, although, according to sources, she did not graduate with a diploma (Usakiewicz, 2019). Elena Lucrezia Cornaro Piscopia was the first woman to obtain a Ph.D. (in philosophy). This happened in 1678 at the University of Padua. Laura Maria Caterina Bassi, on the other hand, became the first woman in European history to hold the position of professor of physics at a university (1735). In turn, the first woman to obtain a higher education diploma (a bachelor's degree) was Catherine Brewer. This happened in 1840, at the first university in the world authorized to award degrees to women, the Georgia Female College (Artis et al., 2018).

When analysing the contemporary European market, it should be noted that in 2022, more than 40% of people aged 25–34 in the EU had higher education. The share of the population with tertiary education is higher in the Nordic and Baltic countries, and women dominate among tertiary-educated people in all countries (Figure 5.1).

In 2022, almost 76 million people aged 15–74 were employed in science and technology in the EU. Of these, 52% were women, and worked mainly in services (except in Malta, where 48% of women employed in science and technology worked in services) (Eurostat, 2023).

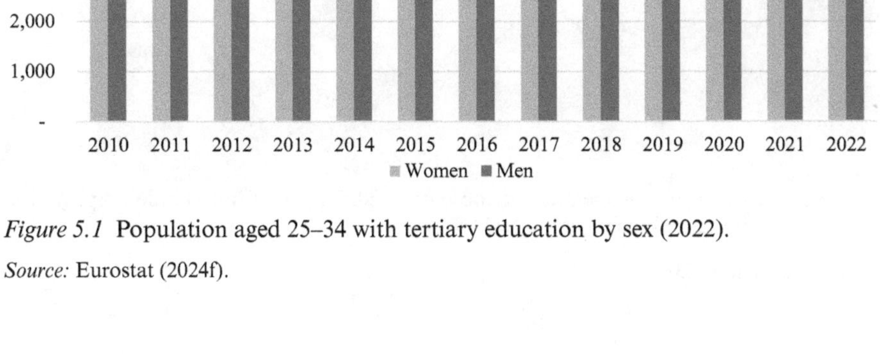

Figure 5.1 Population aged 25–34 with tertiary education by sex (2022).

Source: Eurostat (2024f).

Considering the phenomenon in individual countries, note that the average percentage of women scientists and engineers in 2022 was very diverse, ranging from 52% in Lithuania to 51% in Bulgaria to 31% in Hungary, to 32% in Finland, and 34% in Germany. Among the EU regions (Figure 5.2), the highest percentage of women employed in science and technology in 2022 was observed in Lithuania and Corsica (64% each), as well as in Latvia (63%). At the other end of the spectrum, the lowest share was recorded in the Italian North-West region (45%), followed by Malta and the Italian South and North-East regions (all 46%).

A significant subgroup among R&D professionals are scientists and engineers. They constitute nearly a quarter (24%) of all science and technology employees in the EU. When analysing selected statistics of women scientists, the authors concluded that only one-third of scientists in the EU are women. Only a slightly higher percentage of women are university lecturers worldwide, 35%. In the EU, only 21% of women in academia achieved the highest level of

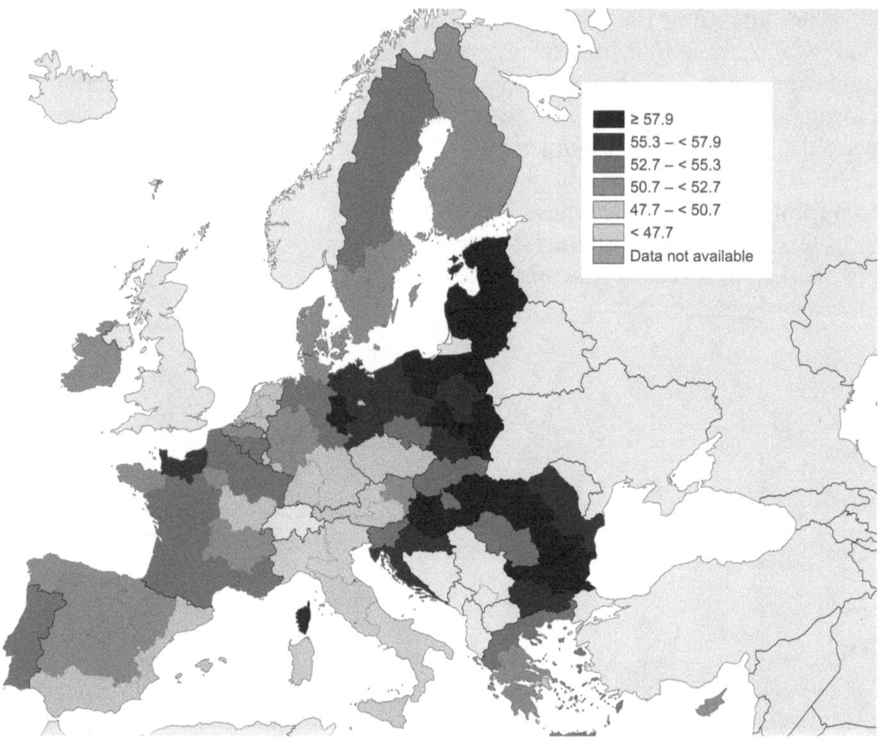

Figure 5.2 Women in science and technology in 2022 (% of total people employed in science and technology, NUTS 1).

Źródło: Eurostat (2023).

their academic career (Gitnux, 2023). Among professors and science managers, men still have a numerical advantage.

In light of the considerations presented, it should be concluded that women's participation in science has evolved. To learn how this process will shape in the future, we must take into account the dynamically changing environment in which women function, including artificial intelligence. It will replace the work of many women and men in the world of science, but on the other hand, it is people of science who will strive to develop artificial intelligence toward its usefulness for the planet Earth and its inhabitants (Vinuesa et al., 2020).

Women in tourism

Europe is the most visited region in the world. Therefore, tourism is an important part of the European economy and a driving force for employment in many countries, such as Italy, Spain, France, or Germany. According to data from the World Travel and Tourism Council (WTTC, 2023), in 2022, the travel and tourism sector contributed EUR 1.37 trillion to the European Union economy (representing 8.7% of EU GDP). It employed 21.8 million people, that is, 1 in 10 employees in the EU. The WTTC forecasts that this sector will grow to almost EUR 1.9 trillion by 2033 (10% of the EU economy) and will employ 26.3 million people. This means that one in eight EU residents will work in the tourist service sector.

Tourism is also an extremely important sector for women (Figueroa-Domecq et al., 2020) as the majority of the workforce in tourism are women. Data from the United Nations World Tourism Organization say that they constitute 54% of all workers in tourism (UNWTO, 2019). In turn, the WTTC (2019) data say that almost twice as many women work in the travel and tourism sector than in other economic sectors.

In the European Union, approximately 5 million women (and approximately one-fifth fewer men) are employed in Section I (accommodation and food service activities) alone – Figure 5.3.

In 2010–2019, this number increased from 4.5 million to 5.1 million (apart from a slight decline in 2012 and 2013, related to the second wave of the economic crisis). The COVID-19 pandemic broke this trend. In 2020, the number of women employed in accommodation and food service activities decreased by 14%, and in 2021 by another 3.5%. However, in 2022, the number increased, and more than 4.8 million women worked in Section I (8.5% more than in the initial year of 2010, but 5.7% less than in the pre-pandemic year of 2019). Note that the predominance of women over men employed in accommodation and food service activities decreased during the period under study – from 18.4% to 11.5%. However, their dominance is still visible.

Among EU countries, most women are employed in accommodation and food service activities in Spain (almost 870,000 in 2022). Germany ranks second (almost 730,000), Italy third (over 700,000), and France fourth (over 550,000) – Figure 5.4. In turn, the fewest women work in this section in Luxembourg (less than 6,000) and Malta (less than 7,000).

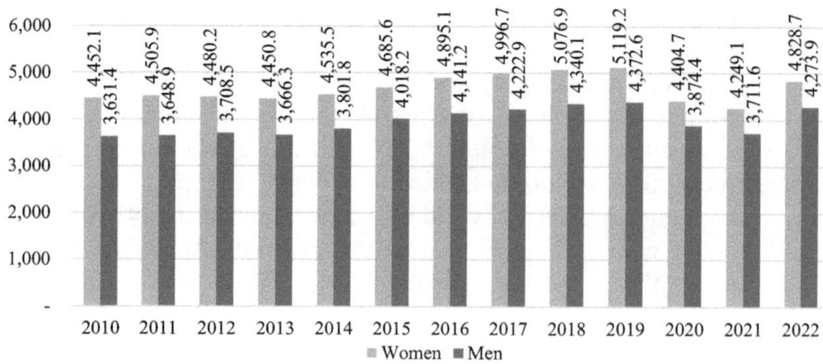

Figure 5.3 Number of women and men in European Union 15 years old or over employed in accommodation and food service activities in 2010–2022 (in thousand).

Source: Eurostat (2024c).

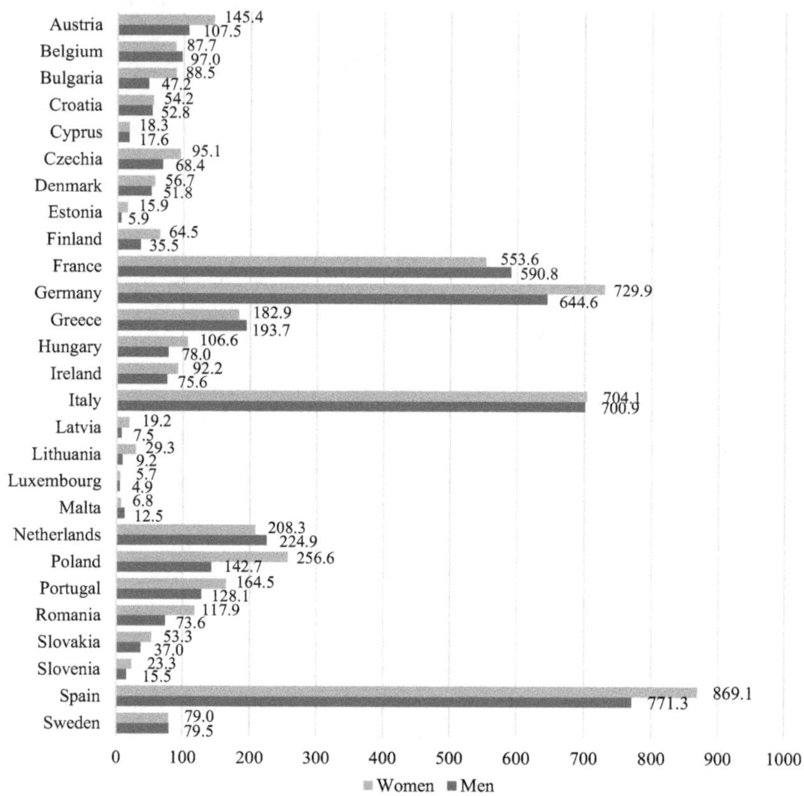

Figure 5.4 Number of women and men in European Union 15 years old or over employed in accommodation and food service activities in 2022 (in thousands, by countries).

Source: Eurostat (2024c).

Note that not in all EU countries, women outnumber men in accommodation and food service activities. Countries with a higher percentage of men include: Malta, Belgium, Netherlands, France, Greece, and Sweden. However, the greatest predominance of women is recorded in the Baltic countries, that is, Lithuania, Estonia, and Latvia, where they constitute 76.1%, 72.9%, and 71.9% of all employees in Section I, respectively.

Women also dominate travel agencies and work as tour guides more often than men. In the case of employment in travel agencies, tour operators, and other reservation services and related activities, their dominance is even greater than in accommodation and food service activities. Approximately 300,000 women work in this NACE[2] class and almost half as many men (Figure 5.5). Although employment in this tourism sector also decreased due to COVID-19 (women by 14.1% in 2020, and by another 18% in 2021, and men by 18.7% and 12.8%, respectively), in the last year under study, there was already an increase, women by 8.7% and men by 5.7%. In total, in 2022, over 40% more women than men worked in travel agencies, tour operators, and other reservation services and related activities, although in the period under study, there was a visible decline in this advantage, from 48.2% to 42.7%.

In terms of employment in travel agencies, tour operators, and other reservation service and related activities, Germany stands out with almost 66,000 women working in this industry (and 43.4% less men) – Figure 5.6. Spain ranks second with over 44,000. women (and 43.9% fewer men), Italy ranks third (over 32,000 women and 50.2% fewer men), and France ranks fourth (over 26,000 women and 32.7% fewer men). In turn, in small island states, that is, Malta and Cyprus, the employment of women in travel agencies, tour operators, and other reservation services and related activities is the lowest (500 and

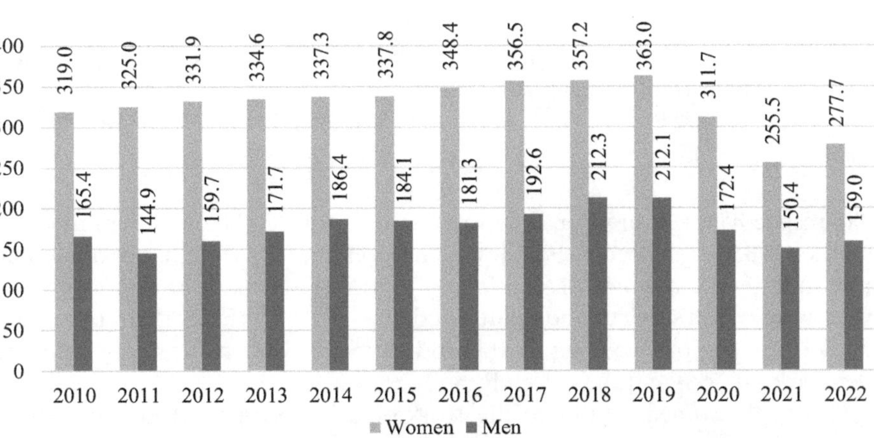

Figure 5.5 Number of women and men in European Union 15 years old or over employed in travel agency, tour operator and other reservation service and related activities in 2010–2022 (in thousand).

Source: Eurostat (2024b).

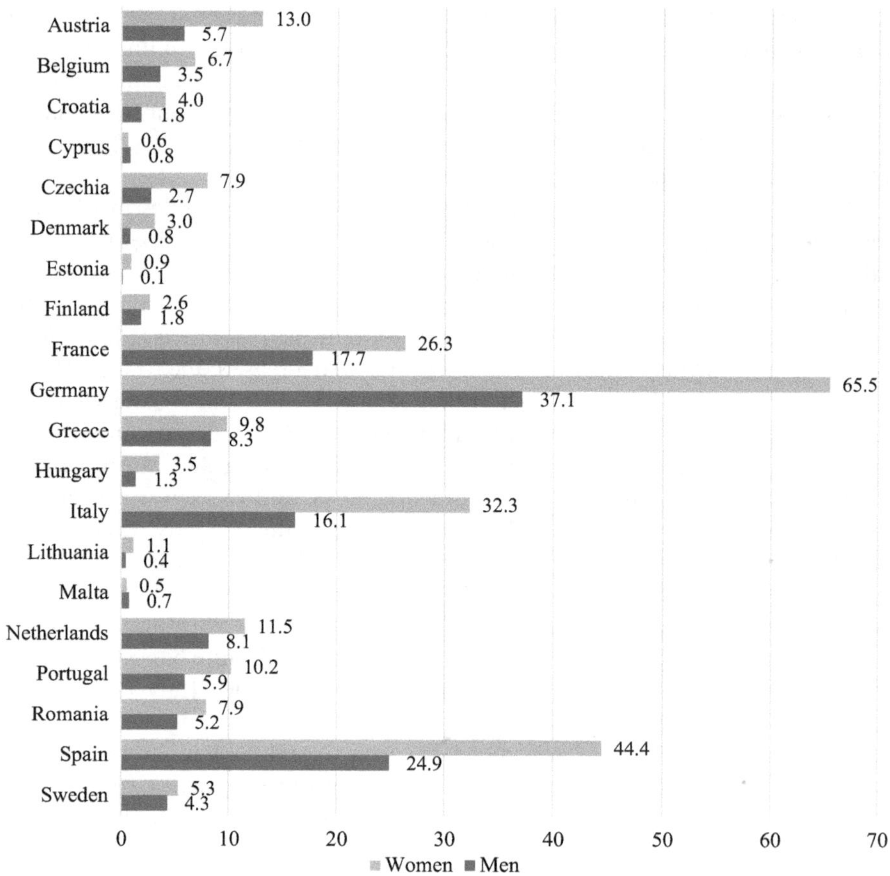

Figure 5.6 Number of women and men in European Union 15 years old or over employed in travel agency, tour operator and other reservation service and related activities in 2022 (in thousand, by countries that provided data).

Source: Eurostat (2024b).

600, respectively). Moreover, they work in this NACE class less than men (by 40.0% and 33.3%, respectively). However, the greatest predominance of women over men in the number of employees of travel agents, tour operators and other reservation services and related activities occurs in Estonia. In this country, 90% of people working in this industry are women. Ranking next are Denmark (78.9%) and the Czech Republic (74.5%).

Although women dominate the workforce in European tourism, gender inequalities are noticeable in this sector. Although women dominate the workforce in European tourism, gender inequalities are noticeable in this sector. The stereotypical division of domestic responsibilities results in the fact that women's work, among other things, is more often casual, seasonal, and temporary than that of men (World Bank, 2017). In the EU, in accommodation and food service activities, this phenomenon affects approximately one-fifth of all employees, that is, approximately 1 million women (and almost 1/3 less men) – Figure 5.7. However, it should be noted that the difference between the number of women and men who work casually in the hospitality and catering industry decreased during the study period, from 31.7% to 23.4%.

Considering the national differences in the temporary employment of women in accommodation and food service activities, it should be concluded that most of temporary workers are found in Italy (over 213,000), Spain (over 205,000) and France (almost 108,000), and the least – in Malta (only 500), Luxembourg (1,000), and Estonia (1,400) – Figure 5.8. The greatest advantage of women over men in terms of casual employment is observed in the Czech Republic. Here, the advantage of women is more than 2.5 times. The countries ranking next are Luxembourg (where the advantage is 2.5 times), Slovenia, and Poland (where the advantage is almost 2.5 times). In turn, in the Netherlands, and especially in Malta, men dominate – 1.2% and 380.0% more men than women work in accommodation and food service activities, respectively.

The greatest advantage in the share of seasonally employed women over men is recorded in Slovenia (by 10.9 pp) and Sweden (by 10.6 pp). In countries such as Malta, Estonia, Denmark, and Germany, the opposite is true: the share of men temporarily employed in accommodation and food service activities s is higher than that of women (by 11.8 pp, 4.8 pp, 0.7 pp, and 0.5 pp, respectively).

Another important issue from the point of view of gender inequality in tourism is that women are employed part-time more often than men. This is

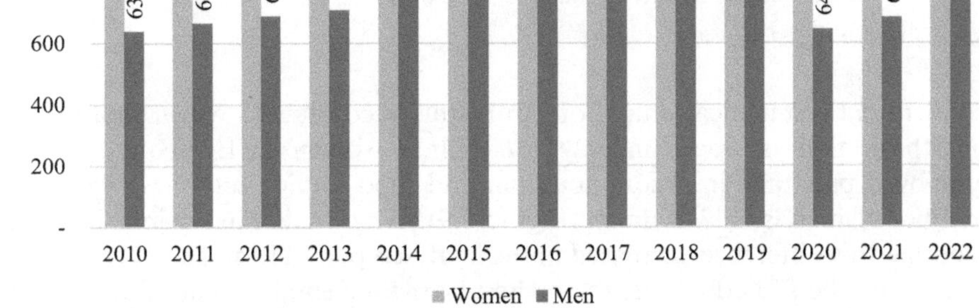

Figure 5.7 Number of women and men in European Union 15 years old or over temporary employed in accommodation and food service activities in 2010–2022 (in thousand).

Source: Eurostat (2024h).

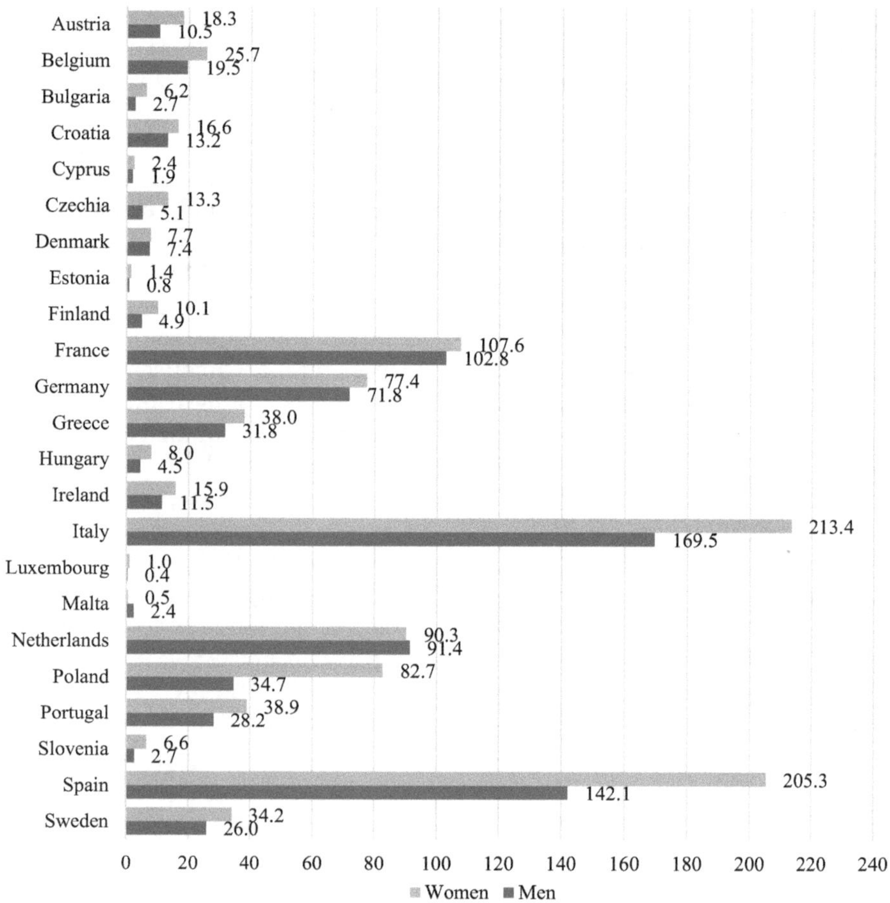

Figure 5.8 Number of women and men in European Union 15 years old or over temporary employed in accommodation and food service activities in 2022 (in thousand, by countries that provided data).

Source: Eurostat (2024h).

confirmed by statistical data from Eurostat, according to which more than one-third, that is, approximately 1.7 million women in EU countries are employed part-time in accommodation and food service activities, while the number of men is half as much (Figure 5.9). What makes us optimistic is the fact that this difference decreased in the analysed period from 58.5% to 47.9%.

Among the EU countries, the highest part-time employment of women in accommodation and food service activities is observed in Germany (over 400,000), Italy (almost 350,000), and Spain (over 266,000). However, the fewest women are employed part-time in Luxembourg (1,500), Malta (2,500), and Cyprus (2,900). It should be noted that in all EU countries, women outweigh men in terms of part-time employment – Figure 5.10.

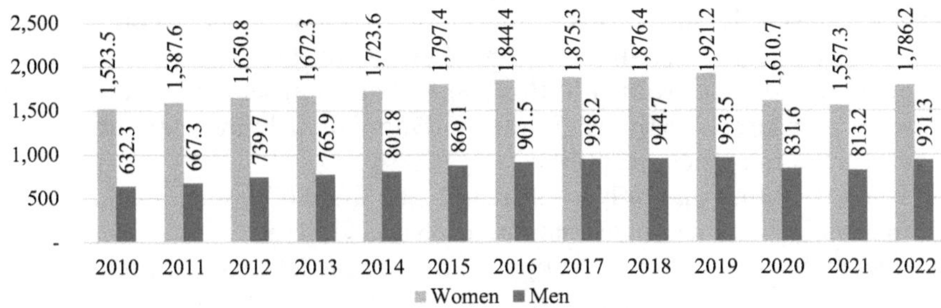

Figure 5.9 Number of women and men in European Union 15 years old or over part-time employed in accommodation and food service activities in 2010–2022 (in thousand).

Source: Eurostat (2024d).

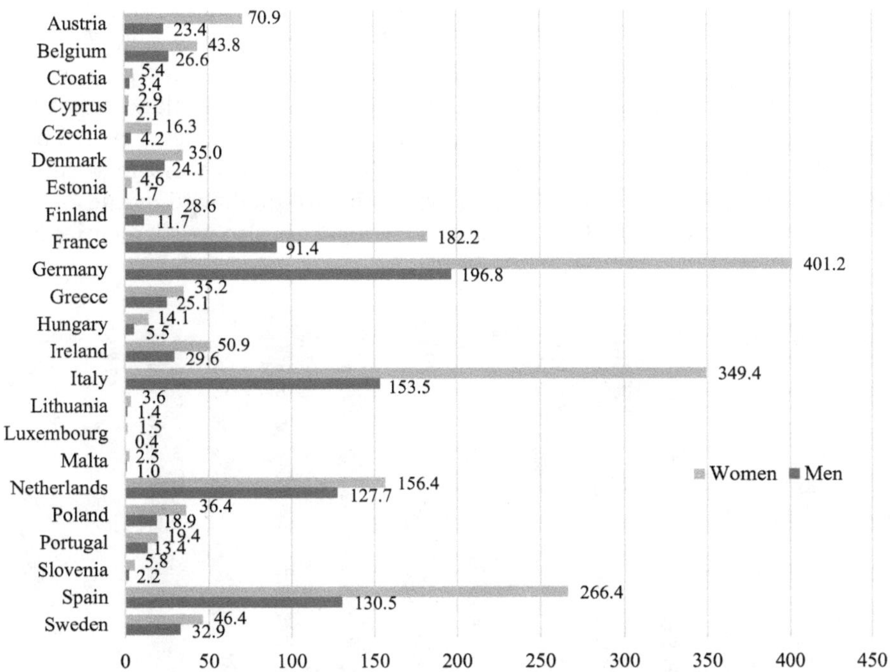

Figure 5.10 Number of women and men in European Union 15 years old or over part-time employed in accommodation and food service activities in 2022 (in thousand, by countries that provided data).

Source: Eurostat (2024d).

The greatest difference is observable in the Czech Republic, where the number of men employed part-time is 74.3% lower than that of women. However, a large domination of women in this respect is also observed in Luxembourg and Austria, where more than 3.5 times and more than 3 times part-time workers are women than men, respectively.

It is worth noting that only in Lithuania, the share of women working part-time in total employment in accommodation and food service activities is lower than the share of men (by 2.9 pp). In other countries, women predominate, especially in: Malta (by 28.8 pp), Italy (by 27.7 pp), and Austria (by 27.0 pp).

Note also the problem of employing women in positions below their qualifications. In the EU, this situation concerns approximately 70% of women working in accommodation and food service activities – Figure 5.11. Among men, this rate is lower (approximately 60%), although it should be emphasized that it increased from 55.5% to 62.9% in the analysed period. Thus, the difference between women and men in terms of underemployment decreased from 11.6 pp to 7.8 pp, that is, by almost one-third.

The highest overqualification rate among EU countries is recorded in Greece, where it amounts to up to 87.7% in the group of women (and 78.9% in the group of men) – Figure 5.12. The country ranking next is Spain, where 86.5% of women (and 79.5% of men) are underemployed. Finland closes the top 3 with a rate of 83.4% among women (and 67.1% among men). At the bottom of the ranking are Lithuania, where 46.8% of women work in positions below their qualifications, and Croatia, where the overqualification rate among women is 48.6%. The Czech Republic and Portugal are also worth mentioning,

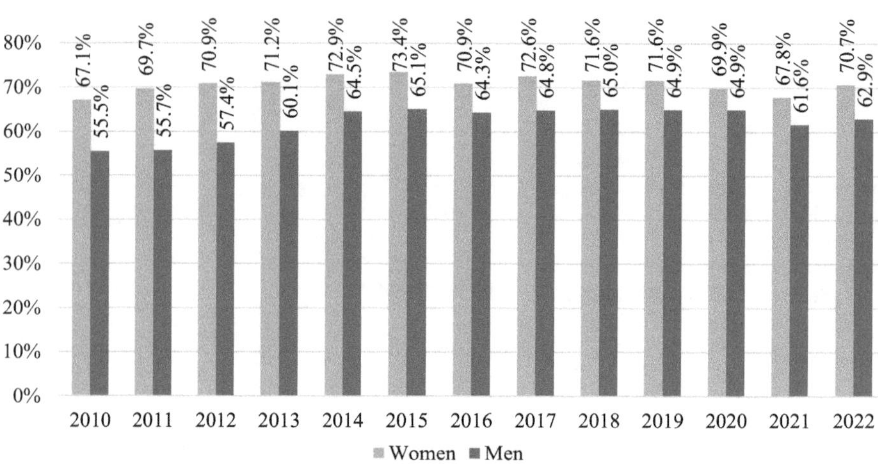

Figure 5.11 Over-qualification rates in accommodation and food service activities among women and men 15 years old or over in European Union in 2010–2022 (in percentage).

Source: Eurostat (2024e).

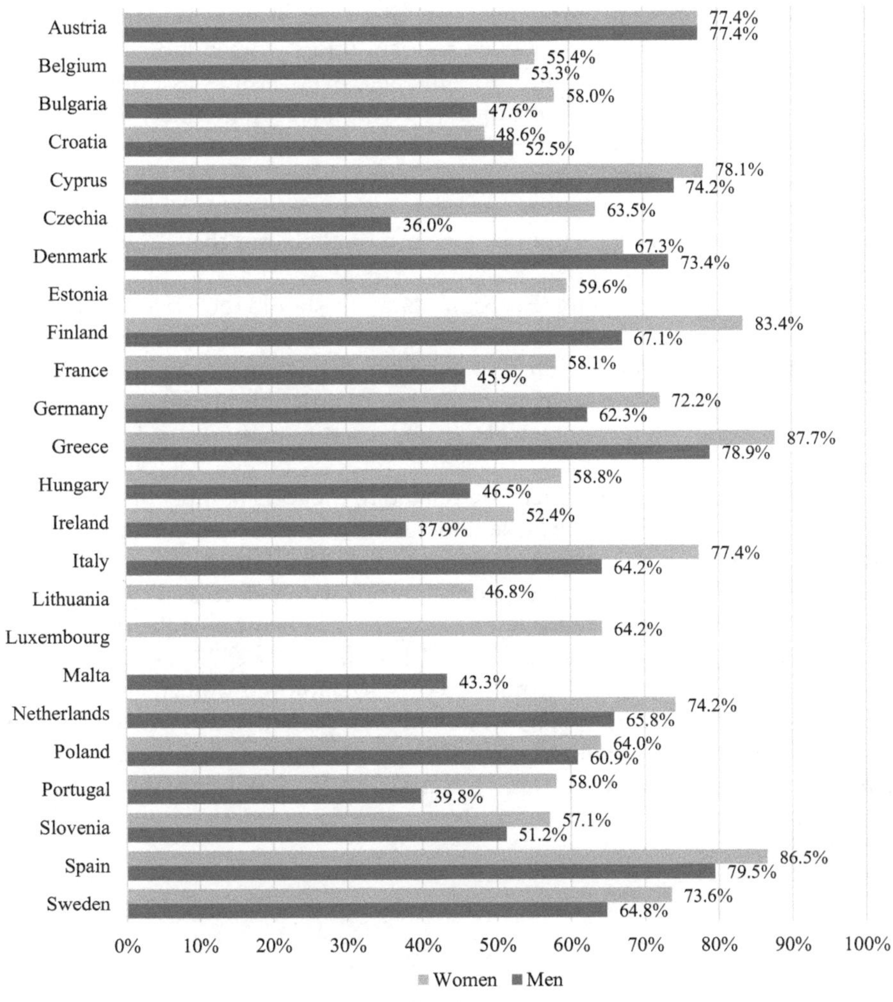

Figure 5.12 Over-qualification rates in accommodation and food service activities among women and men 15 years old or over in European Union in 2022 (in percentage, by countries that provided data).

Source: Eurostat (2024e).

as in these countries the largest positive difference is observed between the over-qualification rate among women and men – by 27.5 pp and 18.2 pp, respectively. In turn, in countries such as Denmark and the above-mentioned Croatia, the percentage of underemployed men is higher than women, by 6.1 pp and 3.9 pp, respectively.

In tourism, women are more often than men employed on a casual, part-time basis and in positions below their qualifications, with lower salaries (they earn 14.7% less than men – UNWTO, 2019), as well as in positions that do not subject to labor laws and protection regarding social security and collective agreements (WTTC, 2019). However, tourism offers women more opportunities than other economic sectors to run their own businesses (World Bank, 2017) and hold managerial positions, as exemplified by the fact that 23% of tourism ministers are women (UNWTO, 2019). This is due to the unique characteristics of the tourism sector, in which there is often less emphasis on formal education and training and more emphasis on personal skills, flexible working hours, and increased opportunities for entrepreneurship that do not require much start-up financing.

However, when analysing Eurostat data, it should be stated that self-employment in accommodation and food service activities is over one-third higher among men (about 900,000) than among women (about 600,000) – Figure 5.13. Progress in balancing gender inequalities in this area is evidenced by the fact that this advantage decreased in the study years from 37.8% to 32.3%.

When data on self-employment are related to the total number of employees in Section I (Figure 5.3), it can be concluded that every fifth man and only every eighth woman in the EU is self-employed. It should also be noted that the percentage of self-employed people unfortunately decreased in the analysed period, although this tendency was smaller among women (from 13.3% to 12.6%) than among men (from 26.2% to 21.0%).

The largest differences in the number of self-employed women and men are observed in Sweden (where 68.7% fewer women than men are self-employed), Malta (63.2%), and Denmark (56.3%). More women than men are self-employed only in Lithuania (over 2.5 times) and Poland, where the difference is minimal (only 0.3%) – Figure 5.14.

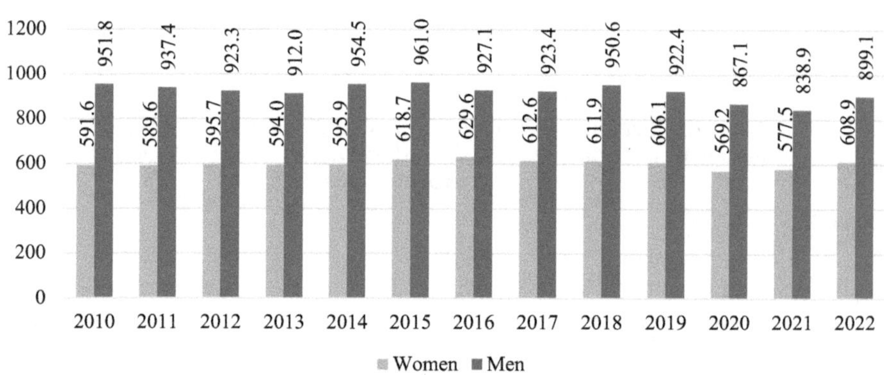

Figure 5.13 Number of women and men in European Union 15 years old or over self-employed in accommodation and food service activities in 2010–2022 (in thousand).

Source: Eurostat (2024g).

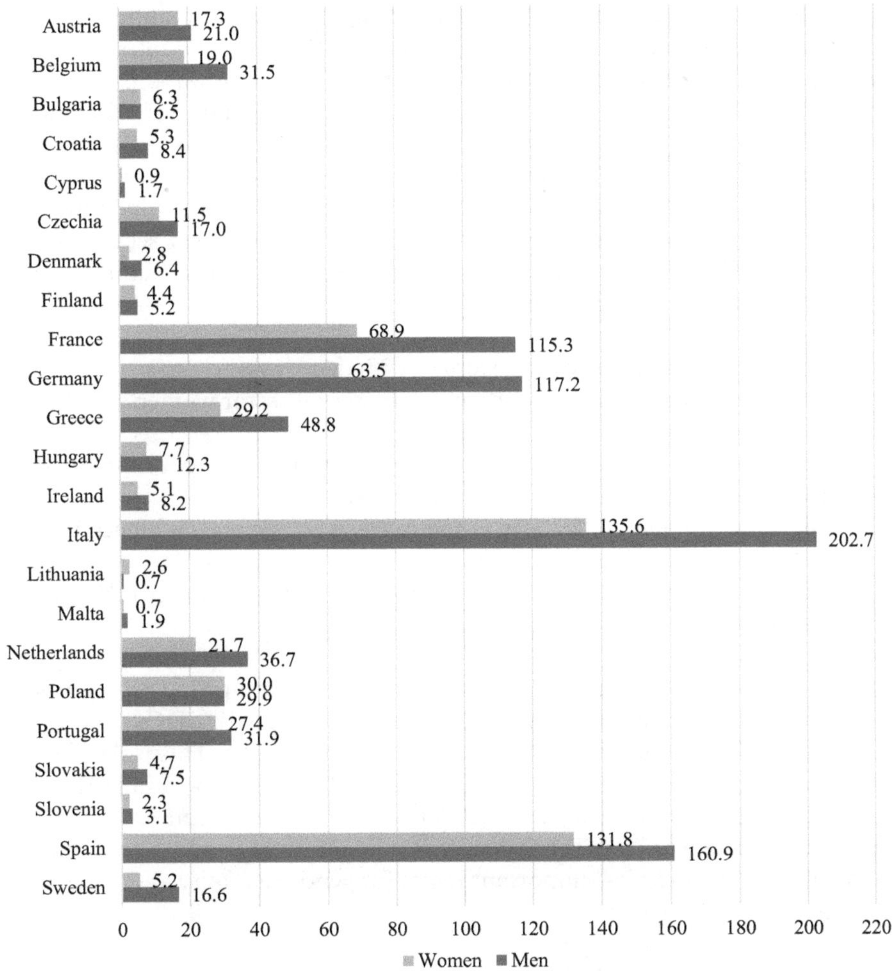

Figure 5.14 Number of women and men in European Union 15 years old or over self-employed in accommodation and food service activities in 2022 (in thousand, by countries that provided data).

Source: Eurostat (2024g).

It should also be emphasized that the share of self-employed women in total employment in accommodation and food service activities is the highest in Belgium (21.7%) and Italy (19.3%), and the lowest – in Cyprus (4.9%) and Denmark (4.9%). The largest difference in the percentage of self-employed women and men occurs in Sweden (by 14.3% in favor of men) and the Czech Republic (by 12.8% in favor of men). Again, only one EU country, Lithuania, has a higher share of women than men working in accommodation and food service activities on their own account (by 1.3 pp).

The analyses conducted prove that significant gender inequalities still persist in the tourism sector, which is in conflict with the principles of sustainable development. Therefore, there is no doubt that tourism has an important role to play in achieving the goals underlying the 2030 Agenda for Sustainable Development, in particular the commitments on gender equality and women's empowerment (Goal 5). Therefore, in 2019, the United Nations World Tourism Organization issued the *Global Report on Women in Tourism*. It identifies the key factors that contribute to gender equality in the tourism sector. In the report, UNWTO (2019) explores five topic areas that ensure equality and empower women in tourism. These are:

1 Employment: tourism provides women with decent work.
2 Entrepreneurship: women's tourism businesses allow for women's economic empowerment.
3 Education: tourism education and training promote gender equality and women's rights to empower them in the sector.
4 Leadership: women are leaders in the tourism sector and influence important decisions regarding it.
5 Community: tourism enables women to work together for gender justice and equality.

Taking into account these five areas, some countries have produced reports to mainstream tourism into the sustainable development goals (SDGs). However, gender inequality remains a persistent challenge in Europe. This is despite the fact that 80% of European men believe that gender equality is important to them personally and 91% say that gender equality is important for a fair and democratic society (UNWTO, 2019). According to the European Institute for Gender Equality, the most important issues for gender equality and tourism in Europe are (EIGE, n.d.):

- gender segregation in the labor market,
- women's low levels of representation in decision-making,
- stereotypes and their relationship with travel and tourism, and
- risks of gender-based violence in tourism.

In conclusion, it should be stated that although Europe is considered a groundbreaker in terms of gender equality, much more work is required on gender equality and tourism. Positive developments to date include a wide range of research on gender equality and tourism in the region, exploring topics such as (UNWTO, 2019):

- reducing gender inequalities;
- elaborating new tools to improve gender-sensitive tourism planning and management;

- gendered tourism behavior;
- education, research, and training.

To close the section, women who changed the tourism industry will be presented. For example, businesswoman and engineer Gwynne Shotwell, who joined SpaceX in 2002 and has since been promoted to president and chief operating officer. SpaceX is a private company that carries out a multi-billion dollar contract with NASA to send astronauts to the International Space Station. Gillian Tans has a similar career. In 2002, she became part of the then small company Booking.com, founded in Amsterdam. Moving through increasingly responsible positions, in 2016 she became the CEO of this company. During her tenure, the global accommodation provider grew into a corporation employing 10,000 people, with 174 offices around the world. In turn, Petra Vaškových joined Kiwi.com in 2014 as the first woman in a company employing less than 5 people and has since grown with the company (Brnáková, Neves, & Mareicheva, 2024).

On the other side of the market, there are fearless women adventurers who, by overcoming new challenges, prove that nothing and no one will stop them. Amelia Earhart is probably the most famous of them. She was the first woman to fly a plane alone over the Atlantic Ocean. In 1910–11, Lilian Bland also made aviation history by designing, building, and then piloting her own model of the Bland Mayfly airplane. Bertha Benz was also one of the women adventurers in modern history. Without its support, Karl Benz might not have won the technological "race" in the automotive industry. Bertha not only financed building the first car in history but also became the first person in the world to travel a long (at that time) distance (106 km, i.e., 66 miles) with the novel means of transport. Jasmine Harrison, in turn, set a record for crossing the Atlantic Ocean in a rowing boat. She achieved this at the age of only 21 and was the first woman to complete such a route by oars. The ocean was also a calling for Laura Dekker. In 2011, at the age of 15, she set off alone from St. Maarten, only to return 518 days later, setting a world record for the youngest person to circumnavigate the globe. Alexis Alford's travel story also made headlines. Known as Lexie Limitless, she managed to visit all 196 countries by the time she was 21, setting a new world record for this. In 2017, Cassie de Pecol established Guinness World Records in two categories: "Fastest time to visit all sovereign countries" and "Fastest time to visit all sovereign countries – Female". Moreover, it is impossible not to mention the unique Air India flight, which ended at the Bengaluru airport. It was the longest nonstop commercial flight ever flown on Earth, operated by an all-female crew. The flight from San Francisco to Bengaluru was almost 14,000 km long and required time zone changes by 13.5 hours (Brnáková, Neves & Mareicheva, 2024). Of course, the list of distinguished female figures in the field of tourism listed here is not exhaustive. The courage, innovation, and determination of those mentioned and many others not mentioned inspire subsequent generations of women. And with them, the travel community and the entire tourism sector are moving forward.

Women in the medical services market

Over recent decades, patterns of women's participation in the labor market have changed significantly in most Western countries. Just a quarter of a century ago, this market was characterized by relative inter-industry segregation based on gender. Men were overrepresented in professions that require physical effort, strength, and analytical and technical skills, while women were more strongly represented in professions that require social and educational skills. Currently, more and more women are entering professional fields previously dominated by men. However, this is associated with a new phenomenon called intra-industry gender segregation. This term means that selected subfields of certain labor market sectors are dominated by men or women (Levanon & Grusky, 2016). An example of such intra-industry gender segregation is the medical labor market.

Medicine has not always been a male-dominated field. In ancient Rome, female physicians practiced in a variety of specialties. One of them was Aspasia, depicted on the fresco above the main entrance to the University of Rome, alongside Socrates, Plato, Archimedes, and Sophocles. In the Middle Ages, monasteries were important centers of medicine. Hundreds of women served there as healers and herbal experts, and perhaps the most famous of them was Hildegard von Bingen (Steiner-Hofbauer et al., 2023). Women have traditionally been responsible for health care in the family and community (Bogusz, 2018), being responsible for obstetrics, among others. However, with the establishment of birthing clinics, long-standing women's extensive knowledge of childbirth was lost, and a male-dominated medical midwifery was born (Steiner-Hofbauer et al., 2023). For many years, women were also denied the right to medical education in universities (Bogusz, 2018). For centuries, they worked outside formal medicine as healers, especially in rural areas (Steiner-Hofbauer et al., 2023).

Currently, women constitute the vast majority of healthcare workers in the EU – their share in department Q86: Human health activities constitute approximately 2/3 of all employees, that is, 3 times more than men (Figure 5.15). Their number (approximately 8.8 million) increased by an average annual rate of 1.3% in the years 2010–2022, while the number of men (approximately 2.9 million) increased by an average annual rate of only 1.1%. As a result, the predominance of women increased in the study period from 66.4% to 67.4%.

The predominance of women over men in the health service is several times higher in all EU countries, except Malta, where there are only two-fifths more women than men. The greatest dominance is observed in the Baltic countries, that is, Estonia, Latvia, and Lithuania, where 8, 6, and 6 times more women than men work in the health service, respectively. Their share in total employment in the Q86 department is 88.8%, 86.2%, and 86.1%, respectively.

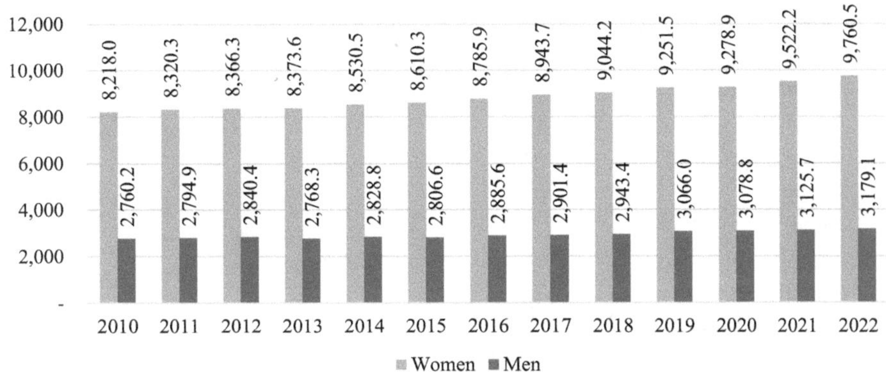

Figure 5.15 Number of women and men in European Union 15 years old or over employed in human health activities in 2010–2022 (in thousand).

Source: Own study based on Eurostat (2024a).

Most women in human health activities work in Germany (over 2.4 million), France (almost 1.5 million), and Spain (over 0.9 million), where they constitute approximately two-thirds of the total workforce – Figure 5.16.

Italy also draws attention, as it ranks fourth in terms of the number of women employed. However, due to the higher number of men employed than in Spain, it has a smaller share of women (66.0%). In turn, in Poland, fifth in the ranking, and Romania, seventh in the ranking, the number of men working in health care is lower than in the leading countries. As a result, the predominance of women is greater: they constitute 79.2% and 82.1% of all employees in the Q86 department, respectively. The fewest women work in health care in Luxembourg and Malta (9,100 and 9,900, respectively), but they still outweigh men – 2.5 times and 41.4%, respectively.

In addition to the female majority in nursing and midwifery – professions traditionally associated with femininity – women are also becoming more and more numerous among doctors. This trend begins already at the point of choosing a study field. Female students choose medical fields more often, and there are also more women among PhD students (Hematoonkologia, 2024).

This is confirmed by available statistical data, which shows that in 11 EU countries, women constitute a higher percentage of doctors than men (Figure 5.17). This dominance is particularly visible in the Baltic countries, that is, Latvia (74%), Estonia (74%), and Lithuania (69%). The predominance of men is observed especially in Luxembourg (where the share of women doctors is only 36%), Italy (42%), Belgium (43%), Ireland (44%), and France (44%), but also in Germany (47 %), Austria (47%), the United Kingdom (48%), and Sweden (48%).

Considering the predominance of women over men among medical students, it is concluded that such a situation already occurs in all EU countries surveyed – Figure 5.18. Litvia (where the difference is as much as 56.5%), Lithuania (54.0%), and Portugal (51.5%) come to the forefront in this

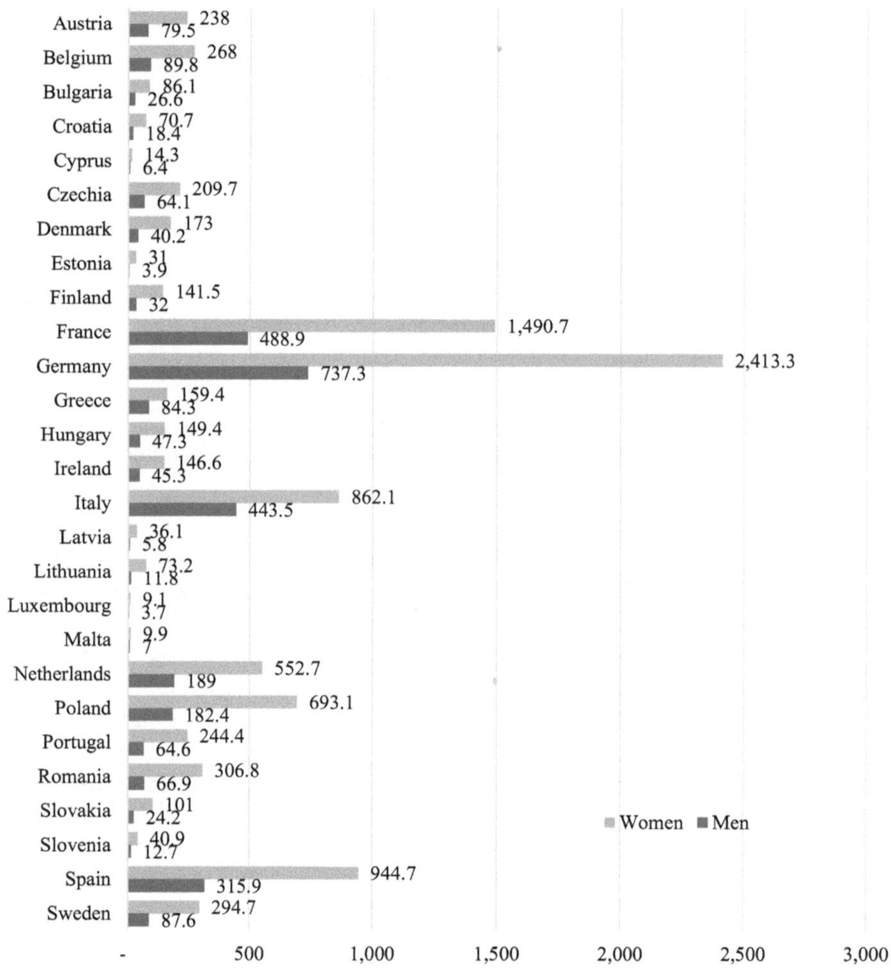

Figure 5.16 Number of women and men in European Union 15 years old or over employed in human health activities in 2022 (in thousand, by countries).

Source: Own study based on Eurostat (2024a).

classification, and at the bottom of the list are Bulgaria (4.6%) and Austria (7.0%). The country where the most women study medicine is France, almost 110,000, that is, over twice as many as in any other EU country, which makes this country ideal for future doctors. Spain is second in the ranking (over 50,000), and Poland is third (over 37,000). The list is closed by Luxembourg (only 92 women students) and Cyprus (less than 400 women students).

It should be emphasized that an increase in the percentage of women is observed in all medical specializations (Stone et al., 2020), but especially in those that are believed to demand more social skills. Therefore, they work much more often as family physicians, internal medicine physicians, and

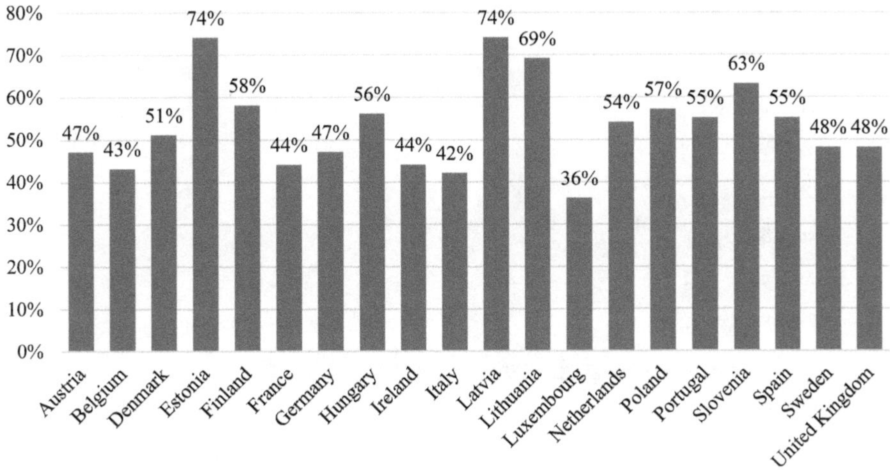

Figure 5.17 Percentage of female doctors in European Union in 2020 (by countries that provided data).

Source: Lenstore (n.d.).

pediatricians (Adar et al., 2022). At the same time, they are underrepresented in surgical positions, which are clearly dominated by men (Abelson et al., 2016). This segregation exists in many countries (Pelley & Carnes, 2020) and could be problematic for the entire society. This happens when women's choices in terms of education and profession do not meet the real needs of the market. But the problem also concerns the career opportunities of women themselves and thus their income situation. Research shows that the barriers to the professional career of these women surgeons, which they themselves identified, are complex. These include personal preferences and social influences, including conflict of social values and concerns about work–life balance (Giantini Larsen et al., 2021). However, among external barriers, women mention ineffective professional mentoring, lack of clear social and professional affiliation of women, inappropriate organizational culture and institutional policy, which negatively affect promotion opportunities and expectations placed on women (Zdravkovic, Neskovic & Berger-Estilita, 2021).

The considerations so far show that the EU is already seeing a reduction in gender inequalities in the number and percentage of doctors, both current and future. However, the situation is much worse when it comes to remuneration. In all countries surveyed, women in health care earn less than men – Figure 5.19. The highest earning women live in Luxembourg, Denmark, and Ireland, and the lowest (over 6 times lower) – in Bulgaria and Hungary. Bulgaria also has the largest gender pay gap, with men earning 50% more than women. There is also a large advantage in Slovakia (48.9%), Estonia (47.2%), and Portugal (47.2%). The most equal wages are recorded in Luxembourg (where women earn only 3.7% less than men) and Belgium (4.1%).

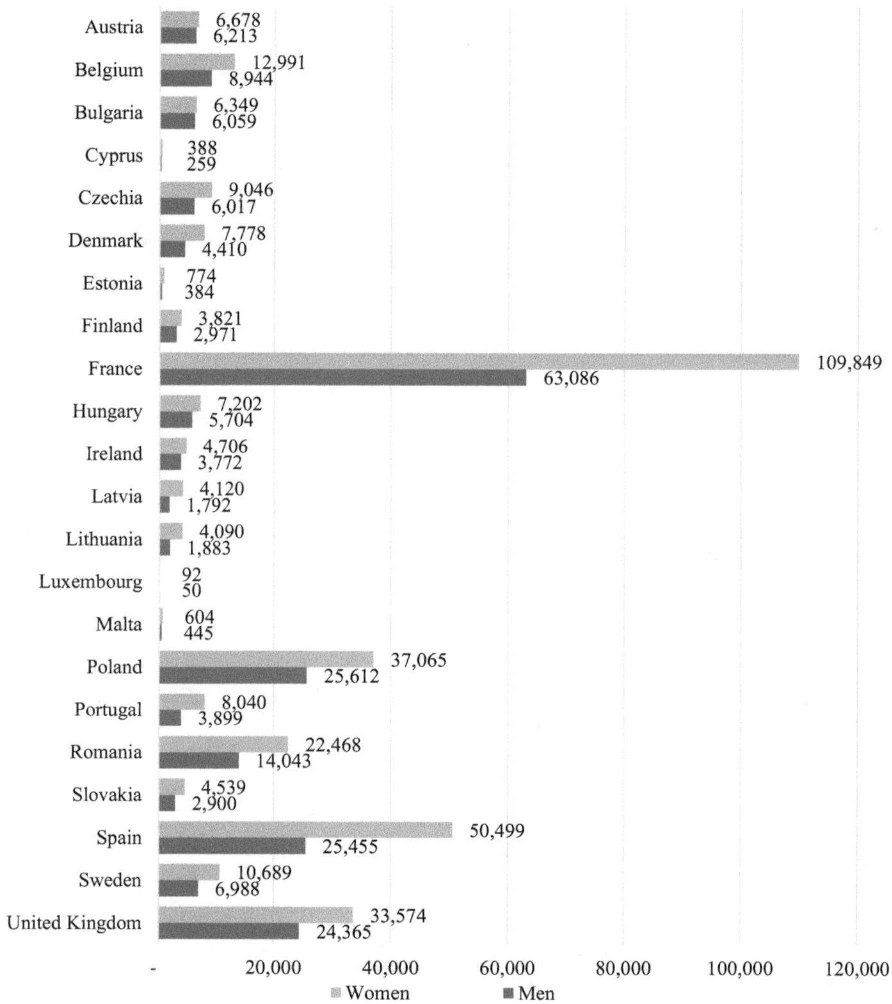

Figure 5.18 Number of women and men studying medicine in European Union in 2020 (in thousand, by countries that provided data).

Source: Lenstore (n.d.).

Using the above statistics (and two additional indicators), the Lenstore team (n.d.) analysed 30 countries in Europe to determine how friendly they are to women in medicine. Thus, taking into account the average annual salary, the number of working hours per week and vacation days per year, the number of women working in the health care sector, the percentage of women doctors, and the number of women in medical fields, it was determined that the best place for women to work in the health service is France. The countries that follow in the ranking are the Netherlands, Finland, Slovenia, and Denmark. The list is closed by Malta, Cyprus, and Bulgaria. However, by analysing the differences in

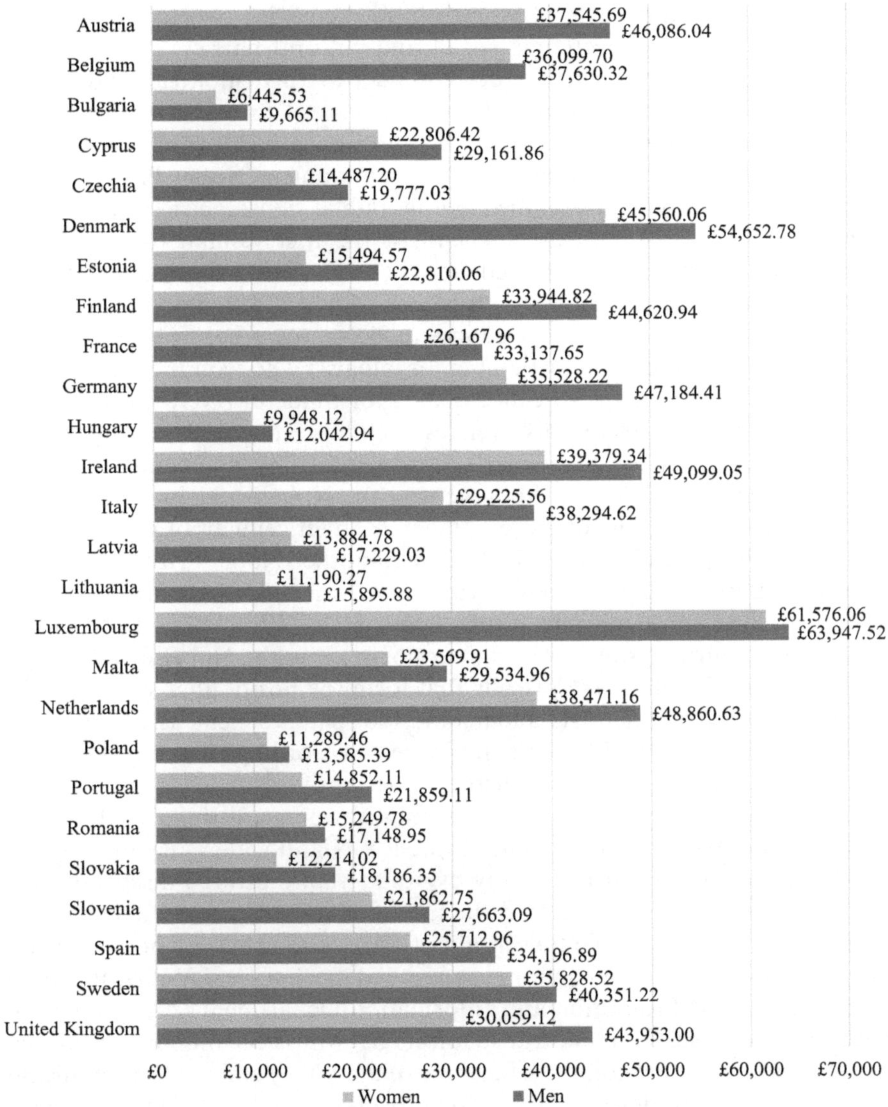

Figure 5.19 The average annual salary of women and men in health care in the European Union countries in 2020 (in £).

Source: Lenstore (n.d.).

salaries, the percentage of women doctors, and the number of women studying medicine, it was found that the countries that offer women in medicine the greatest opportunities and equal opportunities are Romania, Hungary, Sweden, and Denmark. At the bottom of the ranking, interestingly, are France, the United Kingdom, and the Netherlands. This is primarily the result of large pay gaps and disproportionate working hours for women compared to men in these countries.

When discussing the role of women in medicine, it is worth recalling the profiles of those who overcome social and cultural barriers and made an indisputable contribution to the development of this empirical field of science. Despite many limitations and often the lack of formal access to education, they defeated stereotypes by conducting pioneering research and making breakthrough discoveries. Among European women, Nobel Prize winners have become permanently embedded in public consciousness, including: Gerty Cori (Czech-American biochemist), the first woman to receive the Nobel Prize in physiology and medicine. In 1947, she discovered the mechanism of catalytic conversion of glycogen, which is very important in the development of methods of treating diabetes. Another was Rita Levi-Montalcini (Italian neurologist and embryologist) who won the Nobel Prize in 1986 for discovering the so-called nerve growth factor (NGF), which stimulates the growth of nerve cells. Her research has influenced, among others, the search for a cure for Alzheimer's disease, infertility, and cancer. German biologist Christiane Nüsslein-Volhard won the Nobel Prize in 1995 for discovering the mechanism of development of multicellular organisms from single cells during embryogenesis. In 2008, another Nobel Prize winner was Françoise Barré-Sinoussi (French virologist) who discovered the acquired immune deficiency syndrome virus, called HIV. While May Britt-Moser (Norwegian neurophysiologist and neurologist) won the Nobel Prize in 2014 for her role in the discovery of cells that form the positioning system in the brain, which helped scientists understand the spatial deficits associated with Alzheimer's disease. In 1964, British biochemist Dorothy Crowfoot-Hodgkin received the Nobel Prize in Chemistry for determining the structure of penicillin and vitamin B12. Another famous Englishwoman distinguished in medicine was Gertrude B. Elion and Florence Nightingale. The first was a biophysicist and specialist in X-ray crystallography who co-discovered the DNA double helix and pioneered the use of X-ray diffraction. The latter is considered the founder of modern nursing and a reformer of hospital sanitary procedures. Florence Nightingale founded the first secular nursing school in the world (CM Promotion and Information Department, 2022). Last but not least, Polish surgeon and transplantologist Maria Siemionow performed the world's first almost complete face transplant (80%) and made a significant contribution to the development of microsurgery and transplant medicine (CM UMK, 2022).

Conclusions

The situation of women in science, tourism, and health care has improved in the 21st century. However, much remains to be done. Much of the discrimination women experience today is more discreet and harder to detect than before, especially in health care. Although in many EU countries, women constitute a larger percentage of doctors than men, significantly fewer women hold managerial positions in this field. There can be several reasons for this. First, the gender pay gap discourages women from taking up positions where they are likely to earn less anyway. Women's lack of interest in managerial positions is also caused by the frequent lack of opportunities for promotion to these positions. Third, men often have the opportunity to improve their skills in leadership positions, while women do not. Finally, women are largely discouraged from pursuing a career due to the need to combine work and family life. There is also a view that employing women in middle-level positions is sufficient. Thus, although the number of women working in the health care industry has indeed increased, discrimination against them is still widespread (Baltmane, 2023). We should expect the principles of sustainable development to be reliably applied in every industry, including Goal 5 and others indicated in the monograph. Although in reality it is difficult and inspires resistance, there is an awareness that reducing economic differences between the sexes can lead to significant increases in global GDP. It fits the framework of womenomics and helps ensure the well-being of people globally, according to the 5xP principle.

Notes

1 It is also referred to as the Matthew effect, in which outstanding scientists receive disproportionate recognition for their contributions to science, while relatively unknown researchers receive disproportionate little recognition for contributions comparable to those of the former. In this convention, it was noted that grant candidates who had already won other scientific accolades had a greater chance of receiving money for research. Moreover, people who had already won a grant once were much more likely to apply for it again than those who were not among the winners (Bol et al., 2018).

2 NACE (fr. Nomenclature statistique des Activités économiques dans la Communauté Européenne) – statistical classification of economic activities in the European Community.

References

Abelson, J., Chartrand, G., Moo, T., Moore, M. & Yeo, H. (2016). The climb to break the glass ceiling in surgery: Trends in women progressing from medical school to surgical training and academic leadership from 1994 to 2015. *The American Journal of Surgery*, *212*(4), 566–572. https://doi.org/10.1016/j.amjsurg.2016.06.012

Adar, R., Kahalon, R., Ullrich, J., Afek, A., & Eisenberg, V. (2022). Gender bias in the evaluation of interns in different medical specialties: An archival study. *Medical Teacher*, *44*(8), 893–899. https://doi.org/10.1080/0142159X.2022.2046715

Artis, S., Shavers, M., LeSure, S., Spencer, B., & Joshi, A. (2018). Re-framing and reimagining the doctoral student narrative: Black women's experiences in engineering and computer science. *ASEE Annual Conference & Exposition*, Paper ID #23627. https://doi.org/10.18260/1-2-30915

Baltmane, A. A. (2023). *Sexism in medicine – how women are discriminated against in the US and Europe*. Retrieved from https://www.theperspective.se/2023/11/18/article/sexism-in-medicine-how-women-are-discriminated-against-in-the-us-and-europe/

Bogusz, R. (2018). Prestige of the medical profession. Is there a connection between feminization and decreased prestige? *Zdrowie Publiczne*, *128*(2), 85–88. https://doi.org/10.2478/pjph-2018-0016

Bol, T., de Vaan, M., & van de Rijt, A. (2018). The Matthew effect in science funding. *Proceedings of the National Academy of Sciences of the United States of America*, *115*(19), p. 4887–4890. https://doi.org/10.1073/pnas.1719557115

Brnáková, J., Neves, M., & Mareicheva, V. (2024). *Kobieca strona podróży - kobiety i ich innowacje w turystyce* [The feminine side of travel – women and their innovations in tourism]. Retrieved from https://www.kiwi.com/stories/pl/kobieca-strona-podrozy-kobiety-i-ich-innowacje-w-turystyce/

CM UMK. (2022). *Kobiety, które podbiły medycynę* [Women who conquered medicine]. Retrieved from https://www.cm.umk.pl/aktualnosci-2/3497-kobiety-ktore-podbily-medycyne.html

EIGE. (n.d.). *Tourism: Relevance of gender in the policy area*. European Institute for Gender Equality. Retrieved from https://eige.europa.eu

Eurostat. (2023). *Science and technology workforce: Women in majority*. Retrieved from https://ec.europa.eu/eurostat/en/web/products-eurostat-news/w/ddn-20230602-1

Eurostat. (2024a). *Employment by sex, age and detailed economic activity (from 2008 onwards, NACE Rev. 2 two digit level)*. Retrieved from https://ec.europa.eu/eurostat/databrowser/view/lfsa_egan22d__custom_11128287/default/table?lang=en

Eurostat. (2024b). *Employment by sex, age and detailed economic activity (from 2008 onwards, NACE Rev. 2 two digit level)*. Retrieved from https://ec.europa.eu/eurostat/databrowser/view/lfsa_egan22d__custom_10983445/default/table?lang=en

Eurostat. (2024c). *Employment by sex, age and economic activity (from 2008 onwards, NACE Rev. 2)*. Retrieved from https://ec.europa.eu/eurostat/databrowser/view/LFSA_EGAN2__custom_10983234/default/table?lang=en

Eurostat. (2024d). *Full-time and part-time employment by sex and economic activity (from 2008 onwards, NACE Rev. 2)*. Retrieved from https://ec.europa.eu/eurostat/databrowser/view/lfsa_epgan2__custom_11021908/default/table?lang=en

Eurostat. (2024e). *Over-qualification rates by economic activity (NACE Rev. 2)*. Retrieved from https://ec.europa.eu/eurostat/databrowser/view/lfsa_eoqgan2__custom_10977228/default/table?lang=en

Eurostat. (2024f). *Population by educational attainment level, sex and age (%) – main indicators*. Retrieved from https://ec.europa.eu/eurostat/databrowser/view/edat_lfse_03__custom_11414437/default/table

Eurostat. (2024g). *Self-employment by sex, age and economic activity (from 2008 onwards, NACE Rev. 2)*. Retrieved from https://ec.europa.eu/eurostat/databrowser/view/lfsa_esgan2__custom_11037941/default/table?lang=en

Eurostat. (2024h). *Temporary employees by sex, age and economic activity (from 2008 onwards, NACE Rev. 2)*. Retrieved from https://ec.europa.eu/eurostat/databrowser/view/lfsa_etgan2__custom_11001429/default/table?lang=en

Feeley, T. H., & Yang, Z. (2022). Is there a Matilda effect in communication journals? *Communication Reports*, *35*(1), 1–11. https://doi.org/10.1080/08934215.2021.1974505

Figueroa-Domecq, C., Palomo, J., Flecha-Barrio, M. D., & Segovia-Pérez, M. (2020). Technology double gender gap in tourism business leadership. *Information Technology & Tourism*, *22*(1), 75–106. https://doi.org/10.1007/s40558-020-00168-0

Fiorentin, F., Pereira, M. & Suárez, D. (2022). The gender gap in public S&T funding: The Matilda effect in STEM disciplines in Argentina. *IDB Publications*, 11990. https://doi.org/10.18235/0004017

Giantini Larsen, A., Pories, S., Parangi, S., & Robertson, F. (2021). Barriers to pursuing a career in surgery: An institutional survey of Harvard Medical School students. *Annals of Surgery*, *273*(6), 1120–1126. https://doi.org/10.1097/SLA.0000000000003618

Gitnux. (2023). *Must-know women in academia statistics*. Retrieved from https://gitnux.org/women-in-academia-statistics/

Hematoonkologia. (2024). *Kobiety w medycynie: 4 ciekawostki ze statystyk* [Women in medicine: 4 interesting facts from statistics]. Retrieved from https://hematoonkologia.pl/informacje-dla-chorych/materialy-ogolne/id/6864-kobiety-w-medycynie-4-ciekawostki-ze-statystyk

Lenstore. (n.d.). *The best countries in Europe to be a female health professional*. Retrieved from https://www.lenstore.co.uk/research/women-in-health/
Levanon, A., & Grusky, D. (2016). The persistence of extreme gender segregation in the twenty-first century. *The American Journal of Sociology*, *122*(2), 573–619. https://doi.org/10.1086/688628
Nanal, V. (2017). Lise Meitner (1878–1968). A physicist who never lost her humanity. *Resonance*, *22*(3), 193–197. https://doi.org/10.1007/s12045-017-0451-8
Nobel Prize. (2023). *Nobel Prize awarded women*. Retrieved from https://www.nobelprize.org/prizes/lists/nobel-prize-awarded-women/
Pelley, E., & Carnes, M. (2020). When a specialty becomes "women's Work": Trends in and implications of specialty gender segregation in medicine. *Academic Medicine*, *95*(10), 1499–1506. https://doi.org/10.1097/ACM.0000000000003555
Perkowitz, S. (2022). The woman who found hydrogen in the stars. *Physics World*, *35*(3), 39. https://doi.org/10.1088/2058-7058/35/03/31
Rajkó, A., Herendy, C., Goyanes, M., & Demeter, M. (2023). The Matilda effect in communication research: The effects of gender and geography on usage and citations across 11 countries. *Communication Research*, 009365022211243. https://doi.org/10.1177/00936502221124389
Rossiter, M. W. (1993). The Matthew Matilda effect in science. *Social Studies of Science*, *23*(2), 325–341. https://doi.org/10.1177/030631293023002004
Steiner-Hofbauer, V., Katz, H. W., Grundnig, J. S., & Holzinger, A. (2023). Female participation or "feminization" of medicine. *Wiener Medizinische Wochenschrift (1946)*, *173*(5–6), 125–130. https://doi.org/10.1007/s10354-022-00961-y
Stone, A. T., Carlson, K. M., Douglas, P. S., Morris, K. L., & Walsh, M. N. (2020). Assessment of subspecialty choices of men and women in internal medicine from 1991 to 2016. *JAMA Internal Medicine*, *180*(1), 140–141. https://doi.org/10.1001/jamainternmed.2019.3833
UNWTO. (2019). *Global report on women in tourism* – 2nd Edition. Madrid: UNWTO. https://doi.org/10.18111/9789284420384
Usakiewicz, J. (2019). Anna Maria van Schurman (1607–1678) – Ocellus Niderlandów. *Studia z Historii Filozofii*, *10*(1), 171–192. https://doi.org/10.12775/szhf.2019.010
Vinuesa, R., Azizpour, H., Leite, I., Balaam, M., Dignum, V., Domisch, S., Felländer, A., Langhans, S. D., Tegmark, M., & Fuso Nerini, F. (2020). The role of artificial intelligence in achieving the sustainable development goals. *Nature Communications*, *11*(233). https://doi.org/10.1038/s41467-019-14108-y
Wang, X., Dworkin, J. D., Zhou, D., Stiso, J., Falk, E. B., Bassett, D. S., Zurn, P., & Lydon-Staley, D. M. (2021). Gendered citation practices in the field of communication. *Annals of the International Communication Association*, *45*(2), 134–153. https://doi.org/10.1080/23808985.2021.1960180
World Bank. (2017). *Tourism for development, women and tourism: Designing for inclusion*. Washington: The World Bank Group. Retrieved from https://turizambih.ba/en/women-and-tourism-designing-for-inclusion/
WTTC. (2019). *Travel & tourism: Driving women's success*. London: World Travel & Tourism Council. Retrieved from https://wttc.org/Portals/0/Documents/Reports/2019/Social%20Impact-Driving%20Womens%20Success-Mar%202019.pdf?ver=2021-02-25-182742-097
WTTC. (2023). EU travel & tourism sector recovering strongly says WTTC. https://wttc.org/news-article/eu-travel-and-tourism-sector-recovering-strongly-says-wttc accessed on: 26.06.2024.
Zdravkovic, M., Neskovic, V., & Berger-Estilita, J. (2021). Surveys on gender issues among anaesthesiologists: Where do we go from here? *Journal of Gender Studies*, *30*(7), 868–871. https://doi.org/10.1080/09589236.2021.1969225

Index

Pages in *italics* refer to figures and pages in **bold** refer to tables.

FSC
www.fsc.org
MIX
Papier | Fördert gute Waldnutzung
FSC® C083411

Kolibri 360 GmbH
Ferdinand-Jühlke-Straße 7
99095 Erfurt, Deutschland
produktsicherheit@kolibri360.de